The Lieutenant Nun

Transgenderism, Lesbian Desire,

& Catalina de Erauso

The Lieutenant Nun

SHERRY VELASCO

University of Texas Press Austin

Publication of this book was made possible in part by the Program for Cultural Cooperation between Spain's Ministry of Education and Culture and United States' Universities.

Printed in the United States of America

First edition, 2000

Requests for permission to reproduce material from this work should be sent to Permissions, University of Texas Press, Box 7819, Austin, TX 78713–7819.

⊗ The paper used in this book meets the minimum requirements of ANSI/NISO Z39.48–1992 (R1997) (Permanence of Paper).

Library of Congress Cataloging-in-Publication Data
Velasco, Sherry M. (Sherry Marie), 1962–
The lieutenant nun : transgenderism, lesbian desire, and Catalina de Erauso / Sherry Velasco.— 1st ed.
p. cm.
Includes bibliographical references and index.
ISBN 0-292-78745-6 (cl. : alk. paper) —
ISBN 0-292-78746-4 (pbk. : alk. paper)
1. Erauso, Catalina de, b. ca. 1592—In literature. 2. Erauso, Catalina de, b. ca. 1592—In motion pictures. I. Title.
PN57.E68 V45 2000
809'.9335—dc21

00-022196

For my sister Lauri

Contents

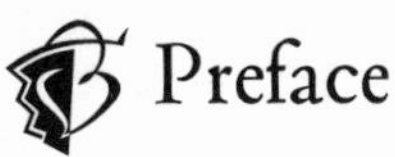

Preface

IN *The Lieutenant Nun* I analyze the various ways in which the early modern Spanish transgenderist Catalina de Erauso, more commonly known as the "Monja Alférez" (Lieutenant Nun), has been constructed, interpreted, marketed, and consumed by the dominant culture and divergent audience groups from the seventeenth through the twentieth centuries in Europe, Latin America, and the United States. This study investigates the cultural function of transvestite narratives through an analysis of the Lieutenant Nun figure presented in literary, theatrical, iconographic, and cinematic adaptations during nearly four hundred years in Spain, England, Latin America, and North America. I argue that the ways in which Erauso's experience has been transformed into a public spectacle help explain the enduring popularity and economic success of transgender narratives as well as how they expose and manipulate spectators' fears and desires. This book explores what happens when the private experience of the transgenderist is shifted to the public sphere and thereby marketed as a hybrid spectacle for the curious gaze of the general audience.

Chapter 1, "Hybrid Spectacles: Lesbian Desire, Monsters, and Masculine Women in Early Modern Spain," provides the necessary background to contextualize the reception and interpretation of transgenderism during the life of Catalina de Erauso. This section reviews the ambiguity and the cultural constructedness of concepts and practices such as hybrid monsters, lesbianism and homoerotic images, cross-dressing, and biological sex assignment during the early modern period in order to understand how a transgendered lesbian figure could gain celebrity status as well as financial compensation and religious affirmation in seventeenth-century Spain. Analyses of sources from official and popular culture demonstrate how Erauso's icon tapped into the early modern fascination with hybrid monsters and the essentialist belief that masculine women were the product of a prenatal transmutation. Likewise, the Lieutenant Nun's popularity during the seventeenth century was a response to the marketability of female transvestism in history, literature, and theater, justified by the need or desire for self-protection (chastity and safety), escapism, adventure, patriotism, the support of patriarchy, romantic and economic motives, and the sex appeal of the revealing garments.

Chapter 2, "Celebrity and Scandal: The Creation of the Lieutenant Nun in the Seventeenth Century," examines the contradictory politics of the Monja Alférez icon as public spectacle during the seventeenth century in Spain and in the New World. This chapter provides an analysis of the different versions of Erauso's life presented between 1618 and 1653 in legal petitions, testimonies, letters, three *relaciones* (news pamphlets), her autobiography, an episode from a picaresque novel, literary and iconographic portraits, and a play. While these narratives reveal a variety of identities—rebellious nun, heroic soldier, deviant criminal, exemplary virgin, and monstrous hybrid spectacle—the one image that is present in the seventeenth-century adaptations but silenced in subsequent periods is that of the lesbian. In particular, this chapter explores the strategies of cultural production and the preferences of the seventeenth-century consumer/spectator involved in the selling and consumption of the Lieutenant Nun celebrity. The manifestations of this icon, represented as both killer lesbian and virgin military hero, also attempt to reveal Catalina de Erauso's reactions to becoming the object of the public's curious gaze. Although the church and state interpreted Erauso's alleged lesbianism, in conjunction with proof of her virginity, as nonthreatening (nonreproductive and nonpenetrative) desire, other popular culture narratives such as the broadsides and a *comedia* linked her same-sex attraction to aggression and deceit. In the end, however, the presentation of Erauso's lesbian desire facilitated official and public approval of her transgenderism: she refrained from heterosexual relations while participating in Spain's project of empire-building. Moreover, the association of her vices with homosexual desire ensured that her personal life would not become an acceptable model for future women.

In chapter 3, "Melodrama and the De-Lesbianized Reconstruction of the Lieutenant Nun in the Nineteenth Century," I discuss the nineteenth-century transformation of the popular icon in Spanish literary journals, a *zarzuela* (Spanish operetta), a Mexican play, and historical novels from Mexico and Spain. While Catalina de Erauso represented a hybrid spectacle that produced admiration, titillation, and shock during the seventeenth century, the nineteenth century was highly critical of the lesbian celebrity. Consequently, writers and critics read the Lieutenant Nun as a demonized lesbian or reconstructed her into a heterosexual or asexual figure who is temporarily transgressive only because of her transvestism and violent nature but not due to her desire for other women. The transformation of the Lieutenant Nun's image from the seventeenth century to the nineteenth century is not surprising considering the dramatic change in how lesbianism was perceived from one period to another. While nonpenetrative sexual activity between women during the early modern period was not seen as a serious threat to orthodox values—especially in comparison to male homosexuality—same-sex relations in the nineteenth century were viewed as a criminal pathology that had to be corrected.

The only nineteenth-century adaptation that presents a more sympathetic image of a lesbian lieutenant nun is found in an anonymous novel from Mexico. This version, nonetheless, portrays same-sex desire as an entertaining erotic spectacle as well as a mechanism that ensures the protagonist's heterosexual chastity.

Chapter 4, "From Cinema to Comics: The Re-Lesbianization of the Lieutenant Nun in the Twentieth Century," builds on the analyses of previous chapters to demonstrate how Latin American, Spanish, and North American films and novels, a play, and various comics and stories for young adults have manipulated the Lieutenant Nun icon for varying and, at times, opposing ideological purposes. An examination of twentieth-century manifestations of Erauso's life reveal a gradual re-lesbianization of the protagonist that reflects the changing attitudes toward homosexuality among certain audiences. The 1944 Mexican film starring María Félix follows the nineteenth-century model by portraying Erauso as the heterosexual femme fatale. Forty years later, however, Javier Aguirre directed a Spanish film that presents Erauso's life as a story of tragic lesbian love, while a year later, in 1987, the North American filmmaker Sheila McLaughlin released the only version to privilege the image of a triumphant homosocial resolution. The twentieth-century prose narratives from the 1950s and 1970s, on the other hand, tend to "correct" Erauso's same-sex desire by portraying her as an asexual protagonist, by rehabilitating the transgressive lesbian, or by presenting homoeroticism in terms of a heterosexual configuration. In other words, in the hetero-biased adaptations the protagonist desires women because she feels like a man.

The twentieth-century sequential art narratives or comic strips likewise propose an asexual reading of the homoerotic episodes in Erauso's life narrative. While those from Spain seek to teach readers about the Basque heroine through both serious and humorous representations, a comic book published in Mexico highlights the action-adventure features of Erauso's life. These three sequential art narratives either suppress homoeroticism or present a historical figure who resisted the sexual advances of other women deceived by the disguise. This chapter, nonetheless, demonstrates the implicit potential for a queer "rereading" of the transvestite narratives (by analyzing the visual impact of the unconvincing disguise in episodes that feature same-sex flirtation) despite the apparent attempt to correct or police lesbian desire in many of the adaptations based on Erauso's experience.

Acknowledgments

SO MANY FRIENDS and colleagues have contributed to the ideas developed in this book that I cannot thank them all. I would, however, like to offer special gratitude to Adrienne Martín, Anne Cruz, Mary Elizabeth Perry, Kristine Ibsen, and Lourdes Torres for providing insightful criticism that helped enrich my thinking about the Lieutenant Nun icon. I also wish to acknowledge my generous colleagues at the University of Kansas. Roberta Johnson, Lee Skinner, Jonathan Mayhew, Isidro Rivera, Danny Anderson, Tony Rosenthal, Luis Corteguera, and Marta Vicente offered perceptive and rigorous comments for which I am very grateful. Special thanks go to Juan Velasco, Jorge Galindo, and Ramón Velasco Moreno for their emotional and critical support as I tracked down yet another obscure representation of the Lieutenant Nun. I am equally indebted to my colleagues at the University of Kentucky, in particular, to Jay Allen, Margaret Jones, and Dianna Niebylski for their counsel on the final revisions. In addition, I would like to express my appreciation for support from the Program for Cultural Cooperation Between Spain's Ministry of Culture and United States' Universities, the General Research Fund at the University of Kansas, and the Tinker Field Research Fund. Finally, I would like to thank Mary Daniels, María José Delgado, Renata Fernández, and especially Lynn Porter, Paula Courtney, and Pam LeRow at the University of Kansas, as well as Rachel Chance, Leslie Tingle, Allison Faust, Alison Tartt, and Ellen McKie at the University of Texas Press for their invaluable assistance in the preparation of the manuscript.

Introduction

CATALINA DE ERAUSO (1592–1650) was a Basque noblewoman who, just before taking final vows to become a nun at age fifteen, escaped from the convent in San Sebastián where she had lived since the age of four. Dressed in men's clothing, Erauso lived successfully as a man for almost twenty years, for a brief period in Spain and later in the New World. As she summarizes in her autobiography: "I was educated there [in the convent], took the habit, became a novice, and was about to be professed when, for such-and-such reasons, I ran away; that I went to such-and-such a place, stripped, dressed up, and cut my hair, went hither and thither, embarked, went into port, took to roving, slew, wounded, embezzled, and roamed about."[1] Although she was distinguished for her fearless deeds as a soldier fighting for the Spanish empire in Peru and Chile, Erauso's memoirs showcase her propensity for violence, which leads to about a dozen murders off the battlefield. Not surprisingly, the cultural representations of this fascinating life are marked by controversy and contradiction. While Erauso's adventurous life was an obvious transgression of the Counter Reformation image of the pious woman enclosed in the domestic sphere of the home (or the convent), as Fray Luis de León recommended in *La perfecta casada* (1583), her masculine character also embodied what Fray Luis referred to as the "woman of value" or the "manly woman" (85). Furthermore, while many versions of Erauso's life highlight her ferocity as confirmation of both nationalistic military sentiment on the battlefield and criminality while engaged in personal conflicts, the life narratives interpret the protagonist's attraction for other women in ambivalent terms. Same-sex flirtation is portrayed as an effective and nonthreatening way to maintain her disguise and to preserve her chastity (in heterosexual terms). At the same time, however, lesbian desire could be viewed as another sign of social and moral deviance.

As one might expect, when describing the life of the seventeenth-century Spanish "Lieutenant Nun," it is difficult not to engage the sensationalist adjectives and verbs commonly featured in popular tabloid accounts. Martha Vicinus, for instance, has described Catalina de Erauso as a "quick-tempered Basque patriot, dressed—and sometimes undressed—as a soldier of fortune, as liable to kill or kiss,"[2] or as Vicki León in her "Uppity Women" series glosses, Erauso was a "nun turned top-gun" and a "Dirty Harry."[3] According to Stephanie Merrim, "Erauso would probably be portrayed in similar terms today by tabloids such as the *National Inquirer* [*sic*]" (1994, 194). However rebellious Erauso may seem, nonetheless, she was rewarded for her gender transgression in 1626 with a soldier's pension from the Spanish monarch Philip IV and dispensation from Pope Urban VIII to continue dressing in men's clothing. In 1630 she returned to the New World and lived the last twenty years of her life in Mexico working as a mule-driver, again dressed in male garb, until her death in 1650.

Despite the historical evidence related to the life of Catalina de Erauso confirming most of the military action recorded in her memoirs (primarily from official testimonies, certifications, petitions, and letters filed on behalf of the Lieutenant Doña Catalina de Erauso), considerable mystery continues to surround her. One of the causes of this uncertainty, or what Rima de Vallbona refers to as the "imaginary spaces," stems from the fact that no autograph or original copy of Erauso's life narrative has been found, even though it was believed to have been submitted to the publisher Bernardino de Guzmán in 1625.[4] The poet and author Cándido María Trigueros (1737–1801) owned a copy of the manuscript, which was then transcribed by the historian Juan Bautista Muñoz in 1784 and deposited in the Biblioteca de la Real Academia de la Historia in Madrid.[5] Muñoz's draft of the autobiography, titled *Vida i sucesos de la Monja Alférez, o Alférez Catarina, Dª Catarina de Araujo* [sic] *doncella, natural de S[an] Sebastián, Prov[inci]a de Guipúzcoa. Escrita por ella misma en 18 de Sept[tiembr]e 1646* [*sic*], was, in turn, copied by others and later edited by the Basque critic Joaquín María Ferrer and published for the first time in 1829 under the new title *Historia de la Monja Alférez, Doña Catalina de Erauso, escrita por ella misma.*[6] According to Ferrer, he obtained a copy of the manuscript from his friend Felipe Bauzá, who was living in exile in London (17).[7] After the first publication in 1829, the autobiography was soon translated and reworked into other languages such as French, German, and English, and was reedited numerous times during the nineteenth and twentieth centuries, frequently published with Juan Pérez de Montalbán's 1626 play, *La Monja Alférez.*[8]

Two additional manuscript copies of Erauso's memoirs were recently discovered by Pedro Rubio Merino in the Archivo Capitular in Seville. Rubio Merino dates these documents to the late seventeenth or early eighteenth century (18). The first of these two manuscripts, titled *Vida y sucessos de la Monja Alférez, Dª Catharina de Erauso* (which I will refer to as the Seville manuscript), contains considerable variations in comparison with the *Vida i sucesos* (1784 Madrid manuscript) and the *Historia* (1829). The second manuscript, housed in the Archivo Capitular in Seville, is an untitled, incomplete, and modified copy of the *Vida i sucesos.* This untitled version ends suddenly at the beginning of chapter 15, which coincides with chapter 14 of the Madrid manuscript and Ferrer's edition. Consequently, it does not include the revelation scene or any aspect of Erauso's public life as the "Monja Alférez." The content of this text is consistent with the other versions, nonetheless, although it does contain minor stylistic variations.

The discrepancies between Ferrer's *Historia* and the 1784 copy of the manuscript in Madrid are restricted to editorial changes in spelling, punctuation, dates, gender markers, and geographical errors. However, while most of the inconsistencies between the Seville manuscript and the 1784 Madrid copy are limited to style and tone, a few episodes show certain modifications in specific plot development. For example, in the last scene of the 1784 text the protagonist merely threatens the two prostitutes who tease her, while in the Seville manuscript Erauso physically attacks the women: "I pulled out my sword and dagger and went toward them with a beating of sword-swipes and they escaped from me by running away. Turning to the women, I gave them many slaps and kicks and I was tempted to cut their faces" (Rubio Merino 92).[9]

Furthermore, at times the Seville manuscript reveals more significant content variations that could encourage scholars to reconsider some of the assumptions and beliefs about Erauso's life narrative. In particular, Erauso's confession of her biological identity in the Madrid manuscript of the *Vida i sucesos* is described as her own decision, unsolicited, whereas in the Seville manuscript it is elicited when the bishop Fray Agustín de Carvajal guesses her secret: "He took me by the hand and asked me closely and in a low voice if I was a woman. I responded yes" (quoted in Rubio Merino 86).[10] In the Madrid manuscript, however, the bishop appears unsuspecting when he asks Erauso about her life: "He asked me who I was and from where, whose son I was and the whole course of my life" (cited in Vallbona 110).[11]

Equally significant for the way in which scholars have interpreted Erauso's life is the absence in the Seville manuscript of the now famous summary of her story narrated for the bishop. In the Madrid manuscript Erauso condenses her autobiography into one brief statement: "I was raised there and took the veil and became a novice, and that when I was about to profess my final vows, I left the convent for such and such a reason, went to such and such a place, undressed myself and dressed myself up again, cut my hair, traveled here and there, embarked, disembarked, hustled, killed, maimed, wreaked havoc, and roamed about" (64).[12] In the Seville manuscript, however, this summation is eliminated: "He asked me truly who I was, from where, and whose daughter I was. I continued to respond. He took me aside and asked me if I was a nun and how and why I left the convent. I told him" (cited in Rubio Merino 86).[13] For Rubio Merino, this episode in Ferrer's text (like the Madrid manuscript) "is more detailed, lively, and intimate. In this version the swashbuckling lieutenant gives in to the venerable personality of the elderly prelate, and down falls the castle of the pseudo-masculine personality in which she had enclosed herself during so many years and she ends up revealing herself little by little" (23).[14] While all early versions of Erauso's memoirs appear, in general terms, to narrate similar events, we can see by the minor variations among the copies that her story has been open to interpretation from the very beginning. Since most critics agree on the historicity of certain episodes and activities in Erauso's life, the personal motivations behind these actions are what seem to both intrigue and frustrate those who attempt to find the "truth" behind the Monja Alférez legend.

Given the various texts and their respective orthographic and factual corrections, as well as content and stylistic modifications, there has been much speculation about the authorship and veracity of the autobiography. Serrano y Sanz and Menéndez Pelayo maintain that Trigueros forged the narrative by refashioning the 1625 *relaciones* (news pamphlets or broadsides) that describe Erauso's adventures, while others have suggested the opposite, that the pamphlets were sensationalized adaptations of the original *Vida* penned by Erauso. Although Vallbona explores the possibility that Pérez de Montalbán's play was the inspiration for the *Vida,* she discredits this option as improbable given the marked differences in the characterization of Erauso in both works (19–22). Other scholars, such as Stephanie Merrim, suggest that Erauso dictated her life story or at least authorized a ghost writer to record her adventures.[15] Consequently, while many readers of Erauso's memoirs have been willing to categorize her as one of the many early modern Spanish women writers, others are more hesitant to consider the autobiography an example of women's literary history: "The interest of this text as feminine literature is diminished since the author and narrator do not coincide; the author doesn't necessarily have to be a woman" (Caballero 482).[16]

The current state of scholarship on the Lieutenant Nun reveals a new stage in Erauso studies at the end of the twentieth century, which in many ways is reminiscent of Dorothy M. Kress's thesis written nearly seventy years ago. Kress's study, *Catalina de Erauso, su personalidad histórica y legendaria,* combines research on Erauso's historical identity with an analysis of the literary representations of her legendary figure as the Monja Alférez. Thanks to the recent bio-bibliographic investigations by scholars such as Rima de Vallbona, J. Ignacio Tellechea Idígoras, and Pedro Rubio Merino, who have researched and published annotated editions of Erauso's *Vida* and other rare documents, critics like Stephanie Merrim, Mary Elizabeth Perry, Encarnación Juárez, and Adrienne L. Martín have analyzed Erauso's life in terms of the cultural significance of her icon.

Erauso's autobiography has also been translated recently into English by Michele Stepto and Gabriel Stepto in a more contemporary prose style than that of James Fitzmaurice-Kelly's earlier translation.[17] Stepto and Stepto's translation has brought Catalina de Erauso's story to the attention of readers outside Hispanic studies, and as a result, the memoirs have garnered such recognition from the gay/lesbian community as a 1997 nomination for the Lambda Literary Award in the transgender book category.[18]

Undoubtedly informed by late-twentieth-century theories on transgenderism, current studies on Erauso reveal a growing division among scholars regarding the gender markers and how female-to-male individuals "should" be represented in texts. While most references to Erauso use feminine adjectives and subject pronouns, scholars and students have recently begun to question what seems to be a privileging of sex-at-birth over gender adoption. In an unpublished conference paper, for example, Chloe Rutter prefers "he" in reference to Erauso since "his actions make him a man, his actions under the guise of a woman could have been impossible . . . present day assumptions of gender to categorize people are used to read early modern texts with little preoccupation over calling figures 'women', even if his life is lived out as a 'man' " (4). Similarly, in a departure from her previously published studies on Erauso, Mary Elizabeth Perry's recent essay on the Lieutenant Nun alternates "he" and "she":

> It seems neither fair nor accurate, however, to use exclusively feminine pronouns to refer to the Nun-Lieutenant, who worked so diligently to make herself into a man. Significantly, most historical sources referring to this person use feminine pronouns and imply that she was basically a female who dressed and lived as a man. Yet it could be argued that Catalina de Erauso should be identified as a male who did not allow his family's mistaken identity of him nor his lack of some of the physiological characteristics of males to undercut his own understanding of himself. . . . I use both feminine and masculine pronouns throughout the essay, alternating them between sentences rather than between paragraphs in order to avoid the suggestion that certain aspects of this person's life were more masculine and others more feminine. (1999, 395)[19]

In her impressive study of female-to-male transsexuals, Holly Devor uses feminine pronouns while referring to episodes in which Erauso was living as a woman and masculine pronouns when she was living as a man (14–15). And yet another response to the gender pronoun dilemma is adopted by Debbie Fraker in her review of Stepto and Stepto's English translation of Erauso's autobiography. Fraker uses "s/he," following the example set by Leslie Feinberg in *Transgender Warriors.*[20]

In addition to the doubt surrounding the authorship of Erauso's life narrative, a comparison of gender usage among the various manuscripts and published texts of the autobiography complicates the issue even further. Rima de Vallbona's annotated edition of the 1784 Madrid manuscript *Vida i sucesos de la Monja Alférez* compares gender markers in the eighteenth-century manuscript to those in Ferrer's 1829 publication of the *Historia de la Monja Alférez doña Catalina de Erauso.* Vallbona notes that both versions of the autobiography use feminine as well as masculine markers but that Ferrer's edition maintains more consistent usage of masculine adjectives. While masculine adjectives also predominate in the 1784 manuscript reproduced by Vallbona, feminine adjectives are more pervasive in the Seville manuscript. With possible editorial changes or errors notwithstanding, other justifications for the gender inconsistencies in the autobiography abound. Roslyn M. Frank proposes that Erauso's native Basque tongue interfered with the gender agreement in Castilian, since there is no grammatical distinction between masculine and feminine in the Basque language (Vallbona 35). Like other critics, Vallbona notes a situational pattern in the dual gender markers. She argues that the narrator adopts either the masculine or feminine forms depending on the nature of the situation in which the protagonist finds herself: "In the passages of courtship, flirtation, and romance she uses the masculine form, as she does in those of war and duels. Nonetheless, when the context is neutral the protagonist-narrator returns to feminine usage" (52).[21] Stephanie Merrim, on the other hand, suggests that the gender variety may also reflect an authorial intention to entertain the readers: "Equally conceivable and in keeping with the rest of the *Historia* is the possibility that its author contrived the adjectival instability for its shock value, to position the text in the space of difference" (1994, 183).

Since the intention of the present study is to analyze the cultural representations of the popular celebrity known as "la Monja Alférez" (without forgetting that there is a "real" historical individual behind the icon), I chose to use feminine pronouns to reflect the fact that the cultural icon of the Lieutenant Nun was defined first as a nun (noun), who happened to become (and modified by) a lieutenant (adjective). Moreover, it would seem that Erauso also manipulated her culture's beliefs and attitudes toward sex, gender, and identity. When she requested a physical examination of her primary sex characteristics, she undoubtedly knew that this information would permanently establish her identity as both "virgin" and "woman" in the minds of those who would control her future. For Holly Devor, Erauso's apparent willingness to present herself in terms of her female identity reflects the financial reality of the popular icon: "The fact that Catalina de Erauso publicly exploited her notoriety as the 'nun ensign' says more about economic opportunities for women than it does about de Erauso's gender. Once exposed, she made the best of her situation until her star faded and she returned to living as a man" (15–16). However, as Paul Bennett quips, "Catalina, despite gender-studies queen Marjorie Garber's assertion, is no RuPaul" (16). Not surprisingly, the representations of Erauso's life are filtered through her icon as the Monja Alférez. The only exceptions to this representational gynocentrism are temporary and undoubtedly intended to shock the reader and to emphasize the success of her transgenderism. For example, in 1626 Pedro de la Valle refers to Erauso with masculine adjectives and pronouns only when relating how others perceived her before she confessed her biological identity: "He acquired a reputation for being brave and because of the lack of beard they took him for and called him an eunuch" (cited in Vallbona 127).[22]

Interestingly, even though the letters, broadsides, and petitions tend to describe Erauso as a woman who performs certain male-gendered activities, her mother was believed by some to have listed her famous child among her sons in her final will.[23] Likewise, in a 1640 lawsuit cited by José Berruezo, the deposition of Captain Juan Pérez de Aguirre (a citizen of San Sebastián) refers to Erauso as a "brother of theirs who was called Don Antonio de Erauso, otherwise known as the Nun Lieutenant" (quoted in Castillo Lara 322).[24] Conversely, J. Ignacio Tellechea claims that Erauso's mother, María Pérez de Galarraga, did not mention Catalina (or Antonio) among either her sons or daughters: "It is significant that her mother does not recognize Catalina among her children. She could have mentioned her and noted her as absent. Perhaps after fifteen years of absence she believed her disappeared or dead? Or does this silence signify a way of willfully eliminating an adventurer from whom she had not heard and who could have been the shame and embarrassment of the family?" (59–60).[25]

In an attempt to contribute to the growing body of scholarship on the Lieutenant Nun, the present study explores how Erauso's life becomes the mirror in which each reader/spectator finds a reflection of his or her own preferences and values. As Marjorie Garber indicates: "In the fascinating and fantastic adventures of the Lieutenant Nun doña Catalina de Erauso, who cross-dressed her way out of a Spanish convent and into the New World, what we read, what we find, *is a version of ourselves*" (1996, vii, emphasis mine).[26] Leslie Feinberg, for example, in her history of other "transgender warriors" like herself includes Erauso in the group of early models of transgenderism, while the Basque historian J. Ignacio Tellechea uses Catalina's story to tell another chapter of his region's past. When Tellechea describes Erauso's baptismal basin, he writes himself into the account: "It's a historical vestige, bound to so many who were born in the shadow of this parish, and in which I myself was baptized" (205).[27] In an otherwise thorough study of the issues associated with Catalina de Erauso, Tellechea's 1992 publication is suspiciously silent about her alleged same-sex desire. In what seems to be the author's attempt to defend his compatriot from accusations of transgressive sexuality, he criticizes certain novelistic and cinematic versions of Erauso's life for focusing on the "diseased" part of the heroine's personality (7).

Even though the cultural reworkings of the Lieutenant Nun reveal a wide variety of transgender spectacles, lesbian desire is the most problematic characteristic associated with her identity during the 400 years since Erauso's birth. Therefore, I began with this source of tension to explore the apparent contradictions and drastic swings in representations across the centuries. When analyzing the cultural narratives based on Catalina de Erauso's life, I discovered that the transgender spectacle enacts the mechanism of fear and desire in society when the transvestite sign is read as both a threat to the fixed nature of gender and sexual identity and an antidote for this disruptive potential. Marjorie Garber posits that transvestism defamiliarizes, denaturalizes, and destabilizes sex and gender categories, or as Annette Kuhn writes, "change your clothes and change your sex" (53). Accordingly, transvestite narratives created for mainstream audiences seek to control and naturalize this potential instability. As one who occupies the space in between traditional gender and sexual boundaries, the cross-dresser's body is proof of the need to police violated borders. It is also the site for the solution to this potential disruption. In this way, the sensational story of Erauso's life can tell us much about seventeenth-century audiences. Her narrative fulfills the public's taste for scandal, which seems to have endured over time. According to a tabloid reporter, "When looking for ideas for stories, it's good to look at *fears,* and it's good to look at real *desires*" (cited in Bird 105, emphasis mine).

Implicit in the discovery of the transvestite's identity is the public's fear of the dissolution of naturalized gender and sexual differences, of not knowing the "truth" in terms of binary categories of male and female. The possibility that the transgender can "pass" permanently without ever becoming a "policed" spectacle undercuts the viewer's belief in the stability of sexual identity and threatens the assurance that s/he is not unwittingly attracted to the "wrong" (i.e., same) sex. In other words, unpoliced (undetected) transgenderism creates a crisis in which the transvestite may be "more woman than a woman" or "more man than a man."[28] When the cross-dresser's experience is made public, however, the transvestism is exploited and transformed into cultural capital that manipulates the panic and attraction evoked by the transgendered body.

One of the keys to understanding how the transvestite spectacle functions on different levels is revealed through an examination of diegetic and extradiegetic spectatorship.[29] While historical accounts of Catalina de Erauso's experience attest to her ability to live successfully as a man, the subsequent narratives based on her actual cross-sex passing are characterized by a diegetic passing. However, the extradiegetic reader or viewer remains unconvinced by the disguise, since s/he knows the "truth" about the absent phallus under Erauso's male clothing. In this sense, transvestite spectacles serve to police gender-bending by reaffirming the body as the location of fixed sexual identity. Once the "truth" of sexual difference is established, the transvestite no longer threatens the "natural" order of things. Mainstream audiences can now enjoy the disguise, anticipating the pleasure of watching the diegetic characters' shock when the "truth" is finally revealed.

Judith Butler argues that "there is no necessary relation between drag and subversion, and that drag may well be used in the service of both the denaturalization and reidealization of hyperbolic heterosexual gender norms. At best, it seems, drag is a site of a certain ambivalence" (125). While Butler analyzes the imitative structure of both drag and heterosexual culture and Garber explores the "category crisis" created by gender crossings, Chris Straayer studies the subversion that arises from privileging the temporary moments of identification with diegetic desire in transvestite narratives.[30] In particular, instead of identifying with the resolution, which seeks to negate the destabilizing function of sexual disguise, the spectator may choose to align himself or herself with those characters duped by the disguise and therefore become attracted to the same sex. Consequently, female transvestism provides more than just the reassurance of stabilized sexual difference. The spectator/reader's knowledge that the disguised man is really a woman, when erotically linked with another woman, can also provide erotic titillation for both heterosexual and lesbian viewers; and if the disguise is unconvincing, the possibility of reading the couple in homoerotic terms is practically unavoidable. Of course, in mainstream representations the opportunities for reading alternative desire are temporary since the masculine woman is seldom allowed to survive as such, and in the end is usually tamed, killed, or abandoned. The "girl gets girl" plot is generally not an option for mass audiences.

While the intimate or personal details of Erauso's final years remain a mystery, the only record of the last few decades of her life features an erotic obsession with another woman. Not surprisingly, Erauso loses her love interest to a man. Even though she is allowed to live dressed in male garb, her biological identity as well as her sexuality are policed in the cultural narratives describing her life. As a result, for nearly 400 years the Lieutenant Nun spectacle has reflected those values (whether they be nationalistic, ethnic, racial, political, religious, or erotic) that each spectator looks for in order to reaffirm his/her own identity or beliefs. And yet, despite the attempt to patrol her icon, Catalina de Erauso ultimately embodies the potential to escape essentializing notions of identity since her long-term passing is a reminder of the unstable and performative nature of gender.

CHAPTER ONE

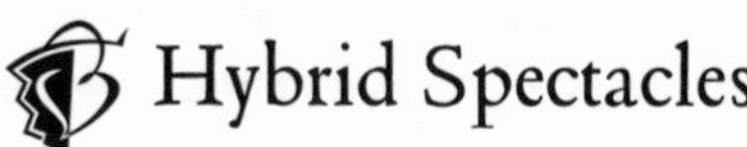

Hybrid Spectacles

Lesbian Desire, Monsters, & Masculine Women in Early Modern Spain

DURING ONE EPISODE of her memoirs, Erauso tells her readers: "She and I were in the front parlor, and I had my head in the folds of her skirt and she was combing my hair while I ran my hand up and down between her legs" (17).[1] This instance of explicit same-sex eroticism is not an isolated case; Erauso frequently expresses romantic interest in various women in the New World that occasionally results in physical caressing but that never leads to the discovery of her anatomical identity. Given the recurrent representations of Erauso's attraction to other women during her lifetime, not only in her autobiography but in a letter, a play, and two news pamphlets, it is significant to note that same-sex desire was defined in multiple ways during the sixteenth and seventeenth centuries in Spain. Although there are fewer documented cases involving woman-to-woman genital contact than there are of male sodomy in early modern Europe, philosophers, lawmakers, and theologians had discussed this transgressive behavior for centuries.[2] Louis Crompton points out that the "Spanish seem to have been preeminent in Renaissance Europe as specialists on the subject of lesbianism and the law" (18). Crompton cites Gregorio López's 1556 revision of *Las Siete Partidas,* which argued that the medieval Spanish law on sodomy applied to women as well as to men.

While many scholars have been working in recent decades to discover and interpret traces of same-sex passion between women in pre-modern societies, agreement over acceptable terminology remains problematic. Some critics argue that "lesbianism" as an identity classification did not exist prior to the nineteenth century. Valerie Traub, for example, prefers "female homoeroticism" when discussing desire between women during the early modern period (156). Likewise, despite her consistent use of the terms "lesbian sexuality" and "lesbian nun" for reasons of convenience, Judith Brown argues that "*lesbian* sexuality did not exist. Neither, for that matter, did *lesbians*" (1986, 17). Since most commonly used concepts, meanings, and connotations have changed over time, other scholars decide not to single out "lesbianism" for erasure from discussion of female desire before the nineteenth century. Emma Donoghue, like Martha Vicinus and Bonnie Zimmerman, defends her use of "lesbian" but notes historical variations nonetheless: "Our foresisters who loved women probably differed in many crucial respects from those of us who love women in the 1990s, but it seems fair to use 'lesbian culture' as an umbrella term for both groups" (7). Similarly, in her discussion of lesbians in the Middle Ages, Jacqueline Murray begins her essay with a review of the terminology debate and an explanation for her stance: "It [the term 'lesbian'] by no means implies consistency over time but rather is used as a convenient term to distinguish those women whose primary relationships, emotional or sexual, appear to be woman-identified" (193).[3] As Harry Vélez-Quiñones summarizes, "It is preposterous to assume that homoerotic affections and behavior can only be given credence, much less critical consideration, if situated within the last hundred years of Western history" (11). It seems that contested terminology is perhaps inevitable, especially given that, even today, we lack any general agreement about what constitutes "lesbian culture." Therefore, in this study I refer to concepts such as "lesbian" and "transgender" in terms of the early modern framework for same-sex desire and gender transgression, which I will explore in this chapter.

And yet despite the controversy in scholarly criticism about whether to use the term "lesbian" when discussing same-sex passion between women in the early modern period, it was used by Pierre Brantôme

(1540–1614) in the late sixteenth century in reference to the growing popularity of "two ladies that be in love one with the other . . . sleeping together in one bed . . . such is the character of the Lesbian women" (128–129), especially in Spain, Italy, Turkey, and France.[4] Describing what were also called *donna con donna,* tribades, and fricatrices, Brantôme concluded that lesbian relations may be less sinful than heterosexual relations outside the confines of matrimony: "Still excuse may be made for maids and widows for loving these frivolous and empty pleasures, preferring to devote themselves to these than to go with men and come to dishonour . . . they do not so much offend God, and are not such great harlots, as if they had to do with the men, maintaining there is a great difference betwixt throwing water in a vessel and merely watering about it and round the rim . . . this alone will make no man cuckold" (133–134).

This relative tolerance of same-sex love between women is presumably based on a male-centered view of female sexuality that assumes that sexually transgressive acts must involve penetration by the phallus or its imitation. Judith Brown argues that even though lesbian sexuality was considered a sin and a crime in early modern Europe, it did not receive the attention given to male homosexuality during the same period since the European view of human sexuality was phallocentric; it was difficult to believe that women could be more attracted to other women than to men (1986, 6). As a result, sexual relations between women have been silenced or minimized in many early modern as well as contemporary commentaries. In the sixteenth century, Gregorio López called female sodomy the "silent sin" (*peccatum mutum*) or "the sin which cannot be named" (Brown 1989, 75). In their study of female transvestism in early modern Europe, Rudolf M. Dekker and Lotte C. van de Pol note that lesbian passion was not taken seriously or was not threatening: "In spite of the prescribed death penalty for tribady, amorous relationships between women, even when these were coupled with physical caresses, were rarely viewed as serious throughout Europe" (57).

On the other hand, Emma Donoghue disagrees with some critics' conclusions about the presumed silence and invisibility of passion between women: "These seventeenth- and eighteenth-century words do not seem to refer only to isolated sexual acts, as is often claimed, but to the emotions, desires, styles, tastes and behavioral tendencies that can make up an identity. . . . A study of this vocabulary suggests that eroticism between women in the seventeenth and eighteenth centuries was neither so silent and invisible as some have assumed, nor as widely tolerated as others have claimed" (3, 7).

There are, in fact, numerous examples of female homoeroticism during the early modern period in literature, theater, legal proceedings, medical treatises, pornographic pictures, songs and anecdotes.[5] Fictional scenes of same-sex attraction between women, even though they most often end with a heterosexual resolution, can be found in works such as Jorge de Montemayor's *La Diana,* Fernando de Rojas's *Celestina,* Ludovico Ariosto's *Orlando Furioso,* Cristóbal de Villalón's *El Crótalon de Cristóforo Gnofoso,* Alvaro Cubillo de Aragón's play *Añasco el de Talavera,* María de Zayas's *Novelas ejemplares y amorosas* and her *Desengaños amorosos,* and the poetry of Sor Violante del Cielo.[6] Whether or not the images of same-sex attraction between women were intended as mere titillation for male readers and spectators, the effect of such images upholds the idea of woman as the object of desire for other women.[7]

Many early modern documents claim that sexual relations between women were much less dangerous than homosexual activity among men. Brantôme comments that "'tis much better for a woman to be masculine and a very Amazon and lewd in this fashion, than for a man to be feminine" (134). When Brantôme appears to associate masculinity in woman with lesbianism, and femininity in men with homosexuality, he assumes that lesbianism may be a sign of virtue, as male characteristics are clearly superior: " 'Tis better far for a woman to be given up to a lustful affection for playing the male, than it is for a man to be womanish; so utterly lacking in all courage and nobility of character. . . . Thus the woman, according to this, which doth counterfeit the man, may well be reputed to be more valorous and courageous than another" (129–130). Even Ambroise Paré in his sixteenth-century study of monsters, argues that it is possible for a female hermaphrodite to transmute into a male but not vice-versa, given that "Nature always moves toward perfection and not the other way around" (42).[8]

This positive image of the manly woman also emerges in certain nongenital flirtation scenes between women. Frequently the concept of desire between women is presented in terms of neoplatonic love and thus serves as spiritual or comical entertainment or both.[9] For example, in María de Zayas's story "Amar sólo por vencer" female homoeroticism is more acceptable than heterosexuality outside the confines of marriage.[10] Only as Estefanía is Esteban free to display his passion for Laurela openly. Moreover, other women in this story join Estefanía in discussing the spiritual advantages of love between women. This neoplatonic expression of same-sex love attempts to define romantic relationships between women as chaste and therefore morally superior to the physically based heterosexual love:

> "Since the soul is the same in male and female, it matters not whether I'm a man or a woman. Souls aren't male or female and true love dwells in the soul, not in the body. One who loves the body only with the body cannot truly say that that is love; it's lust, which brings only repentance after physical satisfaction because that love wasn't in the soul. The body, being mortal, tires of its food, while the soul, being spirit, never tires of its nourishment."
>
> "All right, but for one woman to love another woman is a fruitless love," one of the maids commented.
>
> "No," said Estefania, "it's true love, for loving without reward is the purest kind."
>
> "Well how come men," asked one of Laurela's sisters, "ask for their reward after they've loved for only four short days and if they don't get it, they give up?"
>
> "Because they don't really love," Estefania responded, "if they did love, even unrewarded, they'd never give up. True love is the very substance of the soul and so long as the soul doesn't die, love won't die. Since the soul is immortal, so love will be also. But in loving only with the body, if they don't enjoy the body, they'll soon desist and forget and go seek satisfaction elsewhere. If they do attain their ends, surfeited, they move on to seek more of the same elsewhere."
>
> "Well, if that's the way it is," said another maid, "then nowadays men must all love just with the body and not with the soul." (224)[11]

One central aspect of the defense of love between women is the distancing of female homoeroticism from corporeal lust. The assumption is that lesbian attraction is "amor sin provecho," (fruitless love) and "amar sin premio" (love without reward). Consequently, true (same-sex) love between women does not yield the "provecho" and "premio" associated with phallic-based carnal lust. Regardless of intention, Estefanía's arguments protect lesbian desire from attack since this seemingly "nonphysical" love is exempt from scrutiny based on honor and chastity.

Undoubtedly, the reaction of others is one important indication of the attitude toward female homoeroticism in Zayas's text. When those close to Laurela believe that Estefanía is a woman passionately in love with her, their reaction is jovial, as they find amusement at the idea of lesbian desire:

> For the power of love can also include a woman's love for another woman just as it does a suitor's love for his lady. . . . Estefania's words followed by a deep sigh, made them all laugh at the notion that she had fallen in love with Laurela. . . . Again they all laughed, further convinced that Estefania had fallen in love with Laurela. . . . They all burst out laughing. . . . In spite of the fact that Estefania was always telling her of her love, she and everyone else thought it was simply folly. It amused them and made them laugh whenever they saw her play the exaggerated and courtly role of lover, lamenting Laurela's disdain and weeping from jealousy. They were surprised that a woman could be so much in love with another woman, but it never crossed their minds that things might be other than they seemed. . . . She burst out laughing and her sisters and the other maids joined in. (214–225)[12]

Apparently the idea of passionate love between women was a source of humor and entertainment for the women close to Laurela as well as for the patriarch of the family. Laurela's father entrusts the most intimate aspect of his daughter's care (dressing, undressing, and so forth) to a woman who has openly declared her physical attraction and love for Laurela. Despite this knowledge, Laurela's father finds the situation amusing and is clearly not concerned that this same-sex desire could threaten the family's honor: " 'That's splendid,' don Bernardo responded, 'and we can expect lovely grandchildren from such a chaste love' " (216).[13] The father's joke reflects an underlying sexual code, that honor, chastity, and the control of female sexuality are solely related to issues of reproduction and paternity. According to Valerie Traub, women's desire for other women on the early modern stage, and only when the women were not performing acts that could be construed as phallically imitative, was implausible precisely because it was "non-reproductive" (163).[14]

The association between the manly woman and lesbianism is most explicit in Alvaro Cubillo de Aragón's play, *Añasco el de Talavera.*[15] Cubillo presents the beautiful but rebellious Dionisia, who not only prefers the male gender role but is openly in love with another woman. Nonetheless, Dionisia's love for her cousin Leonor is described in phallocentric terms when the latter argues that lesbian love is "imperfect" because it lacks the reproductive capacity. Dionisia, however, implies that heterosexual love is not as reliable, given that it is motivated by the "premio" of sexual intercourse; while Dionisia loves Leonor without such sexual pretentions: "Only my love is true. Because in the strongest attraction and of the most divine compulsion everyone loves for the reward but I, just to love you" (Act 1).[16] While Dionisia attempts to interpret her romantic interest in her cousin as more sincere than that of men, Leonor confirms the difference between heterosexual and same-sex desire, but implies that there is still a "premio" between women: "Nobody will doubt you, cousin, for the pleasure between two women can hardly be the same [as that between a man and a woman]" (Act 1).[17]

While the protagonist does not need to assume the male disguise to express her feelings of passion for another woman, she is consistently described as a sexy yet masculine femme fatale, embodying both physical beauty and violence. Here we see the recurrent association among the hybrid manly woman, lesbianism, and monstrous bodies. Her character is described by Marcelo: "Not being a woman, she was born a monster of nature" (Act 2).[18] Other witnesses characterize Dionisia as terrible, an animal, cruel, indecent, a lion, arrogant, uncontrollable, a demon, rebellious, and disobedient, as she engages in physical fights and antagonizes others throughout most of the play. Even the *gracioso* (comic fool) Chacón directly calls the audience's attention to the violence of their dramatic roles: "Well, isn't it a bit much that in this entire play the playwright wrote it so that we are always fighting?" (Act 3).[19] Dionisia responds by confirming the popularity of prodigious women who appropriate the male gender role: "Don't be silly! It is so because people today admire women prodigies and their ability to fight or write" (Act 3).[20]

Regardless of Dionisia's uncontrollable nature, one can only imagine the erotic appearance of her costume and actions as she enters the stage: "Woman with a hat, sword-fighting with Chacón" (Act 1).[21] The combination of beauty and strength lures the other men in the play to fall in love with Dionisia, some without having seen her. Diego comments: "Dionisia is quite uncontrollable," to which the Count responds: "Yes, but with extreme beauty and that new combination of beauty and courage is attractive for many souls" (Act 2).[22] Although Dionisia is driven to violence by her jealousy of Leonor and Juan, at the end of the play she displays the appropriate submission and is willing to control her lesbian desire by marrying Juan and instructing Leonor to marry Diego.

Despite her fervent insistence that, in general, theatrical cross-dressing had no homoerotic motivation, Melveena McKendrick does note that Cubillo's lesbian play takes "the concept of the *mujer varonil* [manly woman] to its logical conclusion" (314). As Gail Bradbury concludes: "It is worth remembering, however, that even when she [the female transvestite] first appeared on stage, in sixteenth-century Italy, she was associated, jokingly but openly, with the idea of feminine homosexuality" (577). Based on their studies of female transvestism in early modern Europe, Dekker and van de Pol also argue that cross-dressing is a natural consequence of lesbian desire (58). Donoghue likewise cites numerous cases in seventeenth-century Europe that hint at a connection between cross-dressing and same-sex attraction: "And even if we leave aside the question of intention, we can find evidence that others saw a link between lesbian culture and cross-dressing in a variety of seventeenth- and eighteenth-century texts" (90). Although Donoghue disagrees with Dekker and van de Pol's view that women needed to feel like men in order to love women, she concludes that cross-dressing made lesbian love easier to express in public (61). Like the autobiography of Erauso, the memoirs of female transvestites in the military almost always included flirtation with or courtship of women.[23] In some cases, such as that of the women warriors among the Tupinamba Indians in Brazil during the sixteenth century, the cross-dressed soldiers were married to other women (Perry 1987b, 92).

In his critical response to Carmen Bravo-Villasante's study on female transvestism in the comedia, B. B. Ashcom insists that "the lesbian motif is implicit in most of the plots involving masculine women" (59). Although McKendrick confirms the seventeenth-century public's probable association of lesbian desire and the cross-dressed Erauso ("the object of rumors, suspicions and jokes about her sexual tastes and life" [214]), she argues that the female homoerotic theme was not treated more graphically in Pérez de Montalbán's play based on Erauso's life because the playwright feared ecclesiastical censorship. Moreover, despite the fact that some critics have stripped the female transvestite on the Golden Age stage of any possible lesbian overtones ("it is not prompted by homosexual impulses" [McKendrick 143]), the censors of the period considered the effect of this device on the audience to be primarily erotic. The possibility that this sexual enticement might also be applicable to the female viewer is not usually accepted by early modern or contemporary critics. McKendrick argues that "for the women theatre-goers the *mujer varonil* provided the pleasure of vicarious freedom and adventure" but for the male audience the woman disguised as a man was "blatantly sexual" (320–321). McKendrick does acknowledge, nonetheless, that art may have influenced reality and that some manly women may have taken their cue from the actresses on stage: "It is not impossible that the theatre inspired some real-life *mujeres varoniles* to action or at least suggested to them the form that action might take" (43). In light of the potential influence of female transvestism on women and the erotic nature of the disguise, one should consider the possible erotic effect of women disguised as men for both male and female audiences, especially when reviewing legislation of same-sex desire between women.

According to early modern legal records, the apparent tolerance of lesbian relations seems to be contingent upon the absence of any instrument used as a substitute penis.[24] Antonio Gómez wrote of two nuns who were accused and eventually burned at the stake for sexual relations using a prosthetic phallus, but if lesbian relations did not include an instrument, a more lenient punishment would be considered (Crompton 19).[25] As Jacqueline Murray concludes: "In the absence of either a penis or a substitute, male writers minimized the seriousness of the sin" (199).

The interpretation of the lesbian sexual activity of the seventeenth-century abbess Benedetta Carlini, as well as the consequent sentence of life in prison, clearly demonstrate the lack of tolerance for genital contact between women in the convent: "For two continuous years, . . . after disrobing and going to bed waiting for her companion . . . to disrobe also, she would force her into the bed and kissing her as if she were a man she would stir on top of her so much that both of them corrupted themselves" (quoted in Brown 1986, 162–163).

This concern for same-sex affection among nuns had been an issue in theological works for centuries. St. Augustine warned his sister against similar practices before she took holy vows: "The love which you bear one another ought not to be carnal, but spiritual: for those things which are practiced by immodest women, even with other females, in shameful jesting and playing, ought not to be done" (quoted in Boswell 158). Frequently referred to as "particular friendships" or "particular love," these homoaffective relationships appear as one of the convent sins that must be avoided. Donatus Besançon, in his seventh-century *Regula ad Virginea,* specifies how the nuns could elude the dangerous "particular friendships": "That none take the hand of another or call one another 'little girl.' It is forbidden lest any take the hand of another for delight or stand or walk around or sit together. She who does so, will be improved with twelve blows. And any who is called 'little girl' or who call one another 'little girl,' forty blows if they so transgress" (quoted in Murray 196). These verbal displays of affection among the nuns were also admonished by St. Teresa in chapter 7 of her *Camino de perfección* (The Way of Perfection): "This will be a much truer kind of friendship than one which uses every possible loving expression (such as are not used, and must not be used in this house): 'My life!' 'My love!' 'My darling!' and suchlike things, one or another of which people are always saying. Let such endearing words be kept for your Spouse" (Peers 78–79).[26] Erasmus likewise hints at lesbianism in the convent in his colloquy titled "The Girl with No Interest in Marriage": "Not everything is virginal among these virgins . . . Because there are more who copy Sappho's behavior than share her talent" (quoted in Raymond 1986, 95). Interestingly, even Brantôme in the late sixteenth century suggests that seclusion or women-only communities (convents and prisons, for example) fosters lesbian behavior: "And wherever the women are kept secluded, and have not their entire liberty, this practice doth greatly prevail" (130).

Historical cases of female husbands indicate that the masculine disguise facilitated homoerotic relations between women. The case of Elena de Céspedes (1545?–1588), for example, not only confirms the lack of tolerance for sexual acts interpreted as penetrative but also how both sex and gender were culturally constructed. According to sixteenth-century documents, Céspedes discovered when she was seventeen years old that she had a penis and, as a result, decided to have an affair with the wife of a merchant.[27] Shortly after, she began to dress as a man and later became a soldier. Years later, living as "Eleno" she fell in love with another woman and made plans to get married. While applying for the marriage license, she was assumed to be a eunuch due to her lack of facial hair. To prove she had a penis, she submitted to a frontal examination of her body, which she passed, and was granted the marriage license. When the marriage was later challenged by a former lover, Céspedes again passed two more exams, allegedly by applying an ointment that made her vagina close up. Due to continued gossip, Céspedes was arrested on charges of impersonating a man and soiling the holy sacrament of marriage. During the trial, Céspedes admitted to being a hermaphrodite; during another examination performed by the same officials who earlier found a penis but no vagina, they now discovered the opposite: she no longer had a penis but instead possessed a vagina. Given the discrepancy between examinations, it was determined that Céspedes was involved in demonic activities and was consequently punished by the Inquisition, receiving two hundred lashes and a ten-year sentence to a public hospital. In the end, unable to explain the sexual ambiguities of the case, the courts attributed the unacceptable mutations to magic and the devil.[28] These sixteenth-century documents reveal the flexible and unstable nature of sex assignment as well as the differing attitudes toward homoerotic flirtation that does not involve genital contact.

The great disparity between the apparent tolerance for lesbian desire, cross-dressing, and masculine women in numerous historical and fictional representations and the monsterization of the same themes in other works may help explain the variety of individual responses to Erauso's transgenderism as well as her overall success in soliciting support from the patriarchal order. Despite the tolerance for her transgender identity, her case was highly controlled by the same religious and legal system that often persecuted women for such behavior. However, because there were no signs of penetration or genital contact, neither the church nor the state apparently considered her rumored lesbian activity a threat. Moreover, the fact that she was presented and interpreted as a monstrous spectacle for the curious gaze allayed much fear of a possible epidemic of other "warrior nuns" inspired by Erauso's incredible adventure. The comic scenes of homoerotic flirtation, although they may also provide some women with alternative lessons of female sexuality, seek to trivialize the concept and serve to police the border crossing of transgenderism and nonheterosexuality. Likewise, the link between forbidden practices and that which is monstrous serves to enforce normalized behavior, since the monster "embodies those sexual practices that must not be committed, or that may only be committed through the body of the monster" (Cohen 14).

Hybrid Monsters in Early Modern Spain

Terms such as "shocking," "amazing," "prodigious," "monstrous," "excessive," "marvelous," and "outlandish" are frequently evoked when describing the baroque aesthetic.[29] In a period noted for its fascination and obsession with hybrids and other anomalous "curiosities," it is not surprising that Catalina de Erauso's life was originally interpreted and marketed in terms of a monstrous hybrid spectacle.[30] In Pérez de Montalbán's 1626 play, for example, due to the public's voyeuristic pleasure in watching Erauso, she asks in frustration: "Am I by chance some *monster* never before seen?" (Act 3, scene 3, emphasis mine). Likewise, some critics have continued to describe Erauso as a "monstrous mixture of both sexes" or even a "sex-less monster . . . neither man nor woman" (Morales-Alvarez 18, 34). Although Catalina de Erauso never took her final vows to become a nun, the popular nickname given to her emphasizes the drastic change from the enclosed life in the convent to the open spaces of her travels in the New World. The image of a Lieutenant Nun immediately implies the hybridity of opposite categories, the improbable union of male and female, convent and battlefield.

Despite the absence of any comments related to possible hermaphroditism in Erauso's case, the early modern period did make a connection between the "abnormal" physical condition and same-sex desire, which was attributed to Erauso. The discussion of hermaphrodites and androgynies in Ambroise Paré's 1579 teratology *Monsters and Prodigies* concludes with an explanation of the "monstrous" consequences of hermaphroditism. Paré describes how an enlarged genital protrusion (nimph) in female hermaphrodites can be used in sexual activity with other women: "And there are women who, by using these protrusions (nimphes), corrupt one another. This is as true as it is monstrous and difficult to believe" (40).[31]

The monstrous body has been described in terms of hybridity, a mixed category that escapes classification built on binary opposition: "disturbing hybrids whose externally incoherent bodies resist attempts to include them in any systematic structuration" (Cohen 6). Monsters not only combine incongruent elements (human and animal, male and female, for example) but are also seen as different, both physically and socially, from their spectators (Friedman 1981, 1). In this way, the transgressive and threatening Other of the medieval and early modern periods becomes a monster or a freak, an "embodiment of difference, a breaker of category, and a resistant Other" (Cohen x).[32] Like the observers of the evasive monster body, critics have been trying to categorize Catalina de Erauso for centuries. For many she is a heroic soldier, for others she is either a criminal, an example of Basque or Spanish national pride, a eunuch, an exemplary virgin, a transgressive lesbian, or a combination of all these categories. Despite efforts to assign one fixed label to Erauso, her celebrity sign is unstable precisely because the hybrid nature of her identity as the Lieutenant Nun allows for multiple and contradictory readings. As Stephanie Merrim explains, the representation of Erauso as "monstrous" results in the creation of a "category-conflating textual space" that caters to the popular taste for scandal (1999, 25).

The etymology of the term "monster" (from the ancient Greek root of the word *teras,* which implies both aberration and adoration, as well as from the Latin *monstrum* "to show") indicates the ambivalent and visual nature of the monstrous spectacle. As Lawrence D. Kritzman notes, the deviance from the normative that monsters represent is portrayed as a visual effect—"rarity attributed to the object of the gaze" (173).[33] The visual impact of monster-gazing is manifested through a mixture of fear and pleasure, the repulsion and attraction that explain the cultural fascination with monsters and prodigies (Cohen 17). Accordingly, there are countless references to monsters, prodigies, and hybrid forms in general during the early modern period.[34] In an anonymous tract published in London in 1620 and titled *Hic mulier: or, The man-woman,* the masculine woman is repeatedly described as monstrous because of her clothed and unclothed body: " 'Tis of you I intreat, and of your monstrous deformitie; you that have made your bodies like . . . halfe beast, halfe monster: . . . you have taken the monstrousnesse of your deformitie in apparell" (n.p.). Katharine Park and Lorraine Daston argue that, by far, the most frequent theme in the prodigious events of the sixteenth- and seventeenth-century broadsides was monsters (28). Daston and Park also establish horror, pleasure, and repugnance as the three interpretations and associated emotions provoked by monster narratives (1998, 173–177). In seventeenth-century Spain the accounts of monsters were illustrated more frequently than any other class of news pamphlet while "an essential feature of these relations is that they outdo each other in *admiratio* and, almost by definition, seek to present their subjects as unexampled" (Ettinghausen 1993, 127). Figure 1, for instance, is one example of an illustrated *relación* of a monstrous birth in Spain published around the same time that news of the "Monja Alférez" was also circulated. The illustration and narration of the scale-covered boy provokes the shock that these sensationalist stories of "unnatural" hybridity sought to elicit in the curious readers.

In fact, most descriptions of monstrous bodies emphasize the shocking effect on the spectator and the impulse to share the amazing experience with others. In 1616 Fortunii Liceti claimed that "monsters are thus named . . . because they are such that their new and incredible appearance stirs admiration and surprise in the beholders, and startles them so much that everyone wants to show them to others" (quoted in Huet 6). Likewise, in a news item dated October 24, 1654, of his *Avisos,* Barrionuevo's description of a monster discovered in Cerdania emphasizes the repulsive yet intriguing hybrid nature of the monster for both the reader as well as the king, who would soon see the spectacle in person: "They have caught a monster with goat's feet, human face and arms, with multiple heads and faces, and although it has various eyes and mouths, it only eats through one. They say that it will soon be presented before the king" (262).[35] Not surprisingly, illustrations of this monster were circulating immediately after its discovery. Four days after his first communication regarding the spectacle, Barrionuevo writes: "The portrait of the monster is already in circulation, although not yet published. I have seen it" (262).[36] According to Stephanie Merrim, Catalina de Erauso was able to go from anomaly to cultural icon precisely because of the "monstrous" aesthetic: "She would also remain a cross-dresser—an oddity, a monster, a prodigy.

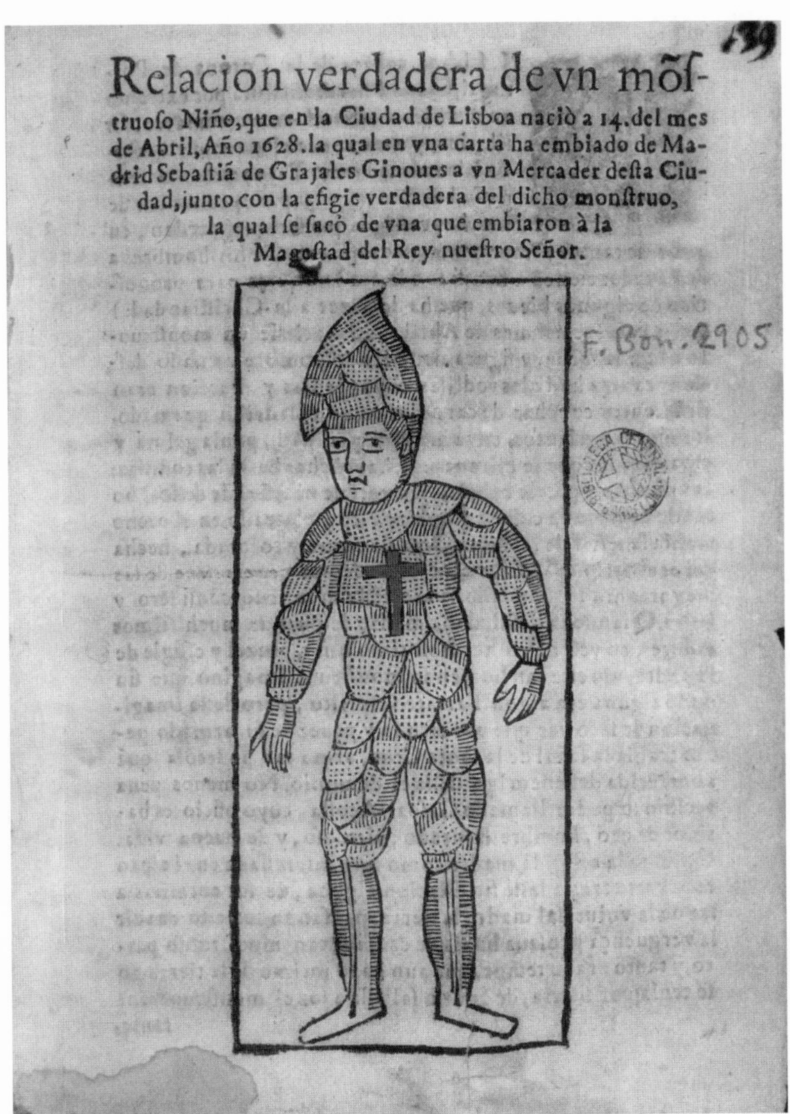

Relacion verdadera de vn mõſ-
truoſo Niño,que en la Ciudad de Lisboa naciò a 14.del mes
de Abril,Año 1628.la qual en vna carta ha embiado de Madrid Sebaſtiã de Grajales Ginoues a vn Mercader deſta Ciudad,junto con la efigie verdadera del dicho monſtruo,
la qual ſe ſacò de vna que embiaron à la
Mageſtad del Rey nueſtro Señor.

FIGURE 1. Illustrated *relación* of "monstrous" scale-covered boy (see Appendix for translation). Barcelona, 1628. Courtesy of Biblioteca de Catalunya, Barcelona.

This double-pronged solution that kept her double edge alive, a fabulous finessing of regulation, reengages with the aesthetic of the bizarre and creatively exploits border-crossing to the gain of all involved" (1999, 26).

Manly Women as Prenatal Transmutations

The scientific rationale for the existence of hybrid and monstrous bodies during the early modern period highlights the unnatural birth of these aberrations.[37] Sebastián de Covarrubias's seventeenth-century definition of the monster, for example, emphasizes its unnatural and hybrid birth: "Monster is any birth against the norm and natural order, like the birth of a man with two heads, four arms, and four legs" (812).[38] Although there are no indications in existing historical documents that Catalina de Erauso was born with any physical irregularities, early modern medical theory based on classical Aristotelian and Galenian concepts attributes masculine physical appearance and behavior in women to an unnatural prenatal transmutation. Juan Huarte de San Juan's medical analysis in *Examen de ingenios para las ciencias* (1575), for example, documents the cultural construction of gender and sexuality as well as the mutability of one's physiological sex.[39] Huarte offers a medical explanation for individuals, like Erauso, whose behavior and appearance do not correspond to their biologically assigned sex. According to Huarte, masculine women, feminine men, and homosexuals were originally destined to be born of the opposite sex, but the temperature of the bodily "humors" changed during gestation and caused the genitals to "transmute" before birth:

> Many times Nature has made a female and, having been in the mother's womb for one or two months, for some reason her genitals are overcome with heat and they come out and a male is created. To whom this transmutation occurs in the mother's womb, it is clearly recognizable later by certain movements he has that are indecent for men: woman-like, effeminate, soft and mild voice; and such men are inclined to behave like a woman and they frequently fall prey to the sin of sodomy. On the other hand, often Nature has made a male with his genitals on the outside, and with an onset of coldness, they are transformed to the inside and a female is created. She is recognized after

birth by having a masculine nature, in her speech as well as in all her movements and behavior. (608–609)[40]

Huarte's essentialist theory, then, concludes that biology determines gender behavior (speech, movements, and actions), transgressive sexual behavior, and anatomical sex assignment. Moreover, the author also specifies three different levels of the bodily "fluids" that determine physiological and behavioral characteristics. Although all women are composed of cold and moist liquids, not all have the same level of these humors. For women, these levels are assessed by observing different categories such as intellectual capacity, habits and behavior, voice tenor, body fat and musculature, coloring, facial hair, and physical beauty or ugliness (613–617). According to Huarte's classifications, if a woman has the lowest level of coldness and humidity, she is more intelligent, but such a woman is also more disagreeable and has an aggressive and conflictive personality (614–616). Likewise, since a strong, deep voice is common to the hot, dry nature of men, a woman with a "masculine" voice also has the lowest level of coldness and humidity, as do women with dark hair and complexion (616–617). Not surprisingly, women who have much facial hair show signs of low levels of coldness and moisture and, according to Huarte, are rarely beautiful (617). Women with more body fat were thought to possess high levels of coldness and humidity but strong and muscular women with little body fat possess low levels of the "feminine fluids" (616–617).

If we apply Huarte's theories to what has been written about Catalina de Erauso by those who came in contact with her during the seventeenth century, we would conclude that she had low levels of coldness and humidity in areas related to both behavior and appearance. According to the seventeenth-century broadsides, letters, and her autobiography, she possessed a disposition for violence and fighting as well as for same-sex attraction. Erauso's physical appearance was likewise described by eyewitnesses as masculine in comparison to that of other women: "Tall and powerfully built, and with a masculine appearance. . . . Her face is not ugly but not pretty either. . . . Her hair is black and short like a man's" (Pedro de la Valle, 1626); "She was of strong build, somewhat stout, swarthy in complexion, with a few hairs on her chin" (Nicolas de la Rentería, 1645).[41]

Throughout the centuries, Erauso has been described as a eunuch, a pseudo-hermaphrodite, and a masculine woman, who could be compared to the *marimacho* described by Covarrubias: "We say mannish woman for the woman who has the mannerisms of a man" (790).[42] Pedro de la Valle, in a letter written in 1626, mentions twice that Erauso was assumed to be a *capón* (eunuch), given the lack of beard. According to Covarrubias, some eunuchs are born that way due to excessive coldness and lack of heat, while others are castrated; "there are others who, without necessity, castrate their children to sell them or to take advantage of them by making them feminine" (295).[43] He goes on to describe a different type of eunuch, nonetheless, who manifests positive attributes such as valor and piety: "There are castrated men who are valiant and eminent in arms as well as in letters, and who are prudent and great servants of God" (294).[44] Ambroise Paré, on the other hand, described eunuchs as those who have "degenerated into a womanish nature, by deficiency of heate," as opposed to mere "manly woemen, which their manly voyce and chinne covered with a little hairinesse doe argue" (quoted in Jones and Stallybrass 83).[45]

In the seventeenth century, Covarrubias used the terms "androgyne" and "hermaphrodite" interchangeably to refer to those who possess both sex characteristics of male and female (118, 530–531).[46] Although Nicolás León described Erauso as a "pseudo-hypospadic hermaphrodite" at the beginning of the twentieth century, there is no evidence from seventeenth-century documents that she was believed to possess primary sexual characteristics of both sexes.[47] In fact, the matrons who examined her found no indication of any physical irregularities (enlarged clitoris, for example) in their analysis. Other observers, nonetheless, described Erauso's secondary sexual traits in terms of maleness. According to Pedro de la Valle, Erauso admitted to having used an *emplasto* (poultice) obtained from an Italian to flatten her chest: "She has no more breasts than a girl. She told me that she had used some sort of remedy to make them disappear. I believe it was a poultice given her by an Italian—it hurt a great deal, but the effect was very much to her liking" (translation from Stepto and Stepto xxxiv).[48] By using a poultice, or mixture spread on a cloth, Erauso rebelled at the "contours that cultural expectations imposed on her body and self as female, and scorning the long hair and developing breasts that so often symbolized the sexuality and availability of unmarried girls in this period" (Perry 1999, 397). This invasive technique testifies to Erauso's intention to live permanently as a man, unlike the temporary male impersonator who sooner or later returns to female garb. Since the female body, clothed or unclothed, is most visibly identified through the breasts, Erauso's conscious decision to permanently eliminate this cultural sign of femininity complicates how she may be read once her anatomical sex is discovered. In this way, using a poultice, instead of merely binding her breasts, further distinguishes Erauso from the popular image of the *mujer vestida de hombre* (woman dressed as a man). In fact, recent studies on female-to-male transsexuals likewise attest to the importance of breast removal for these individuals:

> Of all the medical procedures which participants employed in their achievement of manhood, breast removal seemed to have been the most unequivocally satisfying. . . . The significance of breasts as markers of gender should not be underestimated. When asked, most people say that genitalia are the ultimate arbiters of both sex and gender. However, in the routine activities which fill everyday lives there are few times or places where genitals must unavoidably be displayed. In the normal course of events, sex characteristics are assumed to match the genders displayed by normally clothed human beings. Thus what was of paramount importance to these individuals who were striving to become credible men was to look and act the part. (Devor 400)

Kathryn Schwarz argues that during the Renaissance the breast is "invoked to confine women to specific erotic, domestic, iconographic, and maternal roles" (150). Therefore, when the Amazons, according to myth, deliberately participate in the self-mutilation of breast removal, "they destabilize the categoric processes of reading through the breast" in a process similar to Erauso's attempt to erase the restrictions inherent in possessing breasts (Schwarz 148).

Warrior Women in the Early Modern Period

While anatomical transmutations were frequently used to justify the unnatural aberration of masculine women, another form of cultural hybridity associated with the *mujer varonil* is female transvestism. The male impersonation theme has a long tradition in western culture dating back to classical Greek and Roman mythology and continuing in the Middle Ages with Christian female saints who cross-dressed for pious reasons.[49] One of the most famous of this group of heroic and religious transvestites is Joan of Arc, who undoubtedly served as an inspiration for various heroines on the Golden Age stage, while Virgil's Camilla (*Aeneid* VII and XI) was also one of the main precursors to the many bellicose women, such as Ariosto's Marfisa, found in the epic-romance genre.[50]

Similarly, Catalina de Erauso is not alone in her preference for the male gender role, given the numerous examples in early modern history of women who donned men's garb for a variety of purposes, including both heterosexual and same-sex romantic motives, patriotism, economic necessity, safety while traveling, criminality, desire for freedom and adventure, and so forth.[51] Despite the apparent shock generated by her case, Erauso's military inclination was not unique during the early modern period. Julie Wheelwright, Simon Shepherd, Diane Dugaw, Jo Stanley, Rudolf M. Dekker and Lotte C. van de Pol, and Emma Donoghue are just a few of the recent scholars who document the lives of other warrior women, including soldiers, sailors, and pirates in historical as well as fictional sources. While Wheelwright studies historical cases of sexual disguise, Dugaw examines, in particular, the figure of the transvestite female warrior and its popularity in ballads of the early modern Anglo-American tradition. Unlike Erauso, most of the heroines in these ballads return to female garb and marry the man for whom they left home to search in the first place (Dugaw 139). The popular Spanish ballad titled "La Doncella Guerrera" (The Military Maid), for example, portrays a female warrior who lived disguised as a man for two years in the military and eventually returned to the traditional female gender role after proving to herself and to others that she was capable of fulfilling the masculine bellicose activities expected of the son that her father never had (Menéndez Pidal 203–206).[52] Even though the ballad maintains the traditional heterosexual end, like other medieval and early modern narratives, it develops a subplot that demonstrates one of the consequences of the male disguise, while it also explores the relationship between gender and sex. When the prince is unexpectedly attracted to the young "male" warrior, he immediately suspects that the object of his sexual desire must be a female disguised as a man. In order to discover the truth, his mother designs a series of "gender tests" to prove without a doubt that the prince is not experiencing homosexual impulses and that his love interest must surely fall into the trap of behaving according to the female gender role. The first three tests are based on stereotypical gender behavior, assuming an essentialized relationship between anatomy and social roles. Prepared for her performance, the young woman easily selects the appropriate responses associated with the male gender. Using the name Don Martín, she chooses arms over elegant dress and a staff over flowers; when some rings are thrown toward her lap, she closes her knees as a man was expected to do. Once she passes all three exams, the only way to prove her biological sex is by inviting her to swim unclothed. Seeing no way to maintain her disguise, she decides to reveal her "shocking" identity and allow the prince to pursue her.

The romantic complication resulting from sexual disguise also occurs when other women are attracted to the "handsome young man." In addition to this recurrent theme in the theater of the Golden Age, examples abound in prose and epic narratives: Florinda and Mirnalta in *Platir,* Bradamante and Flordespina in *Orlando Furioso,* Minerva and Duante in *Cristalián de España,* Selvagia and Ismenia, Felismena and Celia in *La Diana,* Lope de Vega's *Las fortunas de Diana,* Cristóbal de Villalón's *El Crótalon de Cristóforo Gnofoso,* and so forth.[53] Although these temporary confusions are quickly resolved in most narratives, in two early modern ballads recorded by Pedro Navarro the women marry, maintain the deceit, and, after undergoing a series of gender/sex tests to satisfy public suspicion, one of the women miraculously acquires the requisite phallus (Marco 283).[54]

Unlike the virtuous transvestite of the "Doncella Guerrera" tradition, other cross-dressed heroines in Spanish ballads featuring female soldiers or bandits (such as Doña Victoria de Acevedo, Doña Josefa Ramírez, and Espinela) are killers who eventually repent or die.[55] Espinela, for example, describes her violent life dressed as a man and how she revealed her true identity before her execution for having committed numerous murders and robberies. The final verses of the ballad, which are narrated after the death of Espinela, summarize the didactic intention of the retelling of the protagonist's story: "Women be forewarned, for those who follow in these evil steps, this is the end that awaits them" (quoted in Durán 367).[56]

Other cases of women in Spain and in the New World who fought or dressed as men, either temporarily or permanently, are found in a variety of "historical" sources and are usually lauded for their bravery. Spanish women such as Inés Suárez and María de Estrada are described in chronicle narratives as valiant and courageous soldiers during the Conquest. Typical of the association between the New World chronicles and the epic or chivalric genres, Mariño de Lobera compared Inés Suárez's military activity to that of famous knights: "Unsheathing her sword, she kills them all with such manly spirit as if she were a Roldan or a Ruy Díaz" (quoted in Pumar Martínez 82).[57] Likewise, Bernal Díaz del Castillo described María de Estrada's military abilities as superior to those of any male soldier: "fighting valiantly with such fury and spirit that she exceeded the strength of any man, however forceful and courageous he may be, and even scared our own soldiers" (quoted in Pumar Martínez 84).[58] Similar to the way in which these military women served as examples of the patriotic fervor manipulated to justify Conquest activities, this nationalistic sentiment was clearly exploited in other versions of female soldiers fighting for Spain's empire in Europe. News items published in Toledo in 1538 describe how the transvestite soldier Juliana de los Cobos was rewarded by the king of Spain for her military service, not unlike reports of Erauso's successful solicitation of financial support from the Crown: "She went to the battlefields of Italy, where she served dressed as a male soldier, and at times on horse, . . . without being recognized as a woman. She went to Barcelona, where, at the time, the Emperor was visiting, to ask for compensation for having served in battle. He awarded her twelve thousand *maravedís* each year for the rest of her life" (quoted in Sánchez Cantón 1948, 106).[59] In fact, Erauso has been cited as the likely inspiration for the colonial chronicle of the "Warrior Maidens" Eustaquia de Souza and Ana de Urinza, "valorous young maidens who dressed and lived as bellicose *caballeros* in the mid-1600s" in Potosí (Herrmann 320). Like many of the narratives based on the Lieutenant Nun's adventures, the story of the "Warrior Maidens" (created by the *criollo* chronicler Bartolomé Arzáns y Orsúa) demonstrates how "cultural, economic, racial, sexual, institutional ambivalence permeates the historical mandate of this New World chronicler" (Herrmann 321).

Given the popularity and frequency of the *mujer guerrera* theme in historical and literary sources during the early modern period, it is not surprising that the topic appears in María de Zayas's story "El juez de su causa," published in the 1637 *Novelas amorosas y ejemplares.* Like Erauso, Zayas's protagonist, Estela, proves her valor and courage on the battlefield as she earns the rank of captain and later a promotion to viceroy of Valencia. In fact, Lourdes Jiménez suggests that the real-life case of Catalina de Erauso may have had a possible influence on Zayas when she drafted "El juez de su causa": "Zayas seems to recreate the most celebrated qualities and virtues of the Monja Alférez in Estela, the perfect example of the manly woman" (120). Alicia Yllera notes that the readers would have made the connection between Estela and Erauso, which had the effect of making Zayas's story more believable (41).[60]

Regardless of whether the cross-dressed women are depicted as murderesses or heroines, the male disguise provides many advantages and almost always empowers the women in men's clothing. In the autobiography of the soldier Diego Duque de Estrada, "Memorias de D. Diego Duque de Estrada" (*Memoirs of Diego Duque de Estrada*), the narrator-protagonist recounts how his lover would travel in male garb for safety but then became so attached to the disguise that she chose to continue living dressed as a man for extended periods (476). Likewise, some actresses, such as Bárbara Coronel, who were known for their cross-dressing roles on the stage, also decided to continue the fashion on the street (McKendrick 41).[61] In fact, Coronel's masculine characteristics were believed to facilitate her theatrical success for roles requiring the male disguise. Casiano Pellicer describes her as a "woman who was almost a man, the Amazon of the actresses of her time. Having the misfortune of belonging to the weaker sex, she usually wore male garb, while almost always riding a horse, which she could control like the most skilled horseman. Her fierce nature, so to speak, greatly helped her to perform certain roles onstage to the positive reception of the audience" (quoted in Díaz de Escovar 218).[62] As Mary Daniels notes, Coronel "became an almost freakish antimodel for womankind" (116–117).

Female Cross-Dressing on the Early Modern Stage

The popularity of the *mujer varonil* motif in Golden Age Spanish theater has been well documented. Despite legal and religious opposition, the device of the *mujer vestida de hombre* was an enormously successful feature on the sixteenth- and seventeenth-century stage in Spain.[63] Lope de Vega employed this theatrical device in 113 plays and confirmed his preference for this crowd-pleaser in his *Arte nuevo de hacer comedias:* "The male disguise is usually very entertaining" (190).[64] Despite the crucial difference between the heterosexual plot resolutions of these early modern plays and the markedly nontraditional ending of Erauso's life, the image of a cross-dressed "warrior nun" proved to be highly marketable due to the overwhelming interest in viewing women disguised as men in popular theatrical representations.

An examination of the moralists' rhetoric of the early modern period points to the central reason why the cross-dressed woman was such a successful device on stage: the display of female body parts, particularly legs, which are usually hidden beneath long skirts, was erotic. Accordingly, critics of popular theater evoked terms such as "repugnant," "lustful," "detestable," "diabolic," "lewd," "perverse," "indecent," "disgusting," "dishonest," and "provocative" to describe the "monstrous" nature of the cross-dressed woman on stage in Spain during the sixteenth and seventeenth centuries.[65]

Several justifications were stated in a 1598 petition sent to Philip II requesting permission for women to appear on stage dressed as men: cross-dressing was acceptable in moderation, it was a necessary device for certain plot resolutions, it fit within the exemplary tradition of holy saints who dressed as men, the garments could be modified so as not to be too provocative or revealing (they would be longer and less decorative), and cross-dressed actresses would be married (and therefore monitored) to a member of the theatrical company (Cotarelo y Mori 1904, 424). A commentary to this petition, written by Fray José de Jesús María in 1600, clearly exposes many of the church's concerns regarding the negative effects of this "sinful" exhibitionism (as opposed to saintly covering-up) on innocent spectators:

> Something so detestable and prohibited by divine and human laws, such as that of a woman dressed in men's clothes. If a woman dressed in feminine clothes on stage causes such danger for the chastity of those who *look at her,* then what could we expect if she wears men's clothes on stage, given that this practice is lascivious and provoking enough

to incite the hearts in mortal concupiscence? . . . And if in the ecclesiastical histories one reads of some women who donned men's garb, *it was not so that they would be seen,* but to be *covered;* not to go on stage to provoke sin, but *to hide* themselves. . . . the Christian virgins who wore men's clothing were *fleeing* from the thieves of their purity and from the destruction of their virginity. (quoted in Cotarelo y Mori 1904, 381, emphasis mine)[66]

This distinction between evil transvestism (used as a heterosexual spectacle) and holy cross-dressing (employed to preserve chastity) undoubtedly influenced the official religious sanction of Erauso's decision to live dressed in men's clothing. Her "saintly" motivations could be proved by her success in maintaining her virginity.

Regardless of actual personal, political, or economic factors that influence a woman's decision to don male garb, in cultural representations these images are specularized and specific articles of clothing and body parts are highlighted as dangerously provocative. The criticisms and regulations regarding women dressed as men on the stage specify particular garments and the different parts of women's legs that become eroticized and therefore should not be exposed: "Women must appear onstage only in garments that are decent for women, and they may not appear in an underskirt alone, but must at least wear clothing, such as an outer-skirt over it, and they may not appear in men's clothing"; "when women dress as men, their dress must cover their knees"; and "women cannot dress as men and their skirts must reach their feet."[67] Despite these attempts to eliminate revealing clothing and male impersonation from the stage, the theatrical device continued throughout the seventeenth century.[68] In Pérez de Montalbán's 1626 play *La Monja Alférez,* for example, when Guzmán (Erauso) first appears on stage in the second act, the playwright intends to use the cross-dressed actress as a dramatic visual spectacle, given the special instructions for Guzmán's specific accessories: "Guzmán with a penache in his hat with white and green feathers" (Act 2, scene 2).[69] Again in scene 7 the directions call for Guzmán to appear "with a penache in his hat,"[70] and later in the third act Guzmán enters wearing boots (Act 3, scene 6). The suggestive nature of boots and feathered hats has endured as a provocative sign of sexualizing the cross-dressed woman. Jo Stanley, for example, notes men's interest in viewing the legs of women pirates: "Western men have long fetishised fragments of women's bodies such as legs or breasts. The nude leg hints that eighteenth- and nineteenth-century men saw women pirates as having an animal sexual availability" (46). Likewise, the fetishized accessories are equally effective in twentieth-century film versions of historical heroines in male garb. Actresses such as Greta Garbo in *Queen Christina* (1933) and María Félix in *La Monja Alférez* (1944), with their tall boots and feathered hats, seem to embody the sexualized male impersonator that was so popular during the early modern period.

The erotic appeal of male impersonation is also documented in "real-life" cases offstage. An episode in the seventeenth-century autobiography of Diego Duque de Estrada reveals the visual pleasure experienced by the male voyeur upon seeing his love interest dressed in masculine garb as he hints at her own pleasure in performing the male gender role. The narrator's description of Francisca's body in men's clothing is clearly sexual, as he alludes to the sensuality of the male disguise:

> [Francisca] wanted to see me practice sword-fighting and after watching she asked me to teach her and to show her how to dance in men's clothing, which I gladly accepted. . . . She dressed in men's garb and she truly looked like a man, since she was just the right height, broad-shouldered, slim-waisted, small-footed, and with a well-proportioned leg, unlike most women; she also had a wide forehead and pretty eyes that were almond-shaped and black, a beautiful and proportionate mouth with very white teeth, a well-shaped nose and good coloring without using cosmetics, black hair that stood out over an unequaled white skin, beautiful face and perfect hands. Her beauty created a sweet and balanced harmony, delightful at the sight and even more for the poor guy who, like myself, was captivated by her grace and each day I discovered something new, the spice for love's appetite. (Duque de Estrada 348–349)[71]

References to a sixteenth-century actress who married the playwright Lope de Rueda offer another example of the attraction to women in male garb. A lawsuit brought against Don Gaston de la Cerda, the third Duke of Medinaceli, claims that he promised to pay the actress for her presence and required that she dress in men's clothing: "The Duke became so addicted to her company, as well as to her singing and dancing, that he had her hair cut and dressed her as a page, in breeches, taking her with him hunting and wherever else he went, and indulging a quite obvious pleasure in seeing her dressed as a man" (Merwin xi). The sensual description of these references, nonetheless, differs significantly from the seventeenth-century literary portraits of Erauso. These texts do not present a sexualized Erauso in male garb, nor do they hint at attraction on the part of the male writers or witnesses, either before or after the revelation, even though many women were believed to be attracted to Erauso. In other narratives recounting the adventures of beautiful women in male disguise, however, men often display sexual feelings for the cross-dressed woman before discovering the impersonation. In addition to the prince in the ballad "Doncella Guerrera" and the sergeant in the ballad "Doña Victoria de Acevedo" ("And he became so attracted to this young man Anselmo that he began to doubt if by chance he belonged to the weaker sex" [Durán 363]),[72] other men in Diego Duque de Estrada's life narrative are attracted to the cross-dressed Francisca before they know she is really a woman. A duke inquires: "Who is this young man who is so handsome? He must come from Heaven; certainly he is like an angel; Beautiful boy!" (355).[73] And later a count asks: "Who is this gentleman who is so small, so handsome, and such a favorite of your Highness?" (356?).[74] Diane Dugaw, observing the traditional belief that sex does ultimately supersede gender, offers two possible explanations for why both men and women fall in love with the female warrior in the early modern period: because "manhood is instinctively undeceived by the womanhood that her disguise cannot conceal" and because these scenes may also hint at homoerotic desire (160).

Despite the possibility for same-sex attraction "unbeknownst" to the voyeur fooled by the garments, detractors of female cross-dressing seemed solely concerned with the heterosexual response of those spectators who know the "truth" about the disguise. Moreover, according to the objections raised by the early modern moralists regarding cross-dressed women on stage, the revealing nature of the costume was not the only danger inherent in the male disguise; the detractors also disapproved of the suggestive actions and movements appropriated by women dressed as men: "Other indecent imitative actions, to which should be added women dressing in men's clothing against the virtue and modesty of their sex, and this before all classes of people and delicate ages: all of which provokes lust in such a way that it is morally impossible that they can resist committing many sins" (Padre Pedro Fomperosa y Quintana, quoted in Cotarelo y Mori 1904, 268).[75]

Likewise, in his autobiography, Diego Duque de Estrada describes how Francisca moves when disguised as a man: "She walked firmly and triumphantly and she wore her hat tipped to the side; her cape was crossed over her sword with one hand over it and the other on the jug and all with such temerity and confidence that nobody took her for a woman" (354).[76] This description mirrors the actions of cross-dressed actresses on the early modern stage as well as the sexy "male" poses of Marlene Dietrich, Greta Garbo, and María Félix during the 1930s and 1940s. The relationship between these actresses' persona offscreen (especially Dietrich's and Garbo's rumored bisexuality) and the male disguise onscreen undoubtedly played an important role in the success of their performances.[77]

The seventeenth-century audience likewise brought knowledge about the actresses's offstage life to their onstage performance. In fact, in 1613 the church criticized actresses of "ill-repute" who played the role of sacred or respected figures: "Who would not react with horror and to whom would it not seem evil and indecent and absurd . . . that a clearly adulterous and vile woman, one of those women who regularly participates in that profession, represents the character of the Holy Virgin? . . . In addition to this, these women perform in men's clothing" (quoted in Cotarelo y Mori 1904, 250–251).[78]

There is no doubt that an actress's offstage persona as well as her physical and personal qualities affect the audience's reception of the performance. Therefore, information about the "primera dama" or lead actress in the seventeenth-century stage production of Pérez de Montalbán's *La Monja Alférez* is significant for the understanding of how Erauso's icon was interpreted for theater.[79] The actress Luisa de Robles played the part of Erauso (disguised during the entire play as "Guzmán").[80] Although there are no specific references to the actress's physical appearance, historical records reveal other details about her private and professional life that may contribute to our understanding of how the "Monja Alférez" was marketed for the preferences of the seventeenth-century audience.

Luisa de Robles was married twice, first to a French actor and later, believing that her first husband had died in a shipwreck, to Alonso Olmedo Rufiño. However, when her first husband eventually returned after having been released from captivity by Moorish pirates, Olmedo agreed to terminate the second marriage. Although her first marriage was recognized as legitimate, Robles did not resume living with either husband, but instead the three remained close friends (Shergold and Varey 523). Perhaps even more indicative of Robles's personality are her actions during a performance in Alarcón's *El Anticristo* when another actor, Manuel Vallejo, was too frightened by the dangerous stunt to continue the scene:

> At the end of the play Antichrist rises towards Heaven but receives a blow from the sword of an avenging angel located above. He falls back to earth, whereupon a trapdoor opens and swallows him up, together with the false prophet Elias, after which flames leap up through the hole. This play is of particular interest, for Vallejo, one of the leading actor-managers of the day, when playing the part of Antichrist in Madrid in 1623, found that at the last moment he dared not make the ascent on the "tramoya," which would presumably have carried him up to a Heaven located at second-floor level. Thereupon an actress, Luisa de Robles, with more courage and a genius for improvisation, snatched his crown and robe and made the ascent in his place, an incident which caused much amusement, and about which Góngora wrote a sonnet. (Shergold 229)[81]

Mary Daniels likewise notes the "irony of the role which this intrepid female assumes. With a woman ascending in the robe and crown of the Antichrist, it is no wonder that the moralists wanted them to keep their skirts on" (118).

Three years later, in 1626, Luisa de Robles performed the role of the Lieutenant Nun in Pérez de Montalbán's version of Erauso's life, and undoubtedly the well-publicized episode of Robles's courageous action in 1623 affected both the company manager's decision to acquire the play and the audience's reaction to Robles as a warrior nun. What Erauso and Robles seemed to have in common was their ability to outperform men in activities traditionally considered more suitable for daring males. Like Erauso's fearless acts in her military career, Robles proved that she was also capable of doing a "man's job" better than another man.

Given the publicity surrounding Robles's bravery, we might speculate about how she was viewed by both the male and female spectators. Equally troublesome for the censors was the possible negative effect of theatrical representations, not only on men but also on the female viewer: "Did you not see your daughter before she saw the play, with her blessed ignorance of these dangers as she lived like an innocent dove? And did you not see her after, having opened her eyes to evil, she learned what should be ignored. Now she asks for new clothes, she now wants to go out, and she wants to see and to be seen" (quoted in Cotarelo y Mori 1904, 83).[82]

While many critics, such as Lisa Jardine, emphasize theater's goal of pleasing the male spectator, others recognize the importance of visual images on the female spectator.[83] In particular, iconographic, literary, or theatrical scenes that portray homoeroticism between women, even when designed for the gratification of the male viewer, could have an impact on the female observer. Kristina Straub believes that female cross-dressing on stage had an erotic effect on women, and Patricia Simons argues that the numerous Renaissance depictions of the goddess Diana engaged in erotic activities with other women (bathing with her nymphs, for example) could prove to be subversive, since they offer an alternative option for how women could relate to other women: "Before a female audience, such paintings become instructions about chastity but they also tell tales about a female world of pleasure" (109).[84]

The power of these classical paintings to arouse female spectators was also noted by Pierre Brantôme in the late sixteenth century. Brantôme describes a sensual painting in which women were "naked and at the bath, which did touch, and feel, and handle, and stroke, one the other, and intertwine and fondle with each other" (33). The reader then discovers that a female viewer was so excited by the painting that she implored her companion to join her in sexual pleasure: "Too long have we tarried here. Let us now straightway take coach and so to my lodging; for that no more can I hold in the ardour that is in me. Need must away and quench it; too sore do I burn" (33). Despite the fact that the woman intends to engage in heterosexual relations with her lover, it was a same-sex erotic image that aroused her uncontrollable feelings of passion. It may not be surprising, then, to note that the female rogue Celestina also engages in same-sex petting and flirtation as a way of preparing the prostitute Areúsa for a client:

> Let my eye take its fill in beholding of thee; it does me much good to touch thee, and to look upon thee. . . . O, how plump and fair is thy flesh! What a clear skin! How fresh to look too. What a breast is here! What sweet smelling paps! What beauty! What fine feature in every part! I did evermore hold thee fair and beautiful, seeing but that which all men might see, but now I must needs tell thee that there are not in all this city 3 such sweet bodies as thine. . . . O that I were a man and might gain so great a part of thee as this to glad my sight. (Rojas 1987, 191, 193)[85]

While these scenes of same-sex desire are ultimately manipulated to depict immoral and transgressive conduct, the commercial success of *La Celestina* during the early modern period indicates the popularity of such representations. Similarly, the fame and celebrity of the Lieutenant Nun icon during the seventeenth century demonstrate the complex relationship to gender, sex assignment, and sexuality according to the state, the church, and popular culture during her lifetime. Erauso's celebrity status tapped into society's fascination with hybrid monsters and their belief that masculine women were biologically programmed. Likewise, Erauso's transvestism responded to the success of this theme in history and literature as well as on the stage, which was justified by the desire for self-protection (chastity), patriotism, adventure, escapism, or the sex appeal of the revealing garment for women. Her alleged lesbianism combined with proof of virginity may have been interpreted as nonthreatening desire, since it was nonreproductive and nonpenetrative. As a result, the Lieutenant Nun's marketability in both high and popular culture allowed for the creation of Spain's first lesbian hero.

CHAPTER TWO

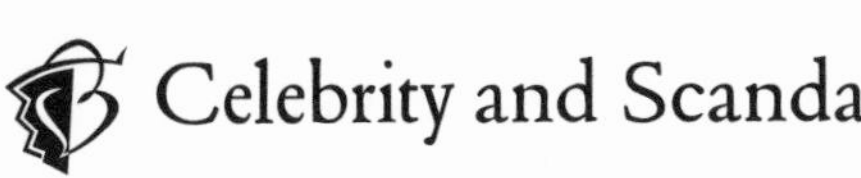

Celebrity and Scandal

The Creation of the Lieutenant Nun in the Seventeenth Century

P. DAVID MARSHALL defines the "celebrity sign" as the cultural representation of a personality or an image that is then circulated as a marketable commodity. Given the ambiguous nature of the celebrity sign, in which "the actual person who is at the core of the representation disappears into a cultural formation of meaning" (Marshall 57), I am less interested in this chapter in revealing the "true" identity of Catalina de Erauso than in analyzing the various multifaceted images of the enigmatic character that are presented during the early modern period. As Mary Elizabeth Perry notes, "She can be analyzed more effectively as a symbol than as a person" (1987b, 90). In particular, this chapter explores the strategies of cultural production and the preferences of the seventeenth-century consumer-voyeur involved in the representation and consumption of the "Lieutenant Nun" celebrity as a criminal, lesbian, virgin, and hero. While analyzing the various narratives based on Erauso's life in official and popular documents (her request for a soldier's pension, letters written by those who knew her, *relaciones* or news pamphlets published in Spain and Mexico, visual and literary portraits, an autobiography attributed to Erauso, a theatrical representation, and an episode in a 1637 picaresque novel), I also explore the public's perceptions of her reaction to becoming the object of the society's curious gaze.[1]

During the seventeenth century, when the legend of the "Monja Alférez" originated, four central images emerged—military hero, criminal, lesbian, and virgin. These images, when juxtaposed, create the hybrid spectacle of the warrior nun. Of these, the lesbian persona undergoes the most radical modification in post-seventeenth-century adaptations. In this chapter I analyze the representation of the Lieutenant Nun in terms of same-sex desire and what cultural function these homoerotic images fulfilled in Spanish society. Undoubtedly, Erauso's instant celebrity status was due in part to the hybrid nature of her life, which shared much in common with many of the popular genres of early modern Spain. While the valiant military hero responds to the popularity of the travel-adventure narratives such as the New World *crónicas* (chronicles), the *novelas de caballerías* (chivalric romances), and the Byzantine novel, the image of Erauso as the delinquent criminal who kills, cheats, and lies while traveling from place to place parallels the successful features of the picaresque novel. Likewise, as I pointed out in chapter 1, the swashbuckling woman dressed as a man was a popular staple of the Golden Age stage as well as ballads, epic and pastoral romances, and a variety of prose narratives.[2] Despite these similarities, which allowed for an instant market for a Lieutenant Nun celebrity, Erauso's military success surfaced at a time when Spain was struggling to maintain control of its empire both domestically and internationally. As a result, the sensational story of a military hero in the New World was easily manipulated for nationalistic purposes.[3]

The Lieutenant Nun as Military Hero

The narratives based on Erauso's life that rely almost exclusively on the courageous warrior image are the petitions requesting recognition for years of military duty on the battlefield. On March 7, 1626, a petition filed on behalf of "Alférez doña Catalina de Erauso" sought compensation for military services rendered to the Crown during the fifteen years that Erauso spent as a soldier in Chile and Peru; the petition also requested permission to continue living as a male. Not surprisingly, given the purpose of such a document, more than half of the narrative is devoted to details of heroic military deeds. The petition articulates Erauso's original motivation for cross-dressing as a particular inclination for military activity to defend the Catholic faith and the Crown (Vallbona 131). This assertion contrasts with other narratives, such as the first *relación* describing Erauso's story (published in 1625 in Madrid and Seville) and the autobiography (not published until 1829), which attribute Erauso's gender transformation to the desire for adventure and the need to escape conflict in the convent.

The brief justification for granting the petition based on Erauso's nobility, valiant service, and the unique and entertaining nature of her life story occupies the first half of the document. The second half alternates requests for financial compensation and other comments related to transvestism. Interestingly, the document concedes that female cross-dressing is transgressive but justifies support of Erauso on the grounds that the past cannot be changed and that she served many years as a brave and valiant soldier for the Spanish Empire.[4] The final sentence of the petition addresses the issue of cross-dressing in the present, since Erauso was not only currently wearing men's clothing but apparently had no intention of returning to women's garb. However, in a supporting testimony from the Consejo de Indias (Council of the Indies), three of the document's four lines confirm her right to a soldier's pension on account of the numerous years of military service, while the last sentence denies support for future cross-dressing: "It is advisable that she return to wearing women's clothing" (quoted in Vallbona 132).[5]

Despite the Council's recommendation to deny permission for permanent transvestism, the petitions manipulate the relationship between cross-dressing and Spanish nationalism to strengthen Erauso's case. An episode from the first petition describing a recent robbery and abuse suffered by Erauso in France is developed with more detail in a second petition to the king, dated April 19, 1626, in which one-fourth of the text is devoted to the assault. This episode emphasizes not only her need for financial support, but it also implies that she suffered physical and verbal abuse as the result of having bravely defended the king's name against the French: "Having heard certain things, she responded out of decorum and reverence to Your Majesty, they mistreated her, both verbally and physically" (133).[6] Although Basque nationalism is frequently evoked in other narratives, particularly in the autobiography, the petitions defend a form of transgender military service to the state that reflects Spain's project of nation-building. It is only through transvestism that Erauso was able to participate in the nation's quest to expand and protect its empire. Not surprisingly, given the function and anticipated readers of the petitions and numerous *certificaciones* (testimonial certifications), these documents silence any mention of crimes, homoerotic activity, violent conflicts off the battlefield, or her gambling habits, which are highlighted in the *relaciones* based on Erauso's life, published just a year earlier.

Similar to the nationalistic spirit of the petitions, the accounts of military activities included in the *relaciones* and the autobiography frequently resemble the chronicle narratives of the colonial period. Henry Ettinghausen's study of seventeenth-century *relaciones* published in Spain focuses on the manipulation of readers that led them to accept the pamphlets as factual sources of news: "They were truly news stories, which, besides providing information, helped structure reality into meaningful fables, performing such other important social functions long associated with literature as entertainment, ideological promotion and moralising" (1993, 118).[7] Given that the majority of events narrated in the *relaciones* reflect the traditional ideology of the monarchy, the military, and the church, it is not surprising that the Monja Alférez's adventures would be seen as a marketable complement to the Crown's numerous successes in 1625, such as the victories over the Dutch at Breda and over the English at Cádiz.[8] The first *relación* concerning Erauso, published in 1625 in Madrid and Seville and again in 1653 in Mexico, begins with a reference to the narratives of the chronicles from the New World—"the victories and deeds that were achieved by the illustrious men in the name of the King and God, and rightly so, the chronicles eternalize their memory and praise their actions" (quoted in Vallbona 160).[9] Having established this male-gendered context and its corresponding literary genre, the text surprises the reader by presenting a contradiction to the culturally constructed belief in the weakness of women: "But that a woman, dressed as a man, since by nature they are all weak and faint-hearted, achieve so much and such manly deeds that even for the most valiant soldier would be memorable, is even more admirable" (160).[10] This provocative introduction is designed to shock and entice the reader to continue the story of this amazing nationalistic spectacle.

Statements such as "the woman fought very valiantly and she killed many Indians by herself" (163) and "she fought like a man, not depending on a harquebus to fight but with a sword and shield, being one of the first to jump forth into the enemy's ship" (168)[11] aggrandize the subject in a manner not unlike some of the marketing techniques used to promote human marvels and monstrosities in freak shows: "Social position, achievements, talents, family, and physiology were fabricated, elevated, or exaggerated and then flaunted. Prestigious titles such as 'Captain,' 'Major,' 'General,' 'Prince,' 'King,' 'Princess,' and 'Queen' aggrandize exhibits" (Bogdan 29). Although her military rank was not fabricated but earned in battle, the dual title of Erauso's icon as the "Lieutenant Nun" capitalizes on the shock value implicit in the sensationalized account of the prodigious military achievements of a religious woman. For Mary Elizabeth Perry, Erauso's celebrity was marketed through the seeming contradiction of the epithet: "What attracted these people who wanted to see the Nun-Lieutenant was his inclusiveness as a hyphenate. Neither simply woman nor man, she was both and all, a sexual anomaly, a circus freak, a symbol of nature undone and amazed, a paradox of boundaries violated but hymen intact" (1999, 407).

The Lieutenant Nun as Deviant Criminal

Both Rima de Vallbona and Stephanie Merrim agree that the autobiography's "largely formulaic chapters showcase Erauso's transgressions with surprisingly little attention to her heroism" (Merrim 1994, 180). While cultural anomalies may have been displayed in terms of the miraculous, another commonly employed strategy used to present monstrous spectacles in carnival exhibits was the "exotic presentation," which places the spectator in a position superior to the object considered. Describing the methods used to attract viewers to freak shows, Robert Bogdan argues that although the aggrandized exhibits and exotic presentations may seem contradictory, they are often used together to enhance the shock value of the anomaly: "In the exotic mode, the person received an identity that appealed to people's interest in the culturally strange, the primitive, the bestial, the exotic. . . . The exotic mode emphasized how different and, in most cases, how inferior the persons on exhibit were" (28–29). The often tabloidesque *relaciones* and autobiography create a similar environment when they present Erauso in terms of the deviant rogue-criminal who commits crimes in faraway places (such as Panamá, Chile, and Peru), similar to the frequent characterization of monsters' habitations as "distant enough to be exoticized" (Cohen 18). Whereas the *relaciones de sucesos* described the "quality" news of military victories or royal visits, the news pamphlets—such as the *relación verissima, relación muy verdadera,* or *notable y prodigiosa relación*—sensationalized human interest stories and are comparable to popular tabloid news in their descriptions of monsters and murders (Ettinghausen 1984, 3–5).[12] As Jerome Friedman notes, the news pamphlets were the "seventeenth-century equivalents of *People* magazine and the *National Enquirer*" (xiv).

Like the inferior position of the exoticized monster or Other, Erauso's numerous jobs and masters, the seemingly constant movement and travel, her affection for gambling and deceiving women for profit, the remorseless crimes, violence, and tricks place the reader in the world of the marginalized *pícaros* (rogues) and criminals of early modern Spain.[13] Erauso's childhood in the convent as well as her life as a cross-dressed page after her escape from convent life are described in picaresque terms, as the young protagonist initially falls victim to society's injustices but gradually emerges as a victimizer. Similar to the first *relación,* which attributes Erauso's desire to escape the convent to a fight with another nun, Erauso's autobiography alludes to a nun's physical abuse: "She was a big, robust woman, I was but a girl—and when she beat me, I felt it" (3).[14]

The same features that characterize the picaresque novel are also present in the soldiers' autobiographies of early modern Spain. For example, in the first chapter of Alonso de Contreras's autobiography, *Discurso de mi vida,* he describes an early criminal incident in which, when he was just a child, he killed another boy by stabbing him with a knife. Likewise, in many of the sixteenth- and seventeenth-century soldiers' autobiographies, such as that of Diego García de Paredes, Diego Suárez Montañez, Domingo de Toral y Valdés, Jerónimo de Pasamonte, Alonso de Contreras, Diego Duque de Estrada, and Miguel de Castro, the picaresque adventures many times overshadow the narration of valiant military deeds. In fact, there are many features that Erauso's autobiography shares with other soldiers' life stories: biographical inaccuracies, mistreatment during childhood, particular interest in clothing, numerous citations of quantitative statistics such as distances, sexually explicit episodes, remorseless crimes, interviews with Pope Urban VIII, and the fact that the early modern soldiers' autobiographies were not published until the late nineteenth or early twentieth centuries.[15]

Erauso's autobiography, then, presents features from the first-person narratives that are distinguished by their exclusively male-gendered nature: soldiers' autobiographies, picaresque novels, and chronicles from the New World. Even though there are various novels with female rogue protagonists (*pícaras*), no picaresque novel penned by a woman from early modern Spain is known to exist. Likewise, Erauso does not follow the cultural expectations (mainly prostitution) of the *pícara*. In her study of the picaresque novel, Anne J. Cruz omits Erauso's autobiography from her analysis because "the fact that she lived undetected as a man justifies my not including it among female picaresque narratives" (243). Curiously, despite the potential impact of Catalina's early years in the convent, her life narrative does not display many features of the numerous nuns' and saints' lives that were written and read by women during the sixteenth and seventeenth centuries. (One exception might be the insistence on her virginity.) In this sense, nineteen years of cross-dressing necessitated the literary act of "cross-writing," or the appropriation of genres not generally adopted by women writers.

The first *relación* concerning Erauso, published in 1625 (*Relación prodigiosa de las grandes hazañas, y valerosos hechos que una muger hizo en quarenta años que sirvió a Su Majestad en el Reyno de Chile y otros del Perú, y Nueva España, en ábito de Soldado, y los honrosos oficios militares que tubo armas, sin que fuesse conocida por tal muger, hasta que le fue fuerza el descubrirse*), narrates Erauso's escape from the convent, her transformation into a boy, and a brief jail term for a few weeks for having thrown a rock at another child. Although the text does not, at first, explicitly specify the violent nature of the protagonist, the reader witnesses the conflictive personality documented in the fights with a nun in the convent and later with the boy. The life narrative repeats similar episodes but includes more details, such as physical abuse from the first master, who "went so far as to lay his hands on me" (5).[16]

Erauso then begins a series of varied jobs as she travels to the New World, which the *relación* documents with a detailed itinerary of names, places, distances, and time periods. She eventually acquires a job managing a store and soon finds herself in more fights while demonstrating a hot temper and predisposition for violence: "with a perforated knife she stabbed him . . . and she wounded Reyes' friend, who fell dead" (162).[17] Again she spends time in jail but is released when her boss posts bail. Most of the first *relación* emphasizes the dramatic action of the criminal transgressions of the protagonist.

The second news pamphlet, also published in 1625 (*Segunda parte de la relación de la Monja Alferes, y dízense en ella cosas admirables, y fidedignas de los valerosos hechos desta muger; de lo bien que empleó el tiempo en servicio de nuestro Rey y señor*), continues the sensationalist version of Erauso's life as it presents the protagonist as heroic soldier, murderer, gambler, chivalrous gentleman, virgin, nun, and cultural legend. One example of this dramatic multiplicity is described in an episode in which the protagonist, while in church, hears the noise of card-playing from a nearby establishment and, true to the picaresque character, goes directly to the gambling house after mass, where she once again finds herself embroiled in violent conflict. In this episode Erauso meets and confronts a dangerous soldier named "El Nuevo Cid." In an attempt to defend her earnings from the card games, she kills him in a fight in which she also is seriously wounded. Overall, the most detail in the second *relación* (about three-fourths of the narrative) is dedicated to action and violence, both on the battlefield and in personal fights in the gambling houses as well as in the streets.

Although the autobiography describes in more detail the episodes included in the *relaciones,* petitions, and letters, it also narrates additional events that are similar in nature, such as military activities, brawls, duels, and gambling-scene attacks resulting from the "cornudo" (cuckold) insult: "He told me I lied like a cuckold. I drew out my dagger and ran it into his chest" (22).[18] Perhaps one of the most significant variations on an above-mentioned event, however, is the murder of Erauso's brother. Only in the autobiography—but not in any of the other seventeenth-century prose narratives—is there mention of Erauso inadvertently killing her brother Miguel de Erauso. She was serving as a second in a duel when, in the darkness of night, she mortally wounds her brother: "My point went home below his left nipple, as I later learned, through what felt like a double thickness of leather, and he fell to the ground. 'Ah, traitor,' he said, 'you have killed me!' " (24).[19] In a rare display of emotion

Erauso recounts how, with much pain, she watched the funeral from the balcony.

Despite the accidental nature of her brother's death, the description of the murder further criminalizes the figure of the Lieutenant Nun. Likewise, the numerous episodes in which she kills with no remorse and at times with little justification or provocation also create an outlaw image that jars with the heroic soldier character presented in all of the seventeenth-century versions of Erauso's life.[20]

The Lieutenant Nun as Early Modern Lesbian

The ambivalence of the hero-criminal is likewise evident in the representations of the Lieutenant Nun's sexuality. While Erauso is frequently presented in terms of homoerotic desire (but never associated with heterosexual impulses) in the seventeenth century, the way in which her lesbian attraction is depicted varies significantly among these representations. Juan Pérez de Montalbán's 1626 play *La Monja Alférez* and a letter written in 1617 by the bishop of Guamanga, Fray Agustín de Carvajal (published in 1618 by Juan Serrano de Vargas in Seville), present Erauso as an exemplary heroine who is attracted to other women.[21] Conversely, in the first and third *relaciones* (1625 and 1653) and in the autobiography, Erauso's same-sex passion is depicted as another example of her deviancy, supporting Lynda Hart's assertion that "lesbians in mainstream representations have almost always been depicted as predatory, dangerous, and pathological" (x).[22] The criminalization of transgressive sexuality associated with female masculinity is likewise documented in Juan Huarte de San Juan's sixteenth-century medical analysis of masculine women as aggressive and more disagreeable (609, 616). As a result, the Lieutenant Nun's same-sex desire is policed through the connection of lesbianism with aggression, while it is also tolerated since it may even facilitate restraint from heterosexual relations.

Comparable with the sensationalist narratives of the twentieth-century tabloid genre, two of the three news pamphlets published in the seventeenth century highlight Erauso's same-sex preferences in terms of sociosexual deviancy. As described in the first *relación,* when Erauso (using the name of Francisco de Loyola) enlists as a soldier in Chile, she meets her brother Miguel. They quickly become friends, given their common Basque heritage, and remain close for three years before a conflict over a woman separates the two siblings: "And one day her brother asked her not to visit the house of a woman he knew, and she refused to cooperate, which caused them to take out their swords and they fought a while until the captain Francisco de Ayllón came between the two" (163).[23] After the confrontation with Miguel, Erauso then proves herself on the battlefield as valiant soldier (earning the rank of lieutenant) and again resumes her friendship with her brother until a conflict over the same woman causes the two siblings to become enemies for the second time: "Later she became a good friend of her brother but due to the same girl from before, they became enemies and in two years they did not speak to each other" (163).[24] The autobiography develops this episode with more detail: "On occasion, I went with him to the house of the mistress he kept in town, and on other occasions I went there without him. It wasn't long before he found out and, imagining the worst, he told me that he'd better not catch me at it again. But he spied on me, and when he caught me there the next time he waited outside, and when I came out he lit into me with his belt, wounding me in the hand" (19).[25] The conflict between the protagonist and her brother over a woman indirectly raises the issue of Erauso's sexuality, and as a result, the reader may either infer that Erauso was attracted to the woman or that her rebellious and competitive nature led her to challenge the mandate of her older brother. Regardless, the text establishes a link between lesbian desire and aggression that results in the subtle pathologization of the protagonist.

Similarly, three different episodes involving attempted arranged marriages associate Erauso's deviant behavior with same-sex flirtation. In chapter 3 of the autobiography, although it is the girlfriend of Erauso's employer who tries, unsuccessfully, to seduce her, the protagonist visits her at night on a number of occasions and is willing to participate in same-sex petting. This apparent complicity makes us question her innocence in the conflict with the woman: "I used to sneak out at night to the lady's house, and there she would caress me, and implore me, supposedly for fear of the law, not to go back to the church but to stay with her. Finally one night, she locked me in and declared that come hell or high water I was going to sleep with her—pushing and pleading so much that I had to smack her one and slip out of there" (13).[26]

Likewise, two concurrent episodes involve efforts to arrange marriages with Erauso and again the protagonist willingly accepts the gifts and then escapes, leaving the women "burladas" (deceived): "And a couple of days later, she let me know it would be fine by her if I married her daughter—a girl as black and ugly as the devil himself, quite the opposite of my taste, which has always run to pretty faces" (28).[27] Although Erauso has no intention of marrying the girl, perhaps in part due to the potential risk of being discovered, she does reveal her racist colonial ideology through her preference for lighter-skinned women.[28] Erauso's extreme repulsion based on race is further emphasized in the subtle variation in one of the eighteenth-century manuscripts deposited in the Archivo Capitular in Seville: "My wife was black and ugly, quite the opposite of my taste, which has always been for pretty faces; which is why one can imagine that the four months that I was with this woman, for me, were like four centuries" (quoted in Rubio Merino 68).[29]

While Marjorie Garber downplays the role of desire in this episode ("The resistance to marriage is more strongly marked by aversions of class, race, and nobility than by gender or sexuality" [1996, xv]), the intersection of race and desire here creates an intriguing contrast to the subsequent ambiguous spectacle of the "Monja Alférez." Instead of eroticizing the exotic Other (as is frequent in early modern representations of Moorish women in Spain), Erauso enacts a sexual demonization of the mestiza ("black and ugly as the devil himself").

Like Erauso's racist characterization of the mestiza, the narrator in María de Zayas's 1637 story "El prevenido engañado" (Forewarned but Not Forearmed) performs a similar textual demonization of Beatriz's black lover Antonio. Antonio is described as "a negro so black that his face seemed made of black silk . . . a fierce devil . . . devilish black face . . . the devil himself couldn't have looked more awful" (1990, 127).[30] Despite this demonization of Antonio, it is the white noblewoman who, like Erauso, selfishly uses the black lover for her own gain. Antonio presents himself as the innocent victim of Beatriz's voracious sexual appetite: "What do you want of me, madam? Leave me alone, for the love of God! How can you pursue me even as I lie dying? Isn't it enough that your lasciviousness has brought me to this end? Even now you want me to satisfy your vicious appetites when I am breathing my last? Get yourself a husband, madam, marry, and leave me in peace. I never want to see you again!" (Zayas 1990, 127–128).[31] Erauso's autobiography presents the narrator-protagonist's point of view and not the mestiza's, but we can assume that the women deceived by Erauso's false promises of marriage might have expressed anger similar to Antonio's in Zayas's story.

Interestingly, just as Erauso demonized the potential object of her affection, her desire for the "pretty faces" of other women is criminalized through her mistreatment of the women in the New World. Michele Stepto, on the other hand, warns against a comparison of Erauso's racist comments about the mestiza to her own victimization as a transvestite spectacle: "It would be a misreading to see her as anything other than the perfect colonialist, manipulative, grasping, and at moments out and out bigoted. To align Catalina, as a cross-dressing 'other,' with the victims of colonialism is to miss the truth that the rewards of her transformation were gained almost wholly at their expense" (Stepto and Stepto xli). In this way, Erauso undoubtedly contributed to the assault on the personal and cultural integrity of mestiza women, which was based on sexual, racial, and class relations.[32] Consequently, Erauso's "romantic" episodes with the women of Peru and Chile are just as much about violence and power as they are about desire and fantasy.[33]

The next episode in which Erauso pretends to favor marriage in order to receive gifts and money indicates that the protagonist now finds the proposed fiancée attractive: "I met the girl, and she seemed good enough" (29).[34] But again, after collecting the valuables, she abandons the girl. Despite many critics' assertion that the protagonist's behavior reflects her desire to be convincing as a man, in the *relaciones* and in the autobiography Erauso's same-sex desire is frequently associated with aggression or criminality. However, what may have neutralized this negative image in the minds of the early modern readers is the fact that the objects of Erauso's disdain were considered inferior both socially and racially to the upper-class European suitor.

While Erauso continues her pattern of deceiving women in the New World, she more often than not expresses physical attraction for the women. In chapter 5 of the autobiography, we see a more explicit homoerotic adventure: "There were two young ladies in the house, his wife's sisters, and I had become accustomed to frolicking with them and teasing them—one, in particular, who had taken a fancy to me. And one day, when she and I were in the front parlor, and I had my head in the folds of her skirt and she was combing my hair while I ran my hand up and down between her legs, Diego de Solarte happened to pass by the window, and spied us through the grate" (16–17).[35] This is perhaps the most direct account of Erauso's preferences and her desire to engage in a physical relationship with another woman. Nonetheless, when the girl suggests that they marry, we can only assume that Erauso would have eventually left her also, just as she abandoned the other women. However, in this case, she was discovered making wedding plans with the sister-in-law of her boss, Diego de Solarte, and was fired as a result.[36]

By 1630 Erauso had already acquired a pension from King Philip IV, received dispensation and permission from Pope Urban VIII to permanently dress in men's garb, and set sail for the second time to the New World. Most of the third *relación* (*Ultima y tercera relación, en que se haze verdadera del resto de la vida de la Monja Alférez, sus memorables virtudes, y exemplar muerte en estos Reynos de la Nueva España*), published in 1653 in Mexico three years after Erauso's death, is devoted to one particular event that reveals the aggressive nature of its lesbian protagonist. When Erauso is asked to accompany a young woman on a trip, she falls in love with the attractive appearance of her companion, "traveling with her, enamored by her beauty" (172).[37] However, when a gentleman also falls in love with the woman, Erauso becomes possessive and tries to convince the woman to enter a convent with her, offering to pay all the expenses. When the woman rejects the offer and decides to marry the man instead, Erauso becomes ill with jealousy. She eventually recovers, affirming that she would rather survive and be envious than be parted from her lover in death—"considering it to be less painful to be jealous in person than die of separation from her beloved" (173).[38] Accordingly, she starts to visit her love interest but becomes so resentful of the other female friends who also visit the young woman that the husband decides to prohibit Erauso from going to the house. Not surprisingly, Erauso becomes irate and challenges the husband to a duel; when the latter refuses, saying that he would not fight a woman, she erupts: "Our traveler exploded volcanos from her eyes" (174).[39] She later confronts the husband but eventually controls her anger and turns her back on her competitor, while those who witness the scene are impressed by her fearlessness: "The bravery of her confidence was well-known and was much celebrated by those who knew her" (174).[40]

Considering that much of the third *relación* focuses on the homoerotic nature of Erauso's actions, it is surprising when critics, such as J. Ignacio Tellechea, make no mention of it in their discussion of the text. On the other hand, the same-sex desire portrayed in the last *relación* can also provoke a strong negative reaction. When referring to its lesbian plot, Lucas Castillo Lara, in his 1992 study, describes the news pamphlet as a "bad third-rate novel . . . a frenetic and brazen lesbianism . . . a string of crude incoherences and lewd nonsense" (325, 327).[41]

Regardless of how modern readers respond to the seventeenth-century text, what the homoerotic episodes from the *relaciones* and the autobiography have in common is the attempt to associate Erauso's lesbian desire with violence and deviance. Erauso consistently reacts to competitors with aggression and many times ends up deceiving or cheating the women with whom she engages in homoerotic flirtation. Nonetheless, this indirect criminalization of lesbian desire present in the news pamphlets and in her memoirs appears to be absent in a letter written in 1617 and in the 1626 play written by Pérez de Montalbán. This variance among adaptations reflects the complexity of the lesbian figure during the period as well as the differences in readership. While the *relaciones* are intended to provide a more sensationalized and dramatic version of Erauso's life, the relatively sympathetic nature of Fray Agustín de Carvajal's letter could be attributed to Erauso's own account given to the bishop or to the religious status of the author and the anticipated preferences of his readers in Spain.

One of the first notices of an ex-nun dressed in men's garb in the New World is found in a letter dated July 18, 1617, and published in 1618 by the Seville printer Juan Serrano de Vargas, who also published numerous *relaciones* in the early seventeenth century ("Capítulo de una de las cartas que diversas personas enviaron desde Cartagena de las Indias a algunos amigos suyos a las ciudades de Sevilla y Cádiz").[42] The bishop of Guamanga, Fray Agustín de Carvajal, sent news from Cartagena de Indias to friends in Seville and Cádiz informing them of a nun who donned men's garb and lived for years as a man before revealing her physiological identity. Carvajal's letter differs significantly from other narratives of Erauso's life in that it does not include any account of serious crimes such as murder (outside the confines of military battle), nor does it describe the numerous gambling scenes and related conflicts found in other interpretations. The letter does mention Erauso's encounter with her brother Miguel, but there is no mention of any physical violence or conflict over another woman that is evident in other versions. Interestingly, Carvajal's letter represents the first written account of the homoerotic desire with reference to the episode in which Erauso was fired by her boss for compromising activity with his sisters-in-law: "because Olarte's sisters-in-law, who were very pretty, were enjoying themselves with her and she with them, so he fired her" (quoted in Tellechea 63).[43] Overall, Carvajal's account describes the most positive aspects of Erauso's life with little personal commentary or emphasis on her possible vices or deviance. Therefore, the brief mention of lesbian flirtation is tempered by the final affirmation of Erauso's virginity, established by the matrons who examined her. Given the absence of any reproval, Carvajal's letter demonstrates the unspoken tolerance for same-sex attraction described in chapter 1 of this study. Since this desire was nonphallic, it may be accepted as part of the performance to protect and preserve chastity.

Few critics have commented on the positive homosocial episodes associated with Erauso's affectionate relationships with various nuns. In chapter 13 of the autobiography, while the protagonist continues to pass as a man, she describes her favorable friendships with the nuns: "I came out of hiding, settled my affairs, and went quite often to visit my little nun and her mother, and some of the other ladies there, all of whom were invariably pleased by my company and made me many gifts of this, that, and the other thing" (47).[44] Likewise, once Erauso has revealed her biological identity and is temporarily living dressed in religious habit in the convent, the nuns and the protagonist express mutual affection: "I kissed the abbess's hand, embraced and was embraced in turn by each of the nuns" (67); "The nuns were beside themselves when they took their leave of me" (68); "The sisters bade me a sad farewell. . . . I left at once for Guamanga to say my good-byes to the ladies of the convent of Santa Clara, and they held me up there for eight days, during which we enjoyed each other's company and exchanged many gifts and finally, when it was time for me to go, many tears" (69).[45] Although affection among the nuns was a common feature in convent narratives, a conceivable homoerotic reading should not be overlooked, especially in light of the numerous same-sex flirtation scenes in Erauso's life narrative as well as the potential for erotic relationships in monastic settings noted earlier in this study. As Michele Stepto notes, the three years spent in Peruvian convents with the friendly nuns were "not altogether unpleasurable, considering her decided preference for the company of other women" (Stepto and Stepto xxxiii). While these episodes in the early modern autobiography are vague with regard to specific erotic details, in some twentieth-century adaptations, such as Javier Aguirre's 1986 film *La Monja Alférez,* Sheila McLaughlin's 1987 film *She Must Be Seeing Things,* and Carlos Keller's 1972 historical novel *Las memorias de la Monja Alférez,* the convent friendships are converted into explicit lesbian relationships.

Pérez de Montalbán's La Monja Alférez

Perhaps one of the most interesting adaptations of Erauso's assumed same-sex attraction is found in the play attributed to Juan Pérez de Montalbán, *La Monja Alférez.* Catalina de Erauso's popularity during her six years in Spain and Italy before returning to Mexico undoubtedly inspired Pérez de Montalbán to write a play based on the highly marketable life of the Lieutenant Nun. The *comedia* was first performed in 1626 in Madrid, precisely at a time when public interest in the story must have been at a peak and perhaps after the audience had an opportunity to see, hear, or read about the celebrity. Like the "docudrama" genre popular today, Pérez de Montalbán's play combines historical fact with theatrical fiction in an attempt to entertain his audience with what the playwright considered the most interesting aspects of Erauso's life. Since his public was familiar with the protagonist, Pérez de Montalbán did not have the freedom to be completely innovative and abandon some of the established "facts" or currently held beliefs about the protagonist, especially after her recent presence in the city. Therefore, the particular aspects of Erauso's multifaceted identity that Pérez de Montalbán chose to manipulate and exploit may provide possible indications of the perceived tastes and preferences of the early modern consumer. As Dorothy Kress proposed in 1931, "Perhaps Montalbán wrote the comedia only because it was such a popular topic in his day and because he knew better than anyone what the public demanded in order to be entertained" (61).[46]

Despite some critics' comments attributing the lesbianism in Pérez de Montalbán's play to an "almost pathological abnormality" and to "abnormal passions" (Parker 670), clearly the playwright created a noble character who is willing to sacrifice what is most important to her for the future of the woman she loves. Although Erauso's transgenderism is often described as "monstrous," Mary Elizabeth Perry argues that Pérez de Montalbán's protagonist "is not portrayed as an unnatural monster representing the mysterious marginal area between both genders" (1987a, 244). And yet other scholars see Pérez de Montalbán's interpretation of Erauso solely in terms of the masculine character of the protagonist. Although the seventeenth-century actress Luisa de Robles performed the part of Guzmán (Erauso) on stage, some critics see this role as that of a man. Julie Greer Johnson argues that Erauso's "complete rejection of her sex left Montalbán no alternative but to cast her as a man" (146); Melveena McKendrick uses the masculine pronoun in reference to Guzmán since "the character created by Montalbán is a man" (215). Similarly, Debbie Fraker suggests that a male actor would be more appropriate for the role of the Lieutenant Nun: "In a movie based on her life, the leading role could be played by Dennis Hopper or Nicholas Cage" (40).

Perhaps an analysis of the characteristics attributed to the Lieutenant Nun in Pérez de Montalbán's play will facilitate an understanding of the believed preferences of Erauso as well as dramatic elements that would please the seventeenth-century audience. The popularity of the cross-dressed ex-nun-turned-soldier flirting with other women is not surprising considering the success of the *mujer vestida de hombre* motif on the Golden Age stage and the erotic nature of exposing women's legs for the male gaze. As Stephanie Merrim notes, "Although much emphasis is placed on Erauso's virginity when she discloses her sex, the implications of homosexual attraction adds yet another layer of ambiguous titillation to the text as it eroticizes the many, even apparently innocent, encounters with other females" (1994, 182). Although Erauso is not forced into a heterosexual resolution, she does not live happily ever after with the woman she loves. While she is not killed off, she will presumably live alone without her beloved, who will receive the heterosexual prize of marriage to Diego.

First, and perhaps somewhat comparable to the petitions and testimonies submitted on behalf of Catalina de Erauso, Pérez de Montalbán's play forgoes the childhood scenes in the convent, so the audience does not see the actress dressed as a young nun onstage. However, unlike the petitions and other supporting documents, the playwright never takes his audience to the battlefields of the New World to witness her courageous deeds, although certain elements of the brave and valiant soldier are presented indirectly through a brief summary of her military career in the third act. Moreover, even though Erauso's quick temper and preference for gambling are easily observed, the numerous murders and deceptions are absent or minimized. The one detail from Erauso's image that comes to the foreground, however, is the same-sex desire that is believed to be part of her identity.

When the play begins, Erauso has already been transformed into Guzmán and, as a result, we are not privileged to the "before" and "after" contrast. The viewers must create this duality mentally as they privately share the secret of Guzmán's true identity. Although it was not uncommon for the early modern audience to observe an actress playfully flirting onstage with another woman dressed as a man, the initial scene in Pérez de Montalbán's play differs in that the audience, due to prior knowledge of Erauso's life, had no reason to believe that Guzmán was behaving as a cross-dressed heterosexual woman who would ultimately win her man, or even abandon male garb. In the opening scene the audience becomes the voyeur of a love relationship between Doña Ana and Guzmán/Erauso. Ana declares: "Could I (being who I am) give you more clear signs of my love?" (Act 1, scene 1).[47] When Ana gives her a chain, Guzmán responds: "I receive this chain because its links demonstrate the prison in which I live due to my love" (Act 1, scene 1).[48] Even though Ana is unaware of Guzmán's true sex, the latter's expression of love seems just as sincere as her own.

Throughout the play, Guzmán insists on keeping her disguise a secret, preferring death to revelation: "I will not identify myself even though it may cost me my life" (Act 1, scene 18).[49] When her brother Miguel, fueled by suspicions, continues in his obsession to confirm the identity of his sister, Guzmán demands that he keep his distance. Miguel does not stop, but instead confronts her and then pleads: "Come back, Catalina, come back" (Act 1, scene 18).[50] Guzmán not only denies the truth but takes offense at being called a woman; as a result, the siblings initiate a knife fight. Guzmán wounds her brother, and the first act ends as she carries him on her shoulders to a nearby hermitage so that he may confess in case the wound is fatal. This climactic end to the first act differs significantly from the sibling rivalry described in the first *relación* and in the autobiography. In these prose narratives, the fight between the two is based on competition over a woman whereas in Pérez de Montalbán's play the episode focuses on Guzmán's reluctance to reveal her identity; consequently the playwright does not pathologize same-sex attraction, as do the broadsides and the autobiography.

When Guzmán attempts to hug Ana after a long separation, she discovers that her girlfriend has suffered an assault to her honor during a night of passion with a man she thought was Guzmán. As Ana describes the tragedy, she emphasizes her suspicions based on the differences between the body of the unidentified lover and that of Guzmán. Because she was in the dark, Ana could only compare through touch: "First his arm, his corpulent body of delicate distinction showed me the difference, and to be sure I touched his face with its masculine signs and I found in him that which your young age does not yet reveal" (Act 2, scene 5).[51] Upon discovering that the deceptive lover who tricked Ana was really Guzmán's friend Diego, the protagonist confronts him, stating that he completed the act that she (Guzmán) dreamed about doing: "I am the man from whom you robbed the opportunity, I was the one who was in the street waiting for the bliss that you enjoyed . . . so I only completed the act in thought while you did it in deed" (Act 2, scene 7).[52] Guzmán declares her love for Ana but is unable to satisfy her desire or Ana's, at least in a traditional heterosexual (phallic) sense.

Guzmán's goal, then, is to force Diego to restore Ana's honor through marriage. Predictably, Diego doubts Ana's chastity—if she was willing to engage in sexual relations with Guzmán once, perhaps it could happen again: "If she gave you her promise to be your wife and that night she opened her doors to you, with this trust, how can I be assured that she would not repeat the same extreme act of love with you again?" (Act 2, scene 7).[53] Since only one fact could convince Diego of Ana's chastity, Guzmán decides to reveal her "true" identity under the condition that Diego marry Ana and that he tell nobody the truth about her sex. This revelation to Diego is particularly significant in the context of Guzmán's radical insistence throughout the play on preserving anonymity and maintaining a male-gendered identity, even when her life is in peril.

Secrecy, then, is established as the central aspect of "passing" and also for the survival of her preferred identity. Therefore, Guzmán's willingness to divulge her secret for the honor of her beloved clearly reveals Pérez de Montalbán's interpretation of Erauso's identity as well as the perceived tastes of the audience.

Although he had not previously doubted the "heterosexual" love between Guzmán and Ana, Diego now confesses disbelief at the possibility of a woman being in love with another woman: "I am to believe that you loved Ana, being a woman, you loved another woman?" (Act 2, scene 7).[54] Sara Taddeo's interpretation of Erauso's sexuality in the play is more cautious, as she argues that "Catalina's possible lesbianism is neither confirmed nor denied in the play, but the issue is raised by Don Diego" (120). On the other hand, Melveena McKendrick overlooks any potential for lesbian passion in the script: "There were good commercial reasons for writing the play, and there were equally good reasons for leaving out of it any insinuations about homosexual tendencies" (216). Mary Elizabeth Perry, however, sees a more serious portrait of same-sex desire: "Her love for another woman does not have to be reduced to the absurdity of a non-phallic woman pretending to be a man" (1987a, 246).

Once Diego knows the truth, Guzmán is free to narrate her own life story beginning with her troubled childhood. Guzmán explains that since she displayed masculine and somewhat aggressive traits as a child, her parents decided to place her in a convent to correct her rebellious nature. This decision had the opposite effect, however, as Catalina grew even more defiant upon being locked up in an enclosed space: "But my parents, seeing my wild nature, put me in a convent, which impedes such spirit: Oh Diego, if only I could explain to you the rage, fury, and anger that grew in my heart during that time" (Act 2, scene 7).[55] This justification for Erauso's rejection of the female gender role, which assigns responsibility to her parents, is significantly different from the explanations offered in the documents, letters, petitions, and news pamphlets examined above. Some of the narratives claim that she left the convent due to a fight with another nun while other texts affirm that she had a special inclination for arms and adventure. Once Guzmán establishes what led to her decision to escape from the convent, her version forgoes the transformation scene in which she sews a male costume out of her nun's habit. Instead, she enters directly into an account of her jobs and military service in the New World. Again, Guzmán confirms that she would rather die than reveal publicly that she is a woman: "Announce that I am a woman, Diego? I would rather die first" (Act 2, scene 7).[56]

Despite Diego's promise to keep Guzmán's secret, after the protagonist kills "El Nuevo Cid" in self-defense during a fight and is subsequently sentenced to die for the crime, Diego reveals his friend's identity to save her life. Guzmán continues to deny the truth, however, and again is unwilling to live in the female gender role: "Me a woman? You liar! Go ahead and execute the sentence your Honor, Diego is lying to save my life. . . . Why would I want to live if they know that I am a woman? (Act 2, scene 15).[57] Thus ends the second act, reinforcing the importance for Guzmán to choose her own gender identity. Being forced to perform the traditional gender role assigned to her anatomy represents the only real threat of death for the protagonist.

In subsequent scenes, we see Ana's resentment toward Guzmán and Guzmán's anger at Diego. Guzmán is furious with Diego for revealing her secret because it denies her the freedom and the privilege of being treated as a man: "I have suffered and continue to suffer only because you did not honor your word that you would keep my secret" (Act 3, scene 8).[58] They start to fight and Diego is told that he should not fight a woman, to which Guzmán responds: "Liar, I am not a woman as long as I take up this sword, which has defeated so many men" (Act 3, scene 9).[59] When Guzmán appears insulted to be called a woman, she is asked: "If you *are* a woman then why do you get offended?" Guzmán then responds: "If I am, I won't admit it nor can I allow that anybody call me one. It is because of Diego that I suffer these insults" (Act 3, scene 9, emphasis mine).[60]

When Ana expresses her anger at Guzmán for deceiving her and refusing to facilitate her marriage to Diego, Guzmán reminds her of the sacrifice she made for the sake of Ana's honor, and in a climactic act of selflessness, Guzmán confesses publicly her true identity to confirm that there was no phallic sexual activity between the two women. Guzmán's statement provides the definitive assurance for Ana's future with Diego. Her confession dispels all suspicions concerning Ana's chastity and eliminates objections on the grounds of sexual promiscuity. Moreover,

Guzmán's revelation implies that lesbian passion was not an issue in the question of Ana's honor, as the public's concern over genital penetration was allayed by proof of Erauso's virginity:

> Listen, madam, it was your gratitude and your honor that were so dear to my heart that only because I wanted to satisfy Diego's doubts did I confess that I was a woman when it was so secret. Now Ana, given that it is public and I am less threatening and have satisfied my anger, the deceit which prevented your marriage ends here. So I will confess it to restore your honor and not spoil the kindness that, at my own cost, I have shown. And so, Diego, it is fair to restore what I owe to Ana, by declaring that only my love filled her heart and you have seen the attempt to deny this love, so give her your hand in marriage, if that's what it takes, and don't pay attention to my offense so that she won't marry someone for whom she has no feelings. And to clarify this situation, for the second time I confess that I am a woman and I am undoing what was done and satisfy with this your offense, since saying that I am a woman is the same as admitting that I could not have insulted you or offended you: And if this does not satisfy you, may my gratitude do what death could not do to this invincible chest (kneeling), by surrendering to you and by confessing myself defeated, I live by your mercy. You are more benefitted and satisfied with this than by killing me. (Act 3, scene 9)[61]

This fascinating speech not only rewards Guzmán with hero status in the final scene but also reiterates the underlying theme of homoerotic love, which Pérez de Montalbán highlights in his version of Erauso's life. Guzmán was not willing to confess her identity to her brother, or even to save her own life, but she is willing, twice, to sacrifice her identity and freedom for her beloved. This is the ultimate "valor" to which the other characters refer in the end. Even though Guzmán admits that she is biologically a woman, this does not mean that she will return to female garb or live as a woman like the protagonists of traditional Golden Age dramas: "Catalina does not return to the status quo (on the most obvious level, wearing skirts) in the finale" (Taddeo 114). The play's final statement, like the resolution of a contemporary docudrama, informs the audience of the actual status of Erauso as she continues traveling (in men's garb): "With this and with your permission, this true story comes to an end, and where the play ends so do the actual events, since today the Lieutenant Nun is in Rome and if more news provides my pen additional material I promise you a second part. The End."[62]

Despite the homoerotic content of Pérez de Montalbán's version of the "Monja Alférez," the story is sympathetic in comparison to the *relaciones* published just a year earlier. The first time we see Guzmán react with force is when she defends her brother Miguel during a card game. Likewise, on other occasions when Guzmán responds with fury, her behavior is provoked or is justified by the need for self-defense. The seventeenth-century audience was able to read Pérez de Montalbán's Guzmán as a hero precisely because of his careful construction of the cross-dressed lesbian. The playwright first rationalizes her transvestism as the logical consequence of the conflict experienced in the convent (which ultimately has a normalizing effect for cross-dressing). Then, insisting that her desire is nonphallic and therefore nonthreatening, and finally showing how she is able to sacrifice everything she values for her beloved, Pérez de Montalbán leads his public to interpret Guzmán as the true hero of the play.

Given the numerous references to homoerotic attraction and activity in various representations of Erauso's life, we might question how this facet of her identity functions in the creation and development of the "Monja Alférez" legend. What was absent in the petitions, testimonies, and the letter written by Pedro de la Valle was mentioned in Agustín de Carvajal's letter of 1617 (published in 1618), suggested in the first and third *relaciones* published in 1625 and 1653, and developed with more detail in the autobiography as well as in Pérez de Montalbán's 1626 play. Surely, as McKendrick postulates, Erauso was "the object of rumours, suspicions and jokes about her sexual tastes and life" (214). It is this connection in the mind of the seventeenth-century public between Erauso's cross-dressing, masculine appearance and behavior, and "manly preferences" that lead Pérez de Montalbán to concentrate the plot of his play on the homoerotic tension. Although the potentially subversive nature of this nonheterosexual attraction is partially neutralized for some spectators (due to Erauso's abstinence from heterosexual relations), the homoerotic identity is ever present for other viewers: "Her celebrated chastity would be corporeal but not in her heart or in her hands" (León 1973, 127).[63]

Many critics, on the other hand, attribute the homoerotic scenes in the various narratives to the protagonist's desire to be convincing in her role as a man. Joaquín María de Ferrer, for example, suggests that the homoerotic passages in Erauso's autobiography may be less sexually motivated than they are mere proof of her desire to pass as a man: "This singular inclination of this woman, that even speaking truthfully with her readers, seems that she wants to continue in her obsession to pass as a man, affecting a clear attraction for the female sex" (quoted in Vallbona 70).[64] Julie Wheelwright argues that the flirtation of female transvestites with other women "is part of a larger wholesale adoption of what are seen as male values" (70). And while Rima de Vallbona associates some of the flirtation scenes with the picaresque genre, she also believes that Erauso only engages in the beginning of a relationship ("petting and flirting") to ensure the success of her disguise as a man (48).[65] Mary Elizabeth Perry also speculates about why Erauso did not develop her relationships with other women: "Possibly Erauso wanted to express sexual feelings, but feared the consequences of revealing not only her female identity, but also her homosexual longings. Perhaps he did not want to commit to long-term relationships, or perhaps he did not describe these relationships because he knew that they would not be acceptable in his society of 'compulsory heterosexuality' " (1999, 400).

As discussed in chapter 1, some scholars oppose the term "lesbian" in reference to Erauso's sexual preferences. Adrienne L. Martín notes that even though lesbianism (understood as a sexual identity and social category) did not exist in the seventeenth century, Erauso probably was a lesbian. Martín also stipulates, however, that if her sexuality is interpreted at all, it is not as lesbian but as an attempt to hypermasculinize herself (36–37).[66] Like Martín, Encarnación Juárez is also hesitant to ascribe to Erauso the label of lesbian: "Although it is very possible that there were sexual motivations, one must consider that during that time the concept of homosexuality as we understand it today did not exist, much less that of lesbianism" (1995, 187).[67] Juárez, nonetheless, notes the dramatic tension created by the homoerotic attraction in various episodes in Erauso's *Vida:* "These episodes that relate her contact with other women constitute the proof of her fraud although they hide more than the mere intention of taking advantage of the situation and of making them seem like just more achievements. They are narrated with the tension caused by the sexual deceit and by the impossibility of consummating the relation, which causes friction with the obvious homoerotic attraction of the protagonist" (1995, 190).[68]

Those critics, on the other hand, who interpret Erauso exclusively in terms of maleness have difficulty identifying "him" as a lesbian. Chloe Rutter, following Judith Halberstam's work on female masculinity, argues that Erauso's "codes of behavior identify him as a man, therefore his desire for women fits into the accepted conventions of male/female relationships" (9). Along similar lines, according to Holly Devor's classifications of gendered sexualities (sexual patterns of fantasy, desire, or practice), Erauso could be described as homosexual and straight. For Devor, terms such as "heterosexual," "homosexual," and "bisexual" consider persons' bodies (their sex) while "straight," "lesbian," "gay," and "bi" consider their genders: "So, a cross-living transsexual man who is sexually attracted to female women is both homosexual and straight" (xxvi).[69]

Conversely, Marjorie Garber reads Erauso's desire for other women as allegorical: "When Catalina flirts with two young women, 'frolicking' and 'teasing,' it might seem intriguing to read this as lesbianism *avant la lettre,* an instance of female homosexuality or, at the very least, love play between women. Yet all these readings are allegorical—that is to say, they are readings of her story as a story *about something else*" (1996, viii). Regardless of how we configure Erauso's sexuality today (homoerotic, lesbian, "woman-loving butch," allegorical, and so forth), the early modern representations of the Monja Alférez's erotic desire reveal the perception that she was a masculine woman who was attracted to other women and not to men. As Michele Stepto concludes, the men "are never potential lovers. The women, by contrast, almost always are" (Stepto and Stepto xxxviii).

Like the cases discussed in chapter 1 of this study, the scenes depicting Erauso's sexual preference serve multiple functions during the early modern period. The subtle criminalization of this desire, through the associations between the protagonist's aggression and same-sex attraction, serves to monitor the gender and sexual border-crossings in the mind of the consumer/voyeur. Since Erauso successfully lived as a man for years without any investigation regarding her biological identity, defenders of naturalized gender roles would undoubtedly invoke her case as evidence for the necessary policing of transgressive behavior and desire. It is not by chance that the only *relación* to silence lesbian desire justifies this exclusion. The subtitle of the second *relación* provides this clarification: "In this paper one will not hear the offensive acts that may cause dishonor to the person about whom they are speaking, as it is not fitting. But rather praiseworthy things will be said in her favor and those things worthy of eternal memory" (165).[70] Since the news pamphlet details numerous violent and bloody murders as well as volatile gambling scenes, one may assume that the phrase "offensive acts" refers to the same-sex flirtation scenes contained in the first *relación*.

Even though young women were certainly not encouraged to dress as men or fall in love with other women, the disguised woman was extremely popular, as the performance provided a sexual object for the visual gratification of certain viewers. Of course, if the homoerotic episodes were believed to be nonpenetrative, then they might actually facilitate female chastity (in heterosexual terms) and could avoid censorship on that account.

The Lieutenant Nun as Orthodox Virgin

Despite the potentially controversial aspect of a lesbian Lieutenant Nun, a more traditional and orthodox reading of Erauso's life could result from the belief that she was a "virgen intacta."[71] For those readers who enjoyed the highly popular narratives of saints' lives and other religious treatises, the story of a warrior nun who maintained her virginity while living among men for nearly two decades provided a contemporary version of the medieval cross-dressed warrior saints, who donned male garb to preserve chastity and to prove their religious devotion.[72]

Fray Diego de Rosales (1601–1677) wrote an account of Erauso's life that addresses most of the same nonincriminating episodes included in Carvajal's letter.[73] However, Rosales's version differs from that of Carvajal in silencing homoerotic details and including a literary portrayal of Erauso as religious figure. As Stephanie Merrim summarizes, Rosales's text may be read as a "hagiographic version of Erauso's life" (1994, 190). Unlike the seemingly more "objective" style of Carvajal's comments, the text attributed to Rosales abounds in personal commentary regarding Erauso's holy nature, her temporary transgression of cross-dressing, and her final repentance. Rosales describes Catalina's childhood activities in the convent as "solitary meditation, spiritual exercises and virtue" (quoted in Tellechea 66).[74] Likewise, her decision to don men's garb is consistently described as tragic, "a powerful sadness and temptation" (66).[75] Accordingly, her life dressed as a man created mental anguish for the protagonist: "extreme torture and struggle that were brought on by her conscience . . . the tortures of her conscience and the battles that wounded her soul internally" (68–69).[76]

Rosales's narrative interprets Erauso's life, even when she is dressed as a man, in terms of the pious humility appropriate for women: "Her purity was great, keeping her eyes lowered and fixed on the ground, her words were composed, her actions virtuous, and although they did not know that she was a woman, she always went about covered with the veil of virginal humility" (68).[77] Consistent with this saintlike presentation of Erauso's life, Rosales's text reflects the popular contemplative tradition for early modern women's spirituality, which emphasized submission, penance, chastity, and humility. Like other cross-dressed saints, Rosales's Erauso diligently continued her spiritual exercises: "She had some devotions for which she maintained her virtue, she would flagellate herself every three days, she fasted a few days of the week, she wore a plain hair shirt that was tight against her skin, she recited the prayers of the Virgin, and through these devotions she conserved and suffered the great patience of our Lord who waits for and calls the sinner with great patience and magnanimity" (68).[78] This mystical interpretation of the "Monja Alférez" continues as the author describes how God disapproved of her transvestism: "The one who mainly gave her these wounds was her divine spouse, who as a lover, wounded her in the chest to penetrate her heart with the wound of love that she had so forgotten, and like a soliciting shepherd, he did what the shepherd does with the lost sheep wandering in the hills" (69).[79] Described in the other narratives as a strategy to save her life, Rosales attributes Erauso's decision to confess her biological identity to her desire to return to God in order to live the life of a penitent (69–70).

Interestingly, Rosales's is the only early modern account containing details related to some of the physiological inconveniences of female cross-dressing in the military, such as bathing, dressing, and menstruation: "She slept at night in breeches and she never took them off nor did she bathe and when she was menstruating she would retreat to the hills until it passed. She always maintained her virginity with distinguished virtue" (67).[80] Again, these details underscore her ability to protect her sexual purity. Clearly, Rosales's intention was to present a religious image of Catalina de Erauso that resembled the figure of the saintlike penitent, emphasizing her virginal status after so many years living among men. Like Carvajal, Rosales was also a member of the Catholic hierarchy, and perhaps their positive portrayals of Erauso reflect the papal decision to support a female transvestite despite the church's prohibition of cross-dressing.

The third *relación* (published in Mexico in 1653), like the version penned by Rosales, ends with a description of Erauso's exemplary Christian death and interprets her life in religious terms, despite its mostly lesbian characterization of the protagonist: "She had the habit of praying every day, for all the professed nuns, she fasted every Easter, Advent, and on vigils, every week on Mondays, Wednesdays, and Fridays she did three flagellations and she went to mass every day" (174).[81] This hybrid creation—the aggressive yet pious lesbian-saint—reflects both the need to rewrite her life to neutralize its transgressive power as well as the public's interest in "seeing the monster not only as the sign of marvel but also of disorder and divine wrath" (Braidotti 84). Along similar lines, Henry Ettinghausen attributes the attention given the individuals featured in the *relaciones* either to their "membership of the ruling caste, their success at war, their achievement of sainthood or—at the other end of society—by their physical malformation or violent crimes" (1984, 14–15). This being the case, the story of the Monja Alférez fulfills the reader's curiosity while demonstrating the worldview according to royal, military, and religious rhetoric.

The Lieutenant Nun as Hybrid Spectacle

The dual nature of Erauso's icon as "lieutenant" (male) and "nun" (female) creates a transgender spectacle that provokes a crowd-pleasing shock effect. In this sense, the presentation of the Lieutenant Nun reflects the highly popular talk show programs today, as they parade transvestites and transsexuals on the stage while projecting "before" photos to emphasize the shocking contrast.[82] Likewise, the transformation and revelation scenes in many versions, portraying Erauso's change from nun to young page and the eventual confession of her biological identity, perhaps best underscore the sensational hybridity of the "Monja Alférez" spectacle. The account in Erauso's memoirs of how she initially cuts her hair and sews her new gender-appropriate costume fulfills the public's interest in watching the preparations of the transformation: "There, I holed up for three days, planning and re-planning and cutting myself out a suit of clothes. With the blue woollen bodice I had I made a pair of breeches, and with the green petticoat I wore underneath, a doublet and hose—my nun's habit was useless and I threw it away, I cut my hair and threw it away" (4).[83] This type of "dress-up" scene is recurrent in both early modern as well as contemporary transvestite narratives.[84] Chris Straayer describes the adoption of the opposite sex's gender-coded costume and its accessories, makeup, gestures, and attitudes as a generic characteristic in films featuring "temporary" transvestites (43–47). The consistent presence of these transgender preparations attests to their enduring appeal for spectators and readers, given that the diegetic characters are seldom witness to the private and usually "secretive" transformation necessary for passing.

While the "dress-up" scene initiates the transvestite's transformation, the revelation or unmasking scene brings an end to the characters' belief in the disguise. Moreover, like the sudden confessions of transgenders to their "unsuspecting" lovers or friends on talk shows today, the revelation scene offers the diegetic spectator as well as the extradiegetic reader/viewer the voyeuristic pleasure of the Baroque shock effect of the hybrid "monster" or carnival attraction.[85] Just as Stephanie Merrim notes that "the phenomenon of Catalina de Erauso had something of the 'monstrous' to it" (1994, 193), Sara Taddeo describes the humiliation that Pérez de Montalbán's Guzmán endures as a " 'freak show' being conducted during the play" (117). When Guzmán (Erauso) finally reveals her true identity in the play, Diego, who believes in a biological correspondence between gender and sex, is shocked: "A woman? With the courage to defeat the enemy in battle so many times, that even exceeds what is expected of the most valiant man, how could this be the product of the delicate arm of feminine weakness?" (Act 2, scene 7).[86]

Once Guzmán's identity has been made public, her reaction to this celebrity status reveals a distaste for the newfound attention and lack of independence. In fact, in a comical scene during the third act (scene 3), Guzmán resists society's attempt to control the cultural product of the Lieutenant Nun that views her as some sort of grotesque spectacle or "monster." When other men try to convince her to wear women's clothing for an important visit from a royal counselor, Guzmán resents posing as the object of others' curious gaze: "Why must he see me? Am I by chance some monster never before seen or am I some wild beast seen in Poland that they invented but who is educated and can fight? Has he never seen a man without a beard?" (Act 3, scene 3).[87] Unlike the rest of society, Guzmán considers her identity to be based on gender selection, not anatomy, even though she is reminded of the rare nature of her status: "To be a woman soldier and a Lieutenant Nun is the most strange prodigy that has been seen in these times" (Act 3, scene 3).[88] When the men keep trying to convince her to wear women's garb, even for just a couple of hours, she becomes increasingly more angry and finally explodes, expressing abhorrence for being a woman and having to perform the female gender role: "I hate myself . . . two hours are two thousand years" (Act 3, scene 3).[89] Besides, Guzmán argues, the official would want to see her in the Lieutenant Nun costume since there is no novelty in seeing a woman dressed as a woman. Reluctantly, Guzmán finally gives in, she "throws off the cape with anger," and asks for the "manteo" (skirt).[90] This scene provides visual humor for the audience, as Guzmán has no idea how to wear women's clothing and must be taught by the men. Guzmán not only places the skirt over her sword but also mistakenly puts the garment on backwards. In addition to pointing out her fashion errors, the men correct her gender agreement:

Guzmán: As a man, I am in the habit.
Machín: You mean "as a woman."
Guzmán: I am also used to referring to myself in the masculine.[91]

The *gracioso* Machín continues to instruct the frustrated Guzmán on how to wear the female garb properly, while Guzmán is told to do a series of turns as if she were a model being dressed for a fashion show. This scene plays with the gender markers of male and female clothing: the cape, sword, and breeches are signs of the male gender role, and the skirt and platform shoes are signs of female performance:

Machín: Now put on this pretty skirt.
Guzmán: The most pretty skirt might as well be the most plain breeches as far as I'm concerned.
Machín: Can't you match the seams?
Guzmán: How am I supposed to match them? The devil himself invented these shackles!
Machín: Turn around to the other side.
Guzmán: Heaven help me, how am I supposed to turn? Can't you see that it is too long for me?
Machín: Well put on these platform shoes.
Guzmán: Platform shoes? Are you drunk? (Act 3, scene 3)[92]

At this comical moment the characters hear the sound of fighting off stage and Guzmán is quick to throw off the skirt ("damn this skirt") as she grabs her sword and prepares to join in the fight.[93] When the men ask her to stop, she replies that the female gender lesson is useless: "What should I wait for? This whole thing is a waste of my time and of your time; it is impossible and foolish to even try."[94] Even Sebastian agrees that teaching her to act like a woman is futile since "the only part of her that is female is her stubbornness" (Act 3, scene 3).[95] One of the most interesting and ironic aspects of this scene is the role reversal of men trying to teach a woman how to dress like a woman, while the woman could easily give these men a lesson on how to behave like fearless warriors: they passively watch while Guzmán does not hesitate to grab her sword and attend to the "male" business of fighting. Pérez de Montalbán seems to intuit that for Erauso, living as a woman would be much more of an unnatural performance than the act of challenging society's conflation of biology and gender by living as a man.

In the revelation scene of the autobiography (chapter 20), when Erauso confesses her identity to the bishop to avoid prosecution for murder, she summarizes her life narrative in one brief passage for the reader, which actually took hours to recount to her listener:

> The truth is this: that I am a woman, that I was born in such and such a place, the daughter of this man and this woman, that at a certain age I was placed in a certain convent with a certain aunt, that I was raised there and took the veil and became a novice, and that when I

> was about to profess my final vows, I left the convent for such and such a reason, went to such and such a place, undressed my self and dressed myself up again, cut my hair, traveled here and there, embarked, disembarked, hustled, killed, maimed, wreaked havoc, and roamed about, until coming to a stop in this very instant, at the feet of Your Eminence. (64)[96]

The narratee's first reaction is described in terms of shock and amazement: "My tale lasted until one in the morning, and all the while that saintly gentleman sat there motionless, without speaking or even batting an eyelid, listening to my story, and when I had finished he didn't say a word but remained there motionless, his face bright with tears" (64–65).[97] Later the bishop confirms that hers "was the most astonishing case of its kind he had heard in all his life" (65) and says, "I'm sure you will understand if I tell you that your strange tale raises some doubts," (65).[98] Since he can hardly believe the story is true, Erauso requests a physical examination to prove her virginity. Once the bishop has proof that she is a virgin, he now enthusiastically believes everything she had said: " 'Daughter,' he said, 'my doubt is gone. I believe you now, and I shall believe from this day on whatever you may choose to tell me—I esteem you as one of the more remarkable people in this world' " (66).[99] Perhaps one of the most telling aspects of their interaction and the subsequent procedures is the manipulation of certain elements of her experiences and the complete erasure of others. Once Erauso's virginity is established, the numerous crimes she has committed suddenly lose significance for the judicial as well as the religious institutions. After Erauso identifies herself as a woman, she is sent to a convent, forced to wear the nuns' habit once again, and is paraded around "through a crowd so huge, it was hard to believe there was anyone left at home. . . . News of this event had spread far and wide, and it was a source of amazement to the people who had known me before, and to those who had only heard of my exploits in the Indies, and to those who were hearing of them now for the first time" (66–67).[100] The shock produced by her story also proved to be entertaining for the general public, and so many spectators gathered to see the Lieutenant Nun that they had difficulty getting past the crowds: "There were more people waiting than we knew what to do with, all come out of curiosity, hoping to catch a glimpse of the *Lieutenant Nun*" (68, emphasis mine).[101] Her fame began to spread first in the New World, and there she became the popular celebrity known as the "Lieutenant Nun."

According to Erauso's life narrative, however, once she returns to Spain she begins to tire of some of the negative consequences of celebrity status, such as the loss of independence and anonymity. In Seville she tries to hide from the crowds, "lying low as much as possible and fleeing from the swarms of people that turned up everywhere, trying to catch a glimpse of me in men's clothing" (73).[102] Numerous passages from Erauso's autobiography reveal her awareness of the public's curious pleasure in the visual images of *before* and *after:* "Those who had seen me *previously,* and those who *before* and *afterwards* heard of my story, were amazed" (quoted in Vallbona 216, emphasis mine).[103]

Given Philip IV's reputation for enjoying sensational marvels, prodigies, and curiosities as well as Urban VIII's enthusiastic support of lavish spectacles, it is not surprising that king and pope seem equally captivated by Erauso's personality.[104] When she explains to the king how she was robbed on her way to Rome, he clearly seems to take pleasure in her character as the Lieutenant Nun when he asks: "Well, how is it that you allowed yourself to be robbed?" (76).[105] Later when she travels to Italy to tell her story to the pope, her account is reduced to a one-sentence summary in her autobiography: "[I] told him in brief and as well as I could the story of my life and travels, the fact that I was a woman, and that I had kept my virginity" (78).[106] Again her listener is astonished by her entertaining story: "His Holiness seemed amazed to hear such things, and graciously gave me leave to pursue my life in men's clothing" (78).[107] In Rome her popularity only increases as she was the guest of the most wealthy and prestigious people in the city: "My fame had spread abroad, and it was remarkable to see the throng that followed me about—famous people, princes, bishops, cardinals. Indeed, wherever I went, people's doors were open, and in the six weeks I spent in Rome, scarcely a day went by when I did not dine with princes. . . . All of them—or most of them—seemed remarkably pleased, even moved, to share my company, and they spoke to me a great deal" (79).[108] Despite some apparent resistance to the publicity, Erauso confirmed her increased fame by sitting for at least two portraits and by retelling her story to numerous listeners who, in turn, recorded their own versions of Erauso's narration.

In 1626 Pedro de la Valle, a member of Urban VIII's circle of intellectual friends, described Erauso's popularity as well as her visits with the pope and other distinguished people in Rome.[109] The last paragraph of de la Valle's letter provides a detailed description of Erauso's physical appearance in the form of a literary portrait. According to the author, Erauso was "tall and powerfully built, and with a masculine air, she has no more breasts than a girl. She told me she had used some sort of remedy to make them disappear. I believe it was a poultice given her by an Italian—it hurt a great deal, but the effect was very much to her liking. Her face is not ugly, but very worn with years. Her appearance is basically that of a eunuch, rather than a woman" (quoted in Stepto and Stepto xxxiii–xxxiv).[110]

Although Pedro de la Valle based his physical description of Erauso on first-hand observation, numerous critics have subsequently commented on her appearance by examining Francisco Pacheco's famous portrait of the "Lieutenant Miss Catalina de Erauso," painted in 1630 (see fig. 2).[111] Many observers emphasize the masculine attributes of the portrait: "Through it we see that she had masculine features, more typical of a soldier than of a young woman" (Serrano y Sanz 390); "her expression is hard and inexpressive. . . . [The portrait] gives us the idea that it pertains to a man and not to a woman" (León 1973, 125); "it seems quite contrary to the idea we have of a woman. Her entire face has the appearance of a man" (Sánchez Calvo 227); "the uniqueness of her physical condition, clearly masculine, . . . is evident in her portrait" (Sánchez Moguel 6–7).[112] While these observers see Erauso as a masculine woman, others view her in terms of an "effeminate man." Basing her analysis on de la Valle's description and Pacheco's portrait, Melveena McKendrick goes so far as to doubt the possibility that Erauso's physical appearance could readily attract women (214). However, given de la Valle's assertion that Erauso resembled a eunuch, her appearance may have held a special attraction for other women. Gail Bradbury, for example, cites a seventeenth-century Spanish ballad to demonstrate "the eunuch's success as a lady-killer" (578). And yet some discussions of Erauso's physical appearance and sexual preferences hypothesize that her abstinence from heterosexuality had less to

FIGURE 2. Engraving made by Fauchery from Pacheco's 1630 portrait of "Lieutenant Miss Catalina de Erauso." Courtesy of Biblioteca Nacional, Madrid.

do with her possible lesbianism than with the fact that men were not attracted to her masculine nature. In 1927 Edmund B. D'Auvergne wrote: "She might, notwithstanding, have been thawed by the ardour of a man's passion; but what man was there to love this tall, harsh-visaged, evil-tempered bravo?" (44).

Some, moreover, have tried to use the portrait together with her memoirs to prove physiological, psychological, and sexual pathology. Berruezo notes that Pacheco's rendition of Erauso was so well done that "we could easily judge it to be a psychological portrait of the Lieutenant Nun" (9).[113] Reminiscent of the early modern link between biology, masculine women, and homosexuality as described by Huarte de San Juan, Sánchez Calvo attributes Erauso's masculinity and lesbian desire to physiology: "Relying on the portrait and on the written memoirs of our heroine . . . the neuro-endocrine pattern described seems to correspond to a hypophysial-suprarenal hyperfunctioning, framed by an excess of masculinity and accompanied by certain erotic abnormalities that are quite frequent in the psychosomatology of such a condition" (224, 228).[114]

Interestingly, some observers of Pacheco's portrait of Erauso express an uneasy sensation of being watched in the act of watching—what Paul Willemen terms the "fourth gaze," Wheeler Winston Dixon the "returned gaze," and James Elkins "the object stares back." The spectator, transformed into the object of the look or gaze, is being watched in the act of watching. For example, Berruezo's analysis of Erauso's portrait attempts to intuit her feelings about being observed: "This portrait that you have just seen, with its clearly mannish appearance, indifferent expression, aquiline eyes, big, sensual lips, insinuating an ironic grin . . . attire that is very military and not at all feminine, with an attitude between absent and introspective as if from the height of her popularity—fame well earned of course—*she looked at us with pure condescension*" (7, emphasis mine).[115] For Berruezo, Erauso's portrait communicates an implied objection to being the object of others' gaze as she seems to reverse the stare back on the spectator.

Like many other early modern playwrights in Spain, Pérez de Montalbán also incorporates the image of the portrait in his version of Erauso's life. While we never see Erauso dressed in nun's garb in Pérez de Montalbán's play, her brother Miguel mentions Catalina's childhood in a letter he reads from his parents. Although this correspondence is conjecture on the part of the playwright, it is interesting to consider the possible consequences of having Erauso's brother suspect the truth about his new friend from his hometown. When their father sends Miguel a letter lamenting the family's dishonor as a result of Catalina's escape, her transvestism, and her trip to the New World, he also includes a portrait of the adolescent Catalina, no doubt in novice's habit. The brother's fury upon reading the letter and his promise to avenge the honor of his family respond to the father's statement that Miguel would know what to do when he found his sister. The father apparently recommends murder, considering that Miguel is explicit about his plan to kill his sister once he has proof of her identity. Of course this episode is not historically documented; neither the brother nor the family knew prior to her confession that she dressed as a man, although they may have suspected it.

Guzmán consequently becomes the object of her brother's investigative gaze as he repeatedly tries to get a closer look at his friend to compare her features with those in the portrait. Not surprisingly, Guzmán tries to maintain distance between the two, but Miguel continues to suspect the truth: "Not only in her voice, face, and figure does she appear to be a woman but it seems that her facial features are similar to those in the portrait, so I need to examine her more closely to compare these features" (Act 1, scene 6).[116] However, not knowing that Miguel has a picture of her, Guzmán cannot imagine that her brother will be able to remember her face, much less with age, experience, and the change of costume.

In addition to relying on the portrait for proof of "Catalina's" true identity, Miguel plans to use a prostitute to test his new friend, assuming that if Guzmán is truly a man, he will naturally welcome the opportunity to enjoy the favors of Teodora: "What I need to confirm that this false Guzmán is my sister Catalina is based on the fact that a young man in his most passionate age should welcome the opportunity to be with a beautiful woman. I swear that it is not believable that he would resist the impulse of Venus' pleasures, even more so when he is not known for his saintly nature" (Act 1, scene 15).[117] Although this scene is not developed further in Pérez de Montalbán's play, it shares certain similarities with the conflict between Erauso and her brother described in the first *relación* and the autobiography. In these versions, however, Miguel did not want his friend (Erauso) to visit his lover, but in the *comedia* Miguel makes the heterosexist assumption that his sister would not be interested in another woman (which, according to other narratives as well as the play itself, would be a false supposition); and if Guzmán were a man, "he" certainly would be interested in a woman (another heterobiased deduction, especially considering the homoerotic confessions of certain early modern soldiers in their autobiographies).[118]

Given the numerous indications of Erauso's perceived resistance to being displayed as a "freak" in a show, it is not surprising that a 1637 picaresque novel written by Alonso de Castillo Solórzano, titled *Aventuras del Bachiller Trapaza,* hypothesizes about the Lieutenant Nun's adverse reaction to her new life as a cultural icon while chronicling a *pícaro*'s plan to take advantage of the commercial success of the popular icon. In chapter 10 of the novel, the *pícaro* Trapaza, having seen a portrait of Erauso and knowing other details that were circulating about her life, decides to pass off his male companion Pernia as the Lieutenant Nun and then charge the public admission to see "her." The success of this ruse, a reversal of the "Victor/Victoria" scam (in this case, a man pretends to be a woman pretending to be a man), depends on the effectiveness of Erauso's original transgender identity. The audience's pleasure comes from the amazing yet convincing appearance of a man whom everyone believes is really a woman dressed as a man. Like the "step right up . . . see the most astonishing aggregation of human marvels and monstrosities" technique used to attract spectators to freak shows, when Trapaza advertises the upcoming Lieutenant Nun exhibition, he promises a visual shock that will entertain the audience: "Your Excellence, my lord, has before your eyes the *portent,* the *prodigy,* the *marvel,* the *terrific miracle* of Spain and I can even say of foreign nations. You have before you the one who . . . has followed her profession with such interest that she has become the *astonishment* of her adversaries, the *shock* of the infidels, the *terror* of those against the Spanish flag" (175, emphasis mine).[119] When Pernia emerges as the Lieutenant Nun merely by using his own male clothing, he responds to Pérez de Montalbán's play (which Pernia attributes to Belmonte Bermúdez), imagining Erauso's resistance to certain interpretations of her transgender identity. In Castillo Solórzano's novel, the character pretending to be the Lieutenant Nun implicitly objects to the playwright's portrayal of her as a criminal-lesbian instead of a skillful and valiant warrior: "The playwright should have informed himself about me first. I could have told him about my true accomplishments to excuse him of having to invent false deeds, like he has done" (177–178).[120] Pernia's convincing performance is so popular that the two rogues take it on the road and proceed to deceive many other spectators desperate to get a glimpse of the Lieutenant Nun in person.[121]

Despite the historical Erauso's apparent willingness to participate in the "celebrity machine" (by posing for at least two portraits and agreeing to visit with numerous rich and famous admirers), her autobiography, like Pérez de Montalbán's play and Castillo Solórzano's novel, reveals signs of resistance to the voyeuristic ridicule that she must no doubt have experienced (Merrim 1994, 196). The last paragraph of the memoirs, in particular, demonstrates the protagonist's strong feelings about not being taken seriously. When two prostitutes mock her, she responds by threatening the two women and anyone else who shares their attitude. The way in which this brief episode is narrated again emphasizes issues of the gaze, or who is seeing and who is being seen:

> I was struck by the tittering laughter of two ladies, who leaned against a wall making conversation with two young bucks. They *looked* at me, and I *looked* at them, and one said, "Señora Catalina, where are going, all by your lonesome?" "My dear harlots," I replied, "I have come to deliver one hundred strokes to your pretty little necks, and a hundred gashes with this blade to the fool who would defend your honor." The women fell dead silent, and then they hurried off. (80, emphasis mine)[122]

In this final episode of the autobiography, the protagonist reappropriates the controlling gaze by converting "they looked at me" to "I looked at them" and then successfully makes the women disappear instead of fleeing herself, as she did repeatedly when she was younger: "For once in the text others leave and Erauso stays" (Merrim 1994, 181–182). Now that she is exposed as a woman dressed as a man instead of being taken for a eunuch, she seems to have a new enemy: those who would ridicule her or fail to take her seriously. Of course, the fact that the women who are the targets of Erauso's anger are distinguished by their transgression in heterosexuality might further antagonize her.[123] Regardless, the protagonist is quick to include in her violent threat anyone who would defend these women.

In this way, perhaps one could examine Erauso's case in the context of Joshua Gamson's theory of how those who live outside the boundaries of heterosexual norms and gender conventions manipulate television talk shows. Gamson argues that while the tabloid programs ridicule and monsterize sexual and gender nonconformists as freaks, these shows ultimately provide a space for transgressive expression in mainstream media. In fact, the frequency of these programs normalize what was originally shocking: "Over time, the talk shows have managed to make homosexuality, and even transsexualism and bisexuality, basically dull. . . . talk shows, through their continual exhibition of the most colorful sideshow figures, make 'deviance' seem 'normal'" (217). Especially given the frequency of the male disguise and the subsequent same-sex flirtation as a result of the device on the seventeenth-century stage, what was once scandalous for the moralists and some viewers must have become standard practice.

During the early modern period, however, in order for the "mujer vestida de hombre" to be commodified, she must either be sexualized by the revealing nature of the male costume or pose as a hybrid spectacle in which both identities are present—the masculine and the feminine, the warrior and the nun. Therefore, even when Erauso does not appear in women's clothing (as in Pérez de Montalbán's play, Castillo Solórzano's novel, and Pacheco's portrait), name recognition is sufficient to create the dual identity. Even Pérez de Montalbán exposes this commercial mechanism as Erauso (Guzmán), when asked to dress as a woman, sarcastically anticipates the preferences of her curious audience: "The judge will want to see me in the same clothing that I am wearing, since this is the novelty that motivates him to see me. But in women's clothing, what is there to see? Since when is it a miracle to see a woman dressed in women's clothing?" (Act 3, scene 3).[124]

Clearly, the multifaceted nature of the Lieutenant Nun phenomenon was able to offer something of interest for a diverse and varied group of spectators. While the Monja Alférez was a nationalistic hero celebrated by the state and a "card-carrying" virgin supported by the church, her same-sex desire and transvestism were policed, not only through the traces of criminalization in her icon but by the mere fact that her "true" identity was revealed and patrolled by the vigilant gaze. In the end, despite (or precisely because of) the observation, exploitation, and commodification of the transvestite warrior nun, a positive image of a lesbian cultural icon can emerge during the seventeenth century.

CHAPTER THREE

Melodrama

& the De-Lesbianized Reconstruction of the Lieutenant Nun in the Nineteenth Century

THE STORY OF the Lieutenant Nun was largely ignored during the eighteenth century, with the exception of a few historical documents from the seventeenth century that were circulated and copied during the eighteenth century (such as works by Salazar de Mendoza and González Dávila, the transcription of Erauso's autobiography made by Juan Bautista Muñoz in 1784 from Cándido María Triguero's copy of the manuscript, and the two manuscript copies of Erauso's *Vida* deposited in the Archivo Capitular de Sevilla).[1] This relative invisibility is not surprising perhaps considering the general trend during the eighteenth century to reject many of the values, themes, and aesthetics of the previous century, clearly embodied in Erauso's story. Dorothy Kress attributes the lack of interest in the Monja Alférez during the eighteenth century to the French influence in Spain and the consequent disdain for old Spanish tradition: "Being a purely Spanish figure, Catalina did not concern any of the writers of the eighteenth century" (63).[2] However, in 1829, when Joaquín María Ferrer published the story of Catalina de Erauso (*Historia de la Monja Alférez Doña Catalina de Erauso, escrita por ella misma*) in Paris, the Lieutenant Nun again resurfaced as a new and different spectacle for nineteenth-century viewers influenced by Enlightenment, liberal, and Romantic values. While Catalina de Erauso represented a hybrid spectacle that produced admiration, titillation, and shock during the seventeenth century, the nineteenth century was highly critical of the lesbian celebrity and as a result the Lieutenant Nun is de-lesbianized and reconstructed into a heterosexual or asexual figure. Moreover, this revised icon is both criticized and celebrated because of her transvestism and gender rebellion, not for her homoerotic desire.[3]

The Lieutenant Nun as Object for an "Enlightened" Gaze

After the eighteenth century, the new scientific and social model of womanhood stressed the reproduction-related function of the female body, her presumed lack of sexual passion, and her role as men's nurturer.[4] This idealized asexual "domestic angel," whose principal motivations are childbearing and meeting the needs of her male partner, contrasts starkly with an independent cross-dresser who not only fails to marry and raise children but is infatuated with other women. Although this image found little acceptance in the ideology of an emerging bourgeois society,[5] the Lieutenant Nun, both in her lesbian incarnation as well as in her asexual and heterosexual reconstructions, served various ideological functions during the nineteenth century. For liberals like Ferrer, who published Erauso's *Historia* from political exile in Paris during the "Absolutist decade" in Spain (1823–1833), the transgressive icon provided confirmation of the need for educational reform in Spanish society (Ortega 7). Although Ferrer is clearly intrigued by his subject (with whom he shares a common Basque heritage), he reads the Lieutenant Nun as a negative example of the consequences of neglecting women's instruction, similar to Leandro Fernández de Moratín's message of educational reform for women in "El sí de las niñas" (1806), which was highly popular during the first decades of the nineteenth century. Given that the domestic mission of women was linked with liberal ideology in the early 1820s, it is not surprising that the introduction to the 1829 publication of Erauso's life is critical of the transvestite lesbian.[6] Ferrer's prologue to Erauso's autobiography again presents the protagonist's history in terms of a hybrid monster or aberration, as he refers to sphinxes, hippogriffs, anomalies, prodigies, a monster with two heads, acephalouses, androgynies, and hermaphrodites (11–12). However, he evokes these images as a reaction against the Baroque sense of wonder and marvel toward the hybrid spectacle and as a result Erauso is now presented as an object for the gaze of "enlightened" spectators whose preferences reflect liberal ideology, with its emphasis on education and a rational, scientific approach to understanding social deviance and criminality: "But unfortunately, Miss Catalina de Erauso is far from being a model to imitate. A strange mix of greatness and of disastrous inclinations, her courage is often blind and ferocious irascibility, her genius is actually mischievous tricks, and without deserving the label of 'great' she must be satisfied with that of extraordinary woman and traveller. She cannot claim the admiration, the kind of hero worship that generations only pay to the useful application of talent, to the just and beneficial use of strength, and to the heroism of virtue" (13).[7] Ferrer claims that Erauso does not deserve the admiration bestowed on her during the seventeenth century, condemning her for "acquiring and feeling inclinations and desires of the opposite sex" (14) and for not having used the superiority of reason in her manly endeavors.[8] On the one hand, the author uses Erauso's history to promote educational reform as a solution to Spain's problems ("Education, Legislators, education should be the most serious business for your consideration, as the primary interest in society, as the only basis of our laws" [14]).[9] On the other, he admonishes the reader against a frivolous and useless consideration of Erauso as mere entertainment. Instead, he claims that his purpose in publishing her life is to provide an object for critical examination to determine the societal influences in her pathology:

> If her intellect had been cultivated by a proper education she may have been led by the piety of a Saint Teresa, inclined to the eloquence and politics of an Aspasia, exalted by the patriotic enthusiasm of a Porcia, or given to the literary ambitions of a Staël. What serious concerns for the legislator who, with this spirit, examines the deeds and the materials of such phenomena provided by history. In order to promote this examination and to call one's attention, instead of pleasing a sterile curiosity or to offer a mere pastime for frivolous and lazy readers, I have found it worthwhile to publish this short work of entertaining episodes that I will relate, combined with the desire to be useful, to

show my country how much I am interested in what can expand its glory or contribute to its improvement. (16–17)[10]

By evoking the classical and contemporary female figures of Aspasia, Porcia, St. Teresa, and Germaine de Staël, Ferrer reveals his ideal model of the pious, patriotic, and educated woman and his disappointment in the "wasted potential" of Catalina de Erauso's life.[11] Ferrer, who is described by José Berruezo as a "delayed product of the Enlightenment" (32), encourages his reader to engage a socio-scientific reading of Erauso's story, as the Lieutenant Nun is now converted into a spectacle for an "enlightened" gaze that pretends to justify its consumption of the manly woman in terms of a useful examination whose results will better society.

Despite Ferrer's appropriation of the Lieutenant Nun for political purposes while in exile, Erauso's *Historia* may have participated in a different literary movement in Paris during the late 1820s and early 1830s. With the emerging success of novels dealing with the transvestite lesbian (which was, according to some critics, a popularity fueled by the public's fascination with George Sand in Paris), the French translation of the Lieutenant Nun's life published in 1830 may also have been read as the story of another exotic yet frequently evil lesbian, who by the end of the century had become a "stock image" in certain French literary works (Faderman 264). Even though Ferrer may have been aware of this possible reception ("a sterile curiosity . . . a mere pastime for frivolous and lazy readers"), he sees in the story of a Basque compatriot his opportunity to participate, from exile, in Spain's ongoing debate about the nation's future reforms for the nineteenth century.

The Lieutenant Nun as Non-Lesbian

By mid-century the Romantic movement and liberal reforms were at their peak in Spain, and the Romantics' preference for spontaneity, feeling, and adventure found support for these ideals in Erauso's legend. Like other Golden Age myths reworked by nineteenth-century writers (such as Zorilla's Romantic adaptation of Tirso de Molina's Don Juan figure), the Lieutenant Nun reappeared in various manifestations with a marked Romantic style.[12] During the summer of 1847, for example, Thomas De

Quincey published in three installments his own Romantic version of Erauso's life under the title "The Nautico-Military Nun of Spain."[13] Unlike the memoirs published eighteen years earlier (as well as Ferrer's reading of Erauso's life), De Quincey's text provides a radically different transvestite spectacle that reflects the changing tastes of the nineteenth-century reader. In contrast to the stark presentation of events in the autobiography, which suppresses any indication of the feelings, emotions, or psychological motivation of the protagonist, De Quincey's version provides all the melodramatic sentiments involved in Erauso's actions as well as emotional commentaries by the narrator. While the original autobiography excludes details of her childhood in the convent (other than a brief mention of a quarrel with an older nun who beat her), De Quincey anticipates his readers' preferences by converting the nuns into loving victims of the mischievous yet gentle novice:

> At times she was even headstrong and turbulent, so that the gentle sisterhood of St. Sebastian, who had no other pet or plaything in the world, began to weep in secret, fearing that they might have been rearing by mistake some future tigress; for, as to infancy, *that,* you know, is playful and innocent even in the cubs of a tigress. But *there* the ladies were going too far. Catalina was impetuous and aspiring, violent sometimes, headstrong and haughty towards those who presumed upon her youth, absolutely rebellious against all open harshness, but still generous and most forgiving, disdainful of petty arts, and emphatically a noble girl. She was gentle, if people would let her be so. (163)

Throughout his narrative De Quincey identifies himself with his protagonist and occasionally inserts himself into Erauso's story. After recounting how Catalina stole money from her aunt before escaping from the convent and then sewed a pair of breeches from her nun's habit, De Quincey interjects his own childhood memory related to coins and gendered garments: "I remember even yet, as a personal experience, that, when first arrayed, at four years old, in nankeen trousers, though still so far retaining hermaphrodite relations of dress as to wear a petticoat above my trousers, all my female friends (because they pitied me, as one that had suffered from years of ague) filled my pockets with half-crowns, of which I can render no account at this day. But what were my poor pretensions by the side of Kate's?" (166–167). In this passage we can sense the humor to which Dorothy Kress refers in her analysis of De Quincey's rendition, which is also evident in his use of the nickname "Pussy" with regard to Catalina (Kress 71).

Sympathizing with his literary subject, he neutralizes the lesbian episodes from her memoirs in order to maintain his own as well as his mainstream readers' identification with Erauso. Although De Quincey includes some of the homoerotic scenes featured in earlier sources, he depicts Catalina as the beautiful but unwilling victim of the passion of other women duped by her disguise: "She was in the course of making up her mind to take Kate for a sweetheart. Poor Kate saw this with a heavy heart" (182); "Catalina, seared as she was by the world, has left it evident in her memoirs that she was touched more than she wished to be by this innocent child" (211). According to De Quincey, Erauso consistently resists the homoerotic complications of the male disguise. Despite his efforts to present a non-lesbian Lieutenant Nun, the ambiguity of Erauso's participation in same-sex flirtation remains apparent: "The sisterly love which Catalina did really feel for this young mountaineer was inevitably misconstrued. Embarrassed, but not able, from sincere affection, or almost in bare propriety, to refuse such expressions of feeling as corresponded to the artless and involuntary kindnesses of the ingenuous Juana, one day the cornet was surprised by mamma in the act of encircling her daughter's waist with his martial arm, although waltzing was premature by at least two centuries in Peru" (212).

Although Catalina does not participate in a heterosexual relationship nor does she return to female garb, the text attempts to reinterpret lesbian desire as "sisterly love" while exposing a Romantic portrayal of her aggression that, by the end, is interpreted as a noble urge for freedom and adventure. De Quincey concludes the story of Erauso's exotic life by describing her travels from country to country, with an open-ended narration that confirms the final mystery of the outcome of the protagonist's adventures: "It has been a secret for more than two centuries; and to man it remains a secret for ever and ever" (237). True, in part, to the "domestic angel" image for women, Catalina is both beautiful and asexual; yet De Quincey's adaptation fulfills his readers' interest in emotion and action while his protagonist is stripped of those qualities (namely masculinity and lesbianism) that may interfere with this identification and admiration.

Reminiscent of De Quincey's effort to neutralize the lesbian aspects of his protagonist, toward the end of the nineteenth century different writers were reacting strongly to the "tolerant" seventeenth-century lesbian image of Erauso in a manner congruent with the changing beliefs about same-sex desire. Nineteenth-century sexologists such as Carl von Westphal, Richard von Krafft-Ebing, and Havelock Ellis developed medical explanations for masculine women and lesbianism in terms of "congenital inversion" or the result of hereditary degeneration and neurosis.[14] In other words, lesbians were cast as pathological and psychotic, or, as Lillian Faderman concludes: "In the popular imagination, love between women was becoming identified with disease, insanity, and tragedy" (252). Consequently, many writers in Spain during the latter part of the century refashioned Erauso into a heterosexual or asexual protagonist, but not all agreed on the historical veracity of her lesbian identity. To celebrate the four-hundred-year anniversary of the "discovery" or conquest of America (as well as the three-hundred-year anniversary of Erauso's birth), the editors of the journal *La Ilustración Española y Americana* used Erauso's portrait for the cover of the July 1892 issue in Spain. Antonio Sánchez Moguel wrote an article to accompany this special issue in which he leveled a ferocious attack against Pérez de Montalbán's play and Ferrer's publication of Erauso's autobiography, strongly denying their authenticity and claiming that the historical figure was much more interesting.[15] For Sánchez Moguel, Ferrer's Erauso was nothing more than a "swordsman or an ordinary bully, better yet a handsome or vulgar braggart, without talent or greatness, even without humor, whose adventures, crudely recounted, are always far from awakening interest much less sympathy. There are passages in this book that are so repugnant, so vulgar that only with solid proof could they be attributed to the real Lieutenant Nun" (6).[16] Interestingly, the author does not take issue with the seventeenth-century *relaciones* that describe the same "scandalous" episodes.[17] Instead, he prefers to describe Erauso in terms of her nobility and virginity: "Daughter of noble and illustrious parents, as she herself tells us, and even her old employers certified knowing her to demonstrate much virtue and chastity" (6).[18] Accordingly, one might wonder to which episodes the author refers when he utilizes the adjectives "repugnant" and "vulgar." Given his defense of Erauso's military service and virginity featured in historical documents, we might assume that Sánchez Moguel opposes the implied lesbianism or the sequences of brawling and murder.

In an attempt to reconcile the transgressive act of cross-dressing, the author compares Erauso's transvestism to that of Joan of Arc in a defense similar to Rosales's seventeenth-century narrative: "Only the Maiden of Orleans is comparable to the Basque Maiden" (7).[19] Moreover, only six years before Spain would lose its last colonies, Sánchez Moguel interprets Erauso's virginity and military valor as religious devotion and national pride: "Faith and patriotism are the great passions that awoke the masculine spirit of that extraordinary woman" (7).[20] Needless to say, this version of Erauso's life silences any of the sensational aspects (fights, murders, gambling, and homoerotic flirtation) included in the *relaciones* and in the autobiography. Predictably, the article includes a warning to the reader that certain versions of Erauso's life—such as Ferrer's edition, Pérez de Montalbán's play, and Coello's *zarzuela* (Spanish popular operetta)—should be considered fictional and thus historically inaccurate. Not surprisingly, the author prefers Coello's heterosexual adaptation: "The most poetic, without a doubt, is Coello's version, with his admirable dramatic instinct, he attributes the secret of the transformation in Catalina to love" (7).[21] This revisionist portrait insists on rewriting the image presented in cultural documents to create a hypothetical heterosexual-nationalistic-virgin spectacle for readers at the end of the century.

The Taming of the Criminal Lesbian

Like Sánchez Moguel's sharp criticism of the characterization of Erauso presented in Pérez de Montalbán's 1626 play and the autobiography published in 1829, José Gómez de Arteche's prologue to Carlos Coello's *zarzuela La Monja Alférez* (first performed in Mexico in 1866 and then in Spain in 1873) is equally disapproving.[22] However, Gómez de Arteche does not question the historicity of the Lieutenant Nun legend but seems mainly concerned with destroying such an identity, whether it is based on fact or fiction. The hybrid qualities that evoked fascination and curiosity in the seventeenth-century audience gave way in the nineteenth century to a more sinister demonization of the protagonist, a savage animal that must be domesticated. As Susan Kirkpatrick notes, "Passion and sexuality were banished from the female psyche and defined as contrary to feminine nature; women who exhibited these attributes . . . were classified as degraded or monstrous" (1989a, 348). For the critic of the *zarzuela,* Erauso's masculine and lesbian (and therefore criminal) traits prove to be signs of her evil nature: "A woman? We are mistaken: she seems like a demon" (Gómez de Arteche vii).[23]

Relying on the autobiography, Gómez de Arteche describes Erauso as a "soldier, gambler, fighter, and even a suitor to a number of beautiful women she meets in her tortuous and always bloody path" (viii).[24] Instead of rewriting Erauso's life to fit the "domestic angel" mold, the critic prefers to strip Erauso of any redeeming qualities. He mentions that numerous women in history have cross-dressed for reasons such as "religious exaltation, the feeling for one's country, a strong passion, a fantasy" (viii),[25] but he excludes Erauso from this pious group. Instead, she was "as cruel to her comrades and her own brother as to the Indians for whom she became a terror and fright. There is a gap between faith and disbelief, between courage and cruelty, between more or less vague but forgivable aspirations and those that nature rejects as being absurd and repugnant" (viii).[26] Like De Quincey's references to Catalina's participation in the Black Legend of Spanish barbarism, Gómez de Arteche seems to be one of the few writers in Spain to interpret Erauso's military deeds as barbarous instead of heroic, undoubtedly due to her transgression of traditional gender roles.

Gómez de Arteche had at hand both Pérez de Montalbán's play and the autobiography, as he cites both sources for his background material on Erauso. Both versions include the homoerotic nature of Erauso's sexuality, and the critic of the *zarzuela* interprets as demonic the "intrigue and love affairs with other women and not infrequently undertaken by the diabolical nun in her new role of capricious and enterprising suitor" (x).[27] Nonetheless, like other critics, Gómez de Arteche also interprets the homoeroticism as a sign of Erauso's successful disguise: "But what most delights Catalina de Erauso above all else is showing to what point she could take her deceit, informing us of the times that she fled from homes, always strange and not infrequently due to her audacity with women who lived there" (x).[28] Even though Erauso was an "object of admiration" during the seventeenth century, Gómez de Arteche describes her as "perverse," as he struggles to find some reason to admire the Lieutenant Nun: "Few were the qualities that adorned Catalina de Erauso to make her recommendable to her contemporaries let alone to posterity. . . . You only have to read her writings and one can see that this boldness was the result of a nature that could not be judged anything less than perverse" (xvi).[29]

Despite his disapproval of the implied lesbianism in the versions of Erauso with which the critic was familiar, he finds himself obliged to defend her status as virgin: "Only one feature enhanced her, that of her chastity. . . . Without this quality, all her care in disguising herself, her manly behavior and her indecency would be ineffective to provide her the freedom to do what she wanted. Love is not, nonetheless, a passion which can be hidden during a lifetime and the Lieutenant Nun must have been completely unfamiliar with it; which is also proof of her unsociable, rude, and inhuman temperament" (xvi–xvii).[30] Even in his defense of her chastity, then, the critic negates Erauso's virginity as a sign of virtue, seeing it instead as the result of her inability to love. Since women's ability to feel and to love was seen as an innate characteristic of their "hypersensitive nervous system," any woman believed unable to do so was categorized as defective (Aldaraca 1989, 404).

The text questions how a figure with such vile qualities could inspire a worthwhile theatrical performance: "Can such characters be used to create a dramatic representation that is interesting and moving? A young girl who is disagreeable, without any of the feelings associated with her sex, living alone in a society of men dedicated to profit and looting, gambling or killing" (xvii).[31] The answer, not surprisingly, is found in Coello's need to modify crucial aspects of his protagonist's life to make his character sympathetic and interesting for the nineteenth-century spectators (xvii). According to Gómez de Arteche, Pérez de Montalbán must have tried to find some positive attribute for his plot to balance the "disgust that his heroine must have inspired" (xvii),[32] for he was more bound by the "truth" and could not completely transform her character. Since these traits were common knowledge to his audience, it would have been impossible "not to attribute to her features that misrepresented the personality known by everyone in the city. He could not risk doing such, while she was alive, even when she wasn't near. On the other hand, without turning his audience's attention away from the defect that was least becoming to her, he adorned her with other disgusting characteristics" (xvii–xviii).[33]

Through Gómez de Arteche's introduction, we learn that Pérez de Montalbán's play was also performed during the nineteenth century in Spain and was well received: "For whomever has read Montalbán's play it will seem impossible yet it is true that it has been performed not long ago in one of the most important theaters in Spain without any protest but quite to the contrary, with encores and clamorous applause. How could the ears of the ladies of the nineteenth century listen to the shameful confession of the protagonist telling Ana that she loved her and was still in love with her purity and charm?" (xix).[34] Clearly, what most concerns the critic is the homoerotic theme in Pérez de Montalbán's version, which minimizes the violence and deviance emphasized in the autobiography. So when he describes the seventeenth-century play as "absurd," "unbelievable," and "repulsive," we must assume that these adjectives refer, in large part, to the sexuality of the Lieutenant Nun icon, similar to his commentary on the "absurd" and "repugnant" aspects in the memoirs "that nature rejects" (viii).

Gómez de Arteche's introduction also discusses the changing tastes of the audience, as he finds it difficult to imagine the popularity of a lesbian plot for the nineteenth century. Therefore, he justifies Coello's radical variation on the events described in Pérez de Montalbán's play and the autobiography, especially in light of the restrictions placed on the seventeenth-century playwright due to historical proximity. According to Gómez de Arteche, the "real" Catalina de Erauso was incapable of love, "for the ex-nun love was repulsive"; but a plot that accurately reflected history would lack the emotions produced by affective relationships and make it difficult for an audience to identify with the characters. Therefore Coello had to remold the Lieutenant Nun "to make her bearable for the spectators" (xix).[35] The basic change to which Gómez de Arteche refers also implies a transformation from lesbianism to heterosexuality, which, according to the critic, is necessary for the nineteenth-century audience, despite his earlier statement confirming the popularity of Pérez de Montalbán's play in the nineteenth century. Given his concern for the effect of lesbian desire on female spectators ("How could the ears of the ladies of the nineteenth century listen to the shameful confession of the protagonist telling Ana that she loved her and was still in love with her purity and charm?"), we might question whether the hetero-sexualization of Erauso reflects the changing tastes of the audience or rather the repression of a potentially dangerous sexuality for alternative gazes. In other words, while the critic argues that the heterosexual Lieutenant Nun merely meets the demands of a new aesthetic, his critique demonstrates a program aimed to educate and condition viewers about "appropriate" gender behavior and female sexuality.

Gómez de Arteche explained the heterosexual plot adjustment as a modification of a mere suggestion in Pérez de Montalbán's play: the friendship between Erauso (Guzmán) and Diego, which in Coello's *zarzuela* becomes romantic love (xx). The critic describes the heterosexual love that Guzmán feels for Lope Dávalos as a necessary fiction, while the "verdad histórica" (historical truth) was a "repugnant and detestable" lesbian love (xxi).

Perhaps the one problem that Gómez de Arteche and other critics found with Coello's work was the popular genre of the *zarzuela.* In general terms, the *zarzuela* has been defined as "musical drama whose text is spoken and sung alternately without breaking from the development of the story line" (García Franco and Regidor Arribas 7).[36] Since the *zarzuela* is popular musical theater, some critics believe it is usually written and performed with the "less sophisticated" tastes of the "common" people in mind (Fernández-Luna 3–20). Considered to be a less serious theatrical genre of the lower classes, the Spanish operetta did not carry the prestige of a classical opera. In his 1934 history of the *zarzuela,* Emilio Cotarelo y Mori at times seems defensive about negative assessments of the inferiority of the popular musical drama. Cotarelo y Mori claims that during the nineteenth century the *zarzuela* was considered entertainment of bad taste and originated from the ignorant common class (1934, 17–18). The critic, in turn, attributes these classist accusations to the "ill-will and jealousy of some and the arrogant stupidity and anti-Spanish attitudes of others" (Cotarelo y Mori 1934, 17).[37] The elitist attitude of the *zarzuela* detractors is also evident in the comments cited by Gómez de Arteche from another critic: "In the 'Monja Alférez' he has created a figure from history and tradition which, if it had been cultivated in more suitable soil than the stage of the *zarzuela* and if it had been accompanied with other more artistic elements, perhaps it would have been one of the most beautiful productions of the writer and one of the most pleasing dramatic creations of our contemporary theater" (xxiii–xxiv).[38] Gómez de Arteche also agrees with the assessment of the *zarzuela* as an inferior artistic form. In particular he notes the less than elegant nature of the popular music, chorus, and stage apparatus required to please the general public (xxiv). Interestingly, Gómez de Arteche concludes his introduction with an apologetic recommendation that Coello not waste his talent on the popular genre of the *zarzuela* but instead concentrate on more serious and important dramatic works (xxv). Despite the critical resistance of the elite to the popular musical theater, Coello thought the legend of the Lieutenant Nun was intriguing and sensational enough to be appropriate for a *zarzuela,* undoubtedly confirmed by the successful production of Pérez de Montalbán's play during the same period.[39]

CARLOS COELLO'S *LA MONJA ALFÉREZ*

The mission of educating young women to become domestic and feminine "angels" is evident from the first scene of Coello's *zarzuela.* The protagonist is initially characterized in a song performed by a blind man about a girl from San Sebastián who was so aggressive that her parents put her in a convent in an attempt to "correct" her behavior. One night she escapes and creates a new identity with a different name and men's clothes. Unlike De Quincey's sympathetic adaptation, in Coello's song Lucifer takes Catalina to hell to make her his wife. The final verses of the song reveal that this incredible tale is the true story of Catalina de Erauso:

> In San Sebastián a girl was born, / and ever since she was young / she was as strong as a castle . . . and as stubborn as anyone. / Hoping to reform her, / her father sent her to a convent / but one night she said / "I'll be right back" and she hasn't returned since. / . . . Suddenly it was discovered / that Lucifer appeared in person / and took her to hell / for his wife. / And this song that I sing / is not made up but the true story / of Catalina de Erauso, / famous around the world. (16–17)[40]

The audience is invited to reprove the strong and stubborn rebel, as she is demonized on account of her gender transgression. The first time the viewers actually see the Lieutenant Nun (Act 1, scene 9), she becomes a source of humor as the chorus mocks her valor: "(jokingly): 'Oh what a valiant young man! / Oh, how he scares us! / Oh, just hearing him, / how . . . we . . . shake!' . . . (The chorus, especially the women, laugh at the words of the lieutenant)" (32, 25).[41] The image of a courageous war hero has disappeared, and now Erauso, disguised as Guzmán, is ridiculed by the other characters.

Despite the protagonist's marginalized status, Guzmán's heterosexual desire provides hope for future integration: "And for Lope I save / all my tenderness. / Just thinking about how deeply / I love him drives me crazy. / If I call it friendship / it seems too little, / and brotherly love is not right either. / Lope means much more to me" (29).[42] To reinforce this heterosexualization of the protagonist, Coello stresses her aversion to other women: "I know them well / and am sure how little they are worth" (36).[43] Guzmán also discusses her childhood and how it shaped her character, implying that environment played a key role in her psychological development. The protagonist blames her parents for a conflictive childhood ("my parents used force against me" [36]),[44] which established a pattern of aggression that would continue for years. Since the other characters believe Guzmán is a man and therefore suspect homosexuality because of an indifference toward women ("In my opinion, the man who does not love, / isn't a true man" [36]), Guzmán assigns blame for "his" disinterest in women to an unloving relationship with "his" mother ("He who did not love his own mother, / how can you expect him to love another woman?" [37]).[45] However, the *zarzuela*'s audience, aware that Guzmán is a woman, understands that a woman could go against "nature" (women's "hypersensitive nervous system") and live a violent life dressed as a man.

Coello's work reaffirms the belief held by many critics that the homoerotic flirtation in various narratives based on Erauso's life is a necessary aspect of the masculine disguise; Guzmán decides to flirt with Elvira so that others will not suspect the truth. When the former is alone and talking to herself, we see her true feelings, not of a woman who lives as a man, but of a heterosexual woman who considers herself a woman who is temporarily dressed as a man: "I must find a woman. / Yes, a woman— / any woman. / Elvira clearly seemed / to be interested in me. . . . Catalina, calm down! / My name is Diego Guzmán; / I will try to acquire vices / and pretend what I do not feel . . . / Who will doubt that I am a man?" (41–42).[46] In accordance with the features common to temporary transvestite narratives, Coello's *zarzuela* includes many of the characteristics described by Chris Straayer, who includes "heterosexual desire thwarted by the character's disguise" and "accusations of homosexuality regarding the disguised character" among the list of generic elements in transvestite films (44). Not surprisingly, in Act 2, the love interests become more complicated as Miguel (Guzmán's brother) loves Elvira, and Guzmán, who pretends to love Elvira, really loves Dávalos, who also loves Elvira. When Guzmán expresses emotion for Dávalos but is later rejected, the former becomes violent and wounds the latter: "Ingrate! And I / thought only of him! . . . What I feel in my heart / is love . . . it's love!!!" (94, 98).[47] The second act closes with this desperate expression of heterosexual love, undoubtedly revealed for the benefit of the audience since again this apparent same-sex desire should alert other characters to Guzmán's apparent attraction for "another" man.

In a heterosexual variation on the final homosexual sacrifice in Pérez de Montalbán's play, Coello's Guzmán is willing to give her life for the man she loves by taking legal responsibility for the conflict between the two (116). Like the praise of Erauso's behavior toward Ana at the end of Pérez de Montalbán's play, in the *zarzuela* Galindo also congratulates the protagonist with "Your action is generous" (117), and later Rivera confirms, "Noble generosity!" (136). However, unlike Pérez de Montalbán's version, Coello's Guzmán willingly renounces any desire to continue living as a man. She triumphantly announces her future plan to return to the female gender role when she learns to love (in heterosexual terms): "Now I am beginning to see the light: / misfortune made me love . . . / love is what made me a woman. / Without my sorrows I would think / that I am waking up in my infancy. . . . / Woman! Oh how far / I have come in one day! . . . I now surrender my military uniform" (117).[48] This capacity for true love is only possible for the domesticated feminine woman; as an aggressive cross-dresser, Erauso is unable to understand her function, but once she is "educated" she attains the peace that had previously eluded her.

Guzmán continues to lie to her brother, nonetheless, as she speaks in the third person to explain Catalina's childhood. Even though she had a masculine predisposition, again her parents' excessive severity and lack of parental love justify her conflictive nature and her subsequent decision to live as a man (125). Like Guzmán's brother in Pérez de Montalbán's play, Miguel intends to find his sister and kill her to avenge his family's honor.

When Guzmán tries to save Dávalos's life by confessing her own guilt, Miguel insists that Guzmán should die if he (she) is responsible. In a climactic and melodramatic moment, Galindo shouts out that Guzmán is really Miguel's sister: "No, you have sentenced your own sister! (General surprise)" (137).[49] Unlike Pérez de Montalbán's play, which sustains the name "Guzmán" for the protagonist throughout the performance, Coello's script now refers to Guzmán as "Catalina." Despite the general support for Catalina among the other characters, Miguel still thinks she should die, as the chorus shouts "No!, No!" (139). Fortunately for Catalina, though the law may apply to men, it does not apply to women. Upon hearing this news, everyone cheers while Catalina tells Dávalos: "Now my life really begins!" (140).[50]

As a humorous note to the celebrations, the *gracioso* Mostacho saddens; when asked why, he laments that if the most masculine person is revealed to be a woman, what does that say about the less valiant men, such as himself: "If my master, who was so admired / for his masculine behavior, / turns out to be a woman, . . . / what does that make me?" (141).[51] This statement proves to be even more significant with regard to gender identity and the believed nature of the sexes than perhaps the writer intended. Like the scene in Pérez de Montalbán's play in which the men try to teach Erauso how to behave as a woman while she performs the male gender role more effectively than the men, Mostacho's joke at the end of the *zarzuela* hints at a similar questioning of whether anatomy actually determines gender identity. For a viewer interpreting against tradition, this scene is ambiguous enough to be transgressive, as it suggests that gender is merely performative. For mainstream viewers, nonetheless, any serious message is negated by the humor and absurd nature of the *gracioso* character. The frequent inclusion of humor in the temporary transvestite narrative points to its function of both revealing and alleviating the unconscious fear that the cross-dresser's success (even if temporary) destabilizes fixed notions of gender and biology.

Of course the resolution of the *zarzuela* also dispels any lingering threat against traditional gender identity. Despite the fact that Catalina is still dressed as a man, her statements and actions reveal a clearly domesticated feminine character by the end of the *zarzuela*. The protagonist closes the performance by reiterating, through a flirtatious song and dance, her intention to return to her ascribed gender role as a woman: "(With charm and flirtation) / I am not a man. / I no longer fence the broadsword, / swish, swish! / I am nothing more / than a gentle woman and lover" (141).[52] By the end of the performance, the protagonist has been tamed and sexualized in an affirmation of heterosexual love and traditional gender roles. This finale contrasts with the end of the seventeenth-century image of Erauso traveling to Rome in men's clothing or even with the autobiography's final chapter in which she threatens the prostitutes who dare joke about her transgenderism.

JUAN A. MATEOS'S *LA MONJA ALFÉREZ*

Rather than employing any historical evidence from the previous versions of Erauso's story, Juan Mateos, in his 1877 play *La Monja Alférez,* created a Romantic heroine in a largely original narrative.[53] In what may be an attempt to participate in the creation of a national cultural identity in Mexico, Mateos does not merely retell a Spanish narrative but invents a new tale that differs so significantly from previous versions that the reader/spectator may question whether the playwright was deliberately reinventing the Lieutenant Nun story or was less familiar with specific details of the original legend. John Brushwood argues that Juan Mateos, like many other Romantic novelists of the Reform era in Mexico, was attracted to historical writing because of his interest in building the nation (95–97). From the very beginning, Mateos's play distances itself from the European historical past, as Erauso is no longer called Guzmán or Catalina but Andrea.

One of the few features that the play shares with other versions is the protagonist's violent nature. Andrea is a nun in the convent at the beginning of the play, but she is uncontrollably violent, insubordinate, and excessively cruel. The sacristan and the abbess characterize Andrea as a nun who terrorizes the other members of cloister: "What violence, what rage; / she is a fury from hell! / Since she set foot in the cloister / there has been tremendous chaos. / She never obeys the rules / and with a severe attitude / she dominates and confuses us. / Well, we are afraid of her" (1).[54] In Mateos's work, Andrea is depicted as evil, demonic, disobedient, and violent; even the priests are fearful of her. Other characters also view Andrea in demonic terms: "The devil dispels you! / Satan counsels you! . . . She is a Catholic demon" (4, 8).[55] Whereas Erauso is seen as demonic in Gómez de Arteche's discussion because of same-sex attraction, in Mateos's play (as well as in Coello's *zarzuela*) Andrea is evil due to her "unfeminine" aggressive nature.

Like Coello's Guzmán, Andrea reveals her heterosexual desire: "I love a man" (2). Details from this relationship are revealed when Andrea allows the abbess to read a love letter she received from her beloved Don Félix de Montemar, who writes about her "beautiful eyes . . . lips like roses . . . white skin like snow . . ." (3),[56] even though he later abandons her in the convent. Juan Mateos's Lieutenant Nun is far from the seventeenth-century image of the masculine eunuch with scars from twenty years of fighting; rather she becomes a beautiful object of the masculine gaze. While we might assume that the actresses hired to play the part of the Lieutenant Nun (beginning with Luisa de Robles in the seventeenth century) embodied an underlying sensual demeanor intended to appeal to heterosexual male viewers, Mateos's play offers one of the first explicit descriptions of the protagonist's physical beauty.

While attempting to regain her beloved's attention, Andrea discovers that her stepmother, the Countess, is also in love with Don Félix de Montemar and that he is about to marry another woman named Beatriz. Determined to confront Félix, Andrea escapes from the convent dressed as a man with sword in hand, as the curtain falls to end the first act. In Act 2, disguised as a man and wearing a mask to cover her face, Andrea plots to regain the affection of Félix, which results in sedating the wedding guests. Just as they are getting groggy, she pulls off the mask and everyone shouts "Sister Andrea!" as the guests slowly fall asleep. She then takes Beatriz in her arms and carries her away as the second act ends.

Act 3 begins in the basement of a tavern where Andrea is holding Beatriz captive. The protagonist tells her that she is Don Carlos and has come to avenge the honor of her sister, whom Félix abandoned in a convent. When Andrea leaves her alone for a brief period, Beatriz talks to a sacristan who informs her that her captor is really Andrea. At this point, Beatriz convinces the priest to dress in her clothes and wait for her captor while she dresses in his garments in order to escape. With the priest now dressed in women's clothing, Don Félix thinks he has found Beatriz, but when he uncovers the face he is shocked to discover an unconvincing disguise. At this moment the curtain falls to end the third act.

Like the episodes of transgender humor in the theatrical versions of Pérez de Montalbán and Coello, Mateos's play also includes a comical scene based on the confusions and complications created by cross-dressing. Having been advised to arrest a woman disguised as a soldier (the Lieutenant Nun), an officer believes he has found the suspect when he sees a sergeant named Machete.

> Officer: This is definitely the Lieutenant Nun, / and now I will take her in my custody. / Come here, lady! . . .
> Machete: Who the hell are you calling "lady"! / I've got a mustache / that is stronger and even more . . . stiff!
> Officer: Your disguise is in vain, / we have guessed your sex.
> Machete: My sex? I swear to Judas! . . . / Shouldn't I know what I have?
> Officer: Two months ago you abandoned / the convent.
> Machete: Mayor . . . I wouldn't have left / if I lived there!
> Officer: Don't exaggerate, ma'am, / this is a serious issue. / You are wearing men's clothing / but I am an expert judge / and I declare that you are the nun / who, without human respect, / abandoned the convent.
> Machete: Cloister! What the hell? / I am really Machete! . . .
> Officer: Ma'am, be quiet. / In the name of the Holy Office / I take you to prison! (58)[57]

They continue arguing about the sexual identity of Machete, and by the end of the scene the officer is still unconvinced that his prisoner is really a man dressed as a man. While it provides humor, this scene also shows traces of the unconscious fear of the arbitrary relationship between gender and sex, as any man on the street could be suspected of being the Lieutenant Nun. Moreover, hearing the officer call the sergeant "lady" and "ma'am" provides as much humor as the sexual references evoked by the suspect in his own defense. However ridiculous this scene may appear, Beatriz makes the same assumption when she sees the police apprehend Machete. While transvestite narratives employ certain strategies to make the disguise believable for the diegetic characters (and unbelievable for the audience/readers), Mateos's play reverses the pattern. The play's characters are mistakenly tricked by the verisimilitude of a "believable" disguise, while the audience knows there is no disguise but enjoys the confusion just the same.

Unexpectedly, the audience observes a sudden change in Andrea's personality when, alone, she expresses emotions not previously displayed. She is depressed and feels hopeless: "I feel like a lost shadow, / like a wandering ghost, . . . without a tender / or loving word to guide me! . . . Dreams that will never return / to my crazy fantasy . . . I feel like a damaged boat / in a wild sea. / I want to choke / the ghost of my destiny; / which still, silent, inert / it sees my rude eagerness doubtful! . . . Death awaits me here!" (29–30).[58] Having arranged a duel with Félix, the protagonist tells her competitor that she is Andrea's brother, who has come to avenge her honor, and when the two fight she assures him that she did nothing with Beatriz to insult his honor; but that if she should die, he is to find the truth on her body: "On my chest / you will find / the proof of her innocence" (31).[59]

Like Guzmán in Pérez de Montalbán's play, Andrea is concerned with proving the chastity of another woman, but not because of romantic feelings for Beatriz. Andrea and Félix begin to fight and the latter quickly wounds the former. Andrea's breasts literally become the "body of evidence" that proves Beatriz's preserved honor in a heterobiased rationale: "Félix looks for the wound and realizes that Carlos is Andrea" (31).[60] Félix is overcome with remorse and begs for forgiveness as Andrea slowly dies. Andrea exclaims, "Oh, I am happy because I die / in your arms! Compassion!" (31).[61] Andrea likewise declares her own repentance for her sins and asks that the gates of heaven open. Now that Andrea has experienced a complete transformation from aggressive and violent "demon" to self-sacrificing ex-girlfriend, she wants to return to the convent from which she was desperate to escape. She then selflessly instructs Félix to love Beatriz as he carries her into the convent. The slow and melodramatic death continues in a final scene with the abbess in which Andrea repents: "In my . . . last breath . . . / I am . . . repentant . . . for my sins!" (31).[62]

In Mateos's play, Andrea dies the exemplary death of a repentant sinner, and like the versions of Pérez de Montalbán and Coello, the Lieutenant Nun is a hero by the end of the performance. In this Romantic yet fatal revision of the "Taming of the Shrew" tale or the "Mujer Brava" story in Don Juan Manuel's *El Conde Lucanor,* she can die the death of a martyr because she repents and sees the error of her violent nature. However, unlike Coello's version of the "Taming of the (Transvestite) Shrew," Mateos's play is less generous to the reformed cross-dresser, since she is killed at the end of the narrative as a lesson to future gender transgressors.

Homoeroticism as Defense of Chastity

An anonymous manuscript written in Mexico during the nineteenth century, "Catalina de Erauso o sea la Monja Alferes," is perhaps the most sympathetic portrayal of Erauso's same-sex passion since Pérez de Montalbán's play and the third *relación* from the seventeenth century.[63] In general terms, the novel follows the plot structure of the autobiography and continues with the information provided from the third *relación* published in Mexico in 1653. However, like De Quincey's text, this novel fills in the psychological silences of the earlier sources with a marked Romantic-style narrative indicating character motivation, thoughts, feelings, and emotions. Referring to the enduring popularity of Romanticism in nineteenth-century Mexico, John Brushwood observes that "Romantic expression persisted because the reading public's taste for tears does not die easily" (114). For Dorothy Kress, the manuscript's importance for nineteenth-century readers lies in the psychological analysis of the protagonist, which became the central preoccupation for those who studied Erauso's life during that period in Mexico (84). While the manuscript provides an interpretation of Erauso's behavior, it also negotiates an approach to female sexuality that perhaps more closely resembles early modern texts than the other nineteenth-century adaptations of the Lieutenant Nun icon.

According to Chris Straayer, an initial element for the successful adoption of the opposite sex's gender-coded costume presented in transvestite narratives includes close study of the gestures, behaviors, and attitudes as well as of the physical disguise (44). Similarly, once Catalina has escaped from the convent and is disguised in male garb, she receives one of her first lessons on what it means to be a man from Don Luis, who teaches her that men are required to participate in sexual relations with women and that these involvements are characterized by their deception: "So you are troubled by having to seduce them and then abandon them when we leave here? It doesn't really matter, everyone does it, so you shouldn't be so surprised by such an unimportant thing. Seduce the woman whom you find most attractive, the one who most interests you and then count on me. When we leave for Madrid, I will introduce you to other prettier women and you will never remember the woman whom you abandon here again in your life, you'll see" (14v).[64] The pressure for Catalina to perform heterosexuality while playing the role of a man is constant throughout this narrative, as she seduces (or is seduced by) Matilde, Teodora, Leonor, Margarita, and Joaquina. The pattern repeated in the text begins with emotional and passionate scenes of same-sex flirtation between Catalina and other women, which are described in terms of an insincere performance on the part of the protagonist. For example, Catalina tells Matilde: "I love you with the greatest tenderness. . . . until today I had never seen such a sweet and charming young woman who inspired so much love and so much interest as you have created in my heart" (42v).[65] However, the narrator consistently describes the lesbian flirtation scenes as difficult but necessary performances for the success of her masculine role ("to maintain such a difficult conversation with Matilde like the one she found herself obligated to continue in order to perform the difficult role that she had accepted" (44v).[66]

Even Catalina, through interior monologues, confirms the falseness of her manly behavior: "How difficult and irritating it is to have to act like someone else! I am a woman and I have tried to become a man! . . . Oh, this is horrible, unbearable, unacceptable" (59v, 60).[67] With Matilde, Catalina describes her true feelings as "false and deceiving"; for Teodora her love is "feigned"; her relationship with Margarita (her brother's lover) is described as a "very sincere and honest friendship" (146v); and the sweet emotions expressed between the protagonist and Joaquina are "for Joaquina true, but for Catalina false and deceptive" (176).[68] Given these protestations against the possibility of genuine same-sex passion, the heterosexual reader can enjoy the frequent titillating scenes that include verbal expressions of love, nonverbal flirtation, and an occasional kiss: "She held her face with both of her hands and gave her a passionate and very loving kiss on the lips" (79).[69] The reader may interpret these homoerotic episodes as nonthreatening since Catalina seems to resist full participation. However, the protagonist's violent reaction to heterosexuality (evident by her consistent and emphatic rejection of men) suggests that her aversion to physical relations with other women has more to do with the anticipated heterosexual (phallic) activities expected of all men. Verbal flirtation seems harmless to the protagonist, but what she most fears in her affairs with women is the inevitable genital contact and the potential discovery of her anatomy: "to talk and talk is easy any time, but today I have come to the conclusion that it is impossible to maintain my fraud since a lie can be concealed up to a certain point, but there always comes a moment in which one cannot continue" (69v).[70] While Catalina is dressed as a man and, as the text describes her, trying to sustain her "performance" without being discovered, the narrator as well as the protagonist consistently reiterate her resistance to intimate relations with other women. Therefore, Catalina's dramatic reconsideration of same-sex love, once her biological identity becomes public knowledge, proves surprising.

Still wearing men's garb with the permission of the pope but now without the fear of discovery, Catalina, for the first time, is able to act in accordance with her own true feelings. We no longer see the emotional interior monologues informing the reader of the contradiction between her sentiments and her actions. Therefore, when Catalina falls in love with Clotilde in an episode derived from the third broadside, their lesbian desire is no longer negated or justified by the text. Catalina celebrates her sincere feelings of passion for Clotilde; she is not fearful of discovery since Clotilde knows she is anatomically a woman, nor is she forced to express her desire according to heterosexual (phallic) expectations: "Catalina was hugging Clotilde lovingly . . . whom she loved passionately with all her heart" (316v, 317v).[71]

When Catalina explains to Clotilde the difference between their same-sex love and the love between men and women, the reader notes a similarity between her description of heterosexuality and her previous performance of such desire: "Men only know how to deceive poor women. . . . Men's love is almost always feigned, deceptive, pretend, and selfish . . . but my love is sincere, real, and true" (319, 319v).[72] When the two women exchange the promise of eternal love, the narrator comments that if someone had seen them hugging and kissing (not knowing that the man was really a woman), he or she would be scandalized. In this hypothetical case, the diegetic voyeur would not have the privileged knowledge of Catalina's sex, as the reader does; however, unlike twentieth-century mainstream transvestite plots, here heterosexual eroticism is more scandalous than homoeroticism. The narrator's comments are reminiscent of the apparent tolerance during the early modern period of lesbian desire that was believed to be nongenital. Catalina's affection for Clotilde is described by the narrator as "inoffensive and without any danger" (320). This text views lesbianism as a strategy to protect the chastity of both women. Dorothy Kress, on the other hand, sees Catalina's declarations of desire for Clotilde ("I love her ardently! I love her passionately!") as the kind of "thoughts that only a real man would be capable of feeling" (92).[73]

Although Rima de Vallbona characterizes Catalina's love for Clotilde as platonic, I would argue that all indications in the text point to lesbian desire that is conceived by the narrator as both passionate and physical but nonpenetrative and therefore nonthreatening.[74] In the final statement of the novel the narrator insists on the protagonist's heterosexual purity: "Having lived intimately among men of all types and conditions, with all this, nonetheless, she was able to protect herself and remain firm and constant in the purity of her feminine behavior, without even the slightest thought that would have stained her honor and reputation" (367, 367v).[75] An ending that Vallbona describes as "ironic" once again shows how honor and reputation are solely related to penetration, reproduction, and paternity. While the text sharply condemns the imitative and potentially genital-physical passion between Catalina and other women who believed her to be a man, the sincere love that the protagonist feels for Clotilde is represented as pure, eternal, and free of deception. Catalina's insistence that Clotilde never marry a man and the former's willingness to relinquish her freedom to spend the rest of her life in a convent at the side of the woman she loves are only two of the many actions that characterize the last third of the manuscript. Even though Catalina's attraction to women may provide titillation for some readers, the potential risk of a lasting lesbian relationship is policed in the end as the protagonist loses the woman she loves to another man. Like the popularity of the lesbian theme in underground literary pornography during the 1860s in France, the appeal of same-sex exoticism is undoubtedly manipulated for readers' arousal in this anonymous manuscript from Mexico.[76] Nonetheless, while Catalina is a virgin and alone at the end of the text, her lesbian passion and her transgenderism are not denied or corrected with a heterosexual, domestic resolution. This ambiguity creates an environment for alternative readings that acknowledge and celebrate the story of a lesbian transgenderist.

Homoeroticism as Performance

In Spain at the end of the nineteenth century Eduardo Blasco published a two-volume historical novel titled *Del claustro al campamento o la monja Alferez* (From the Cloister to the Battlefield or the Lieutenant Nun), which is based loosely on Erauso's life with the addition of extensive narratives highlighting nonhistorical characters and details unrelated to the historical personage.[77] While the anonymous Mexican novel from the same period ultimately does not question the sincerity of Erauso's homoerotic passion, Blasco's 1892 novel interprets her same-sex flirtation as proof of her intention to pass as a man and to avoid discovery: "Carrying the necessary precautions to an extreme so that her true sex would not be discovered, she thought that nothing would be better than a love affair" (1:193–194).[78]

In what almost appears to be a conflict between the historical figure's actions and the opinions of the author, Blasco consistently denies the possibility of genuine lesbian desire, despite Erauso's behavior. When Catalina expresses her love for another woman, the narrator reinterprets her words for the reader: "Catalina could not have been in love with Perales's daughter" (1:210).[79] Despite the text's attempt to de-lesbianize Erauso, she is not heterosexualized as she is in the versions by Coello and Mateos. Although the author cannot imagine or will not permit a lesbian heroine, the text is sufficiently ambiguous to allow an open reading. When forced to describe the protagonist's actions while dressed as a man, the author expresses his own repugnance, questioning Erauso's motivations: "Catalina had wanted to fool the world with false appearances and in order to maintain her deceit, she found that she had to perform actions that we prefer to believe were, in her heart, repulsive to her. Whatever the case may be, whether with disgust or not, she performed the role to perfection" (2:516).[80] Likewise, although Blasco cites fragments of an account of Erauso's life as a mule-driver in Mexico, he omits the final lesbian episode as well as the relation of her exemplary death. Instead, the author invites readers to create their own end to Erauso's life according to personal preference: "At this point we know nothing else, nor could we tell our readers more about the strange and curious protagonist. . . . Let's allow our reader to conclude, with regard to the question in point, what he or she prefers" (2:774–775).[81]

The nineteenth-century interpretations of the Lieutenant Nun share a conflictive relationship with the seventeenth-century narratives related to Erauso. The function and stylistics of the transvestite narrative shift, whether they are used for didactic purposes and social reform for liberal readers or as material for the Romantics' interest in reviving and readapting Golden Age legends and national myths. With minor variations, the trend in the nineteenth century is to "correct" seventeenth-century sources by converting the transgender lesbian narratives into temporary transvestite stories of heterosexual or asexual lessons on how to tame the aggressive and rebellious She-devil into a repentant and submissive woman. In this way, the adaptations and critiques of Erauso's life, whether they be lesbian, heterosexual, or asexual, ultimately reflect the bourgeois ideal of domestic womanhood during the nineteenth century.

CHAPTER FOUR

From Cinema to Comics

The Re-Lesbianization of the Lieutenant Nun in the Twentieth Century

A COMPARISON of the numerous adaptations of the Lieutenant Nun figure in the twentieth century reveals a variety of interpretations dependent upon both context and genre. Within the group of cinematic representations, for example, Catalina de Erauso is depicted as a heterosexual femme fatale in the 1940s while in the 1980s she reappears as both a melancholy lesbian whose love interest dies and a voyeuristic lesbian whose narrative ends with the optimistic image of the protagonist accompanied by the object of her sexual desire. On the other hand, those versions aimed largely at adolescent or female consumers—mainly prose narratives and comics—demonstrate a more consistent attempt to neutralize Erauso's same-sex attraction through the aegis of edifying their impressionable readers. While other prose and theatrical adaptations vary with regard to the protagonist's choice of sexual object, the common thread joining these versions is the pattern of marketing the Lieutenant Nun as a transvestite spectacle, whether through the selling or the silencing of desire.

The Continuation of the Heterosexualized Lieutenant Nun: María Félix as La Monja Alférez (1944)

Rebecca Bell-Metereau begins her study on male impersonators as historical figures in mainstream cinema by emphasizing that the studios' interest in the past has more to do with spectatorship and the marketing of lead actresses than it does with a sincere attempt to represent "truth": "Hollywood's treatment of the historical female figure almost never lets us know what the real person was like in any sense, but its portrayals of masculine heroines tell us a great deal about what audiences wished or feared about women of the day. For the most part, film depictions of history's female cross-dressers are simply intended to highlight the attributes of a particular star, using readily obtainable material with the built-in exotic appeal of the past" (73–74).

Not surprisingly, Emilio Gómez Muriel's 1944 film *La Monja Alférez* (starring María Félix) demonstrates, perhaps more than any other adaptation, the importance of stardom and the selling of desire through Erauso's life. As I discussed in chapter 1, the association between an actress's offstage persona and her character onstage was already debated by theater opponents during the early modern period. All famous actors or actresses bring additional meaning to their characters through their own personal and professional reputations, private lives, previous roles, physical appearance, and so forth. Paco Ignacio Taibo, for example, notes the similarities between the personalities of María Félix and Catalina de Erauso that facilitated the Mexican actress's portrayal of the seventeenth-century icon. Taibo cites De Quincey's characterization of Erauso as "arrogant" to show how the role was suited to Félix's personality, given public opinion about the actress in her private life and in her film roles (67). Moreover, in accordance with María Félix's popularity in Mexico as the rebellious and sexy "devourer of men," her performance as a warrior nun has more to do with the commodification of desire through the film's star than it does with Catalina de Erauso.[1]

The story of the Lieutenant Nun, interpreted as a temporary transvestite narrative, possessed precisely those elements that would potentially enhance the actress's function as cultural icon. Although the script was adapted by Max Aub and Eduardo Ugarte from the autobiography, the producers insisted on a story that would exploit Félix's appeal as the strong, masculine, and sexy femme fatale. The Spanish writer Max Aub, one of the most important antifascist intellectuals in exile in Mexico after the Spanish Civil War, did not hesitate to express his disappointment with the final script regarding its inability to explore the more interesting aspects of Erauso's life: "It was merely a diversion, a chance for María Félix to appear as a well-dressed and extravagant swordsman. . . . The woman who dresses in men's garb always carries within her a very serious drama, a story that deserves to be studied and written with care. The real Lieutenant Nun was not a folkloric character but rather a passionate woman who could motivate an entire literary exercise and a theatrical or cinematic adaptation that would be of great interest to me" (quoted in Taibo 66–67).[2]

Although some critics argue that Gómez Muriel's film was a "flat, static, slow, dull, and confusing" star vehicle for María Félix (García Riera 124),[3] the adaptation again shows how certain aspects of Erauso's story are easily manipulated for the marketing of (heterosexual) desire for a variety of spectators. When Taibo describes Erauso as aggressive, cruel, and difficult, he, like the critic of Coello's *zarzuela,* confesses that the script writers had to "soften" the figure of Catalina; what remained of the historical Erauso in the film was "truly a handsome figure, a beautifully designed wardrobe, and the ambiguous beauty of María accented with a feathered hat, form-fitting pants, and riding boots" (69).[4] In fact, reminiscent of the apparent obsession with women dressed in form-fitting breeches on the early modern stage, María Félix also became famous for her onscreen as well as offscreen preference for "seductive" pants. The film producers in Mexico discovered after the success of Félix's 1943 movie *Doña Bárbara* that the "public wanted a María Félix dressed as a man. They knew it since they saw her in *Doña Bárbara* wearing pants" (Taibo 67).[5] Consequently, it would seem that one of the most important factors motivating the Mexican cinematic adaptation of the Lieutenant Nun was the image of an aggressive yet sexy María Félix dressed in pants, not unlike her counterparts on the early modern stage. Taibo describes Félix's relationship with pants in symbiotic terms: "María and her pants were so closely associated with each other in such a way and so frequently that they were converted, with few other elements, into one of her most enduring symbols" (71).[6] In fact, like the Golden Age actresses who became so attached to the male disguise that they con-

FIGURE 3. María Félix posing in her sexy male disguise in Emilio Gómez Muriel's 1944 film, *La Monja Alférez*. Publicity still courtesy of Dirección General de Actividades Cinematográficas, Mexico City.

tinued to dress as men offstage, Félix changed her offscreen wardrobe after playing the part of Catalina: "Her encounter with the Lieutenant Nun opened up a series of perspectives to her. . . . Throughout her social life she would appear in swashbuckler's hats, flashy feathers, leather pants, tall boots above the knee, belts from which weapons were hung, and gauntlet-style gloves. An entire paraphernalia that began with this film would periodically and more or less subtly enhance the actress in her private life" (Taibo 69).[7] These elements of Félix's new masculine wardrobe are reminiscent of Pérez de Montalbán's Guzmán (as well as the protagonists of Coello, Mateos, and, as we shall see, Domingo Miras), who appears on stage in male costume, accessorized with a panache (plume) in her hat with white and green feathers, a sword, and boots (see fig. 3).

This sexualized manly woman is intended to be the object of the male gaze (despite her possible appeal for other women), both on the early modern stage as well as in twentieth-century cinema. Many critics have questioned the appeal of the manly woman for the male voyeur. Taibo, for example, ponders the male spectator's interest in seeing a masculine María Félix: "It seems curious and appropriate for psychoanalytic inquiries the fact that the sight of a manly María Félix, in her pants and with her gestures of a swashbuckler or scourger of Venezuelan men, would increase the male viewer's pleasure in Mexico" (65).[8] Many psychoanalytic explanations, frequently in reference to fetishism and castration anxiety, argue that male spectators' fascination with these "sexy demons" is based on the idea that these "phallic women" represent the penis that the male viewer would like to possess or, conversely, confirms what he does not lack.[9] Taibo, nonetheless, suggests that the film *La Monja Alférez* might represent a cultural revenge of the "machismo" tradition, since the "macho" is embodied by a woman who comes to defeat these men at their own game. The Mexican film critic García Riera, however, argues that what actually happens in the movie is a self-conquest, since the "devourer of men" seems to be devouring women: "The devourer of men is converted into the object of their own desires, and before her masculine transformation, it was the women who were ready to be devoured" (124).[10]

Regardless of the possible subconscious motives, the representation of the masculine woman in popular culture frequently results in the erotic undressing of women. Of course this "historical tease" must be temporary within the narrative to allow for a more traditional resolution supporting the status quo for "feminine" women. When discussing the popularity of the femme fatale version of the manly woman in film, Jo Stanley argues that this phallic woman must be punished in the narrative; her power must be mediated either through her death, an unconvincing marriage resolution, or by "taming" the aggressive personality (9).[11] The traditional narrative closure is reflected in the punishment of the transgressive manly woman in the nineteenth century in both Coello's *zarzuela* as well as in Mateos's play. However, unlike the nonheterosexual versions of the seventeenth century in which Erauso is not prematurely killed, married off, or "tamed," the Mexican cinematic version implies that Erauso will return to female garb permanently to marry her childhood love interest.

The Mexican film begins with the "Nuevo Cid" episode, which por-

M.A.125.
OA.

M.A.149.
OA.

FIGURE 4. (opposite top) María Félix defending her earnings in the "Nuevo Cid" episode of Gómez Muriel's *La Monja Alférez.* Publicity still courtesy of Dirección General de Actividades Cinematográficas, Mexico City.

FIGURE 5. (opposite bottom) María Félix dressed as a nun in Gómez Muriel's *La Monja Alférez.* Publicity still courtesy of Dirección General de Actividades Cinematográficas, Mexico City.

FIGURE 6. (above) María Félix and a female admirer in Gómez Muriel's *La Monja Alférez.* Publicity still courtesy of Dirección General de Actividades Cinematográficas, Mexico City.

trays the cross-dressed Félix gambling in a bar. Soon the protagonist must defend her earnings by fighting, which is only resolved when she kills her opponent (see fig. 4). In a subsequent scene, Catalina is in jail talking to a priest as she begins to tell her life story in the form of a flashback. Unlike other versions, Catalina is not raised in the convent but at home, where her father teaches her the male-gendered activities of fencing and horsemanship. As a young girl, Catalina is already cross-dressed and proves to be better than the boys at masculine pursuits. When her father dies, she is sent to the convent and dressed in nun's garb (see fig. 5).

Nonetheless, Catalina soon plans her escape from the convent in order to recover her inheritance and prevent an arranged marriage between Beatriz and her childhood sweetheart Juan, who years earlier promised to marry the protagonist. The transformation from nun to young man, however, is different from that described in the autobiography. In the film, she acquires the male garment from Juan, and the audience is not allowed to witness her preparation; we merely see a brief shot of her nun's habit left behind and then a jump cut to the beautiful actress unconvincingly disguised as a man called don Alonso de Guzmán. Like Pérez de Montalbán's play, the Mexican film minimizes Erauso's military career, although there are numerous fight scenes with swords, knives, and verbal insults. After a shipwreck, Erauso and Roger (who was sent to find Catalina but, not knowing her true identity, becomes her servant) eventually settle in Trujillo. "Don Alonso" is now working for a boss who tries to arrange a marriage between his new employee and his girlfriend Lucinda. In Trujillo there are a series of homoerotic episodes involving Cristina (the boss's wife), Lucinda, and the cross-dressed protagonist that seem to condense certain details from the autobiography but are altered, nonetheless, to relieve Félix's character of any true homoerotic interest.

In the 1944 film, Cristina flirts with "Alonso" (see fig. 6), and Lucinda, portrayed as a ridiculous and somewhat unattractive woman, becomes comically aggressive in her pursuit of the handsome newcomer. The "progression toward slapstick comedy and increased physicality," common in temporary transvestite films, is evident in the same-sex flirtation scenes in the Mexican film (Straayer 44). Lucinda becomes so obsessed with "Alonso" that she chases her around the latter's bed, pushes her down, jumps on top of her, and tries to kiss her, at which moment Erauso's boss (Lucinda's lover) enters and proceeds to fire his employee.

Even though Catalina appears to reject or ignore the women's flirtations, she is willing to participate in the expected activity with Roger as the "men" flirt with other women who also find them attractive (see fig. 7). Later, jealous of Juan's flirtations with a woman named Elvira, the protagonist decides to seduce Elvira. Although these scenes display a strong heterosexual motivation on the part of Catalina, the other women are completely attracted to "Alonso's" beauty. Just before the hanging scene, Catalina's flashback narrative ends and again the female witnesses of her impending execution lament the death of such a handsome young

FIGURE 7. María Félix joins Angel Garasa in flirting with other women in Gómez Muriel's *La Monja Alférez*. Publicity still courtesy of Dirección General de Actividades Cinematográficas, Mexico City.

man. Consistent with other narratives, the protagonist does not attempt to stop the hanging by confessing publicly her true identity but is rescued by Juan and Roger, who escape with her to Elvira's house. In order to avoid arrest and to facilitate their escape, both Roger and "Alonso" cross-dress as women. Even though María Félix is now dressed as a beautiful woman, within the diegesis the film's characters believe that she is Alonso dressed as a woman, a device comparable to both the "Victor/Victoria" plot (a woman pretending to be a man who is pretending to be a woman) and to Trapaza's scheme in Castillo Solórzano's *Aventuras del Bachiller Trapaza* (a man pretending to be Erauso, who is living as a man). In fact, since Juan is the only character who discovers Alonso's true identity, in the final scene of the film, Roger displays shock and confusion upon seeing "Alonso" (dressed in women's garb) and Juan kissing. Although the film's audience knows that the kiss is exactly what it appears to be (a heterosexual display between a man and a woman in their socially prescribed gender costumes), the film's character assigns a homosexual reading to the spectacle, a comical misreading of a nonparadoxical kiss that is not corrected by the film's end.[12]

At no point is it possible for the audience to mistake María Félix for a man, even though one 1944 review of the film in *El Redondel* suggests that Félix's feminine beauty is a deterrent to verisimilitude: "How beautiful she looks dressed as a man! Too beautiful, in fact, because with that face it is impossible to mistake her for a lieutenant" (quoted in Taibo 71).[13] Verisimilitude, nonetheless, was not the purpose of showing actresses dressed as men on the early modern stage or in films portraying historical figures (such as Gómez Muriel's *La Monja Alférez* or Rouben Mamoulian's 1933 film *Queen Christina,* starring Greta Garbo). Rebecca Bell-Metereau points out that Hollywood's treatment of historical manly women inevitably serves the tastes of the audience at the expense of accuracy. In fact, Garbo wanted to embody a less sexy and more "realistic" Queen Christina: "Garbo wished to appear with a large nose and massive, masculine eyebrows" but the director insisted on a "feminine" manly woman, no doubt for the pleasure of mainstream audiences (Bell-Metereau 74).[14]

Like cross-dressed women on the early modern stage, the historical figure of Queen Christina of Sweden (1626–1689) captured the popular imagination of seventeenth-century Spain. Raised in a traditional masculine gender role to facilitate her succession to the throne, she was known to dress as a man and allegedly had affairs with both men and women.[15] In his *Avisos* (1654–1658) Barrionuevo frequently mentions Queen Christina and the fascination that Spaniards displayed for her transgression of traditional gender roles: "The Queen of Sweden arrived at Antwerp dressed as a man, on horseback with a retinue of her people. . . . They say she mistreats a horse as if she were a man, and therefore the King sent her those horses, and they also say that she is more than a woman, not that she is a hermaphrodite but that she is not the marrying type" (quoted in Bravo-Villasante 144–145).[16] Further evidence of Spain's fascination with the Swedish monarch is the fact that Philip IV commissioned a portrait of Christina in 1653 and that Calderón's play *Afectos de odio y amor* was roughly based on the Queen Christina figure.[17] Given the similarities between the historical figures Queen Christina and Catalina de Erauso, the affinity between the stars' personas and that of the seventeenth-century icons whom they portray, as well as between Garbo's and Félix's performances of the two women, it is not surprising that Félix admits to a special admiration for Garbo: "The only person in movies whom I admire is Garbo. I was a fan of hers ever since she started making films, and after her . . . nobody!" (quoted in García Fernandez).[18]

The entertainment value of these cross-dressed women, both onstage as well as on celluloid, comes from their seductive male garments, their provocative poses and actions, the success of their deceit, and the subsequent shock within the diegesis. The audience is an accomplice in the disguise and enjoys the superior position with regard to the other characters who are duped by the costume. In fact, very seldom are cross-dressed characters designed to trick the audience (especially given the interference of star recognition), as was the desired effect in the 1992 film *The Crying Game.* Most temporary transvestite films revel in the transformation contrast of "before" and "after": *Some Like It Hot* (1959), *Tootsie* (1982), *Mrs. Doubtfire* (1993), *To Wong Foo, Thanks for Everything, Julie Newmar* (1995), and *The Birdcage* (1996) are just a few of Hollywood's commercially successful portrayals of cross-dressed men. One might also wonder, of all the recent mainstream Hollywood films based on cross-dressers, why only a few, such as *Victor/Victoria* (1982) and *Yentl* (1983), feature female cross-dressers. While the cross-dressed woman was a common source of entertainment, especially in the drama of the early modern period, precisely because of its alluring and shocking nature, in the late twentieth century it is no longer "curious" to see a woman dressed in pants, suit jacket, and tie, whereas a man wearing a skirt, wig, and makeup still provides the humorous shock effect for mainstream audiences. Despite the general agreement among some critics regarding male cross-dressing, the nature of female cross-dressing seems more ambivalent. Mary Ann Doane, for example, argues that "male transvestism is an occasion for laughter; female transvestism only another occasion for desire" (234); while Janice Raymond highlights the practical advantages for women who wear men's attire: "a woman putting on a man's clothes is, in a sense, putting on male power status, whereas a man putting on women's clothes is putting on parody" (1996, 217).[19]

The marketing strategy for the 1944 film *La Monja Alférez* did not utilize the "before" and "after" contrast for the shock effect (since María Félix is immediately recognizable in men's garb) but rather to enhance the actress's sex appeal. One advertisement distributed in Spain, nonetheless, does take advantage of the hybrid image of the Lieutenant Nun: a photo of Félix dressed in men's garb and in face-to-face conflict with José Cibrián is superimposed on a larger photo of the actress in nun's habit (see fig. 8).

In contrast, other film publicity in Mexico emphasized both the heterosexual attraction of Félix in pants for the interested spectator and the homoerotic complications that result from the disguise. An advertisement in the magazine *México Cinema* (July 1944) uses a photograph of the actress with a feathered hat, long cape, sword, and tall leather boots; accompanying the photo is a poem designed to sell the film by summarizing the most appealing aspects of the protagonist and of the plot: "A sullen girl with steed and sword, / felt desolate in the convent. / She was ordered there by an aunt, / secretly urged by a dark infamy; / but she jumped the walls of the convent / and escaped to recover a will. / First Catalina changed her clothing / by adopting a masculine appearance. / And in the lands of Peru, sweet women / sighed out of love for the lieutenant" (quoted in Taibo 65).[20]

The studio is marketing the attraction of the mysterious woman who cross-dresses to achieve a specific goal that would be impossible within the traditional female gender role. Instead of concluding the poem with the heterosexual "girl gets boy" resolution, the mention of homoerotic flirtation serves to "tease" the public, who must already assume that the ending will fulfill their expectations for the orthodox marriage plot. Likewise, Taibo interprets another photograph used to advertise the movie as a clear example of the lack of passion communicated by the two actors who are supposedly in love with one another in the film. The photo depicts a closeup of Félix wearing women's garb and holding a black lace fan while her love interest (José Cibrián) is portrayed looking away, showing his profile. As Taibo notes, "Sex has disappeared from both attitudes and what remains is a pose for the benefit of a keen observer who would be shocked at the double hedonism, far from the passion that should be aroused by such beauty in the opposite sex" (70).[21]

Although the film is clearly a heterosexual adaptation designed specifically for María Félix, the suggestion of homoeroticism is likewise present either as titillation for the male viewer or as an unintended subversive message for those spectators who are willing to watch the image out-

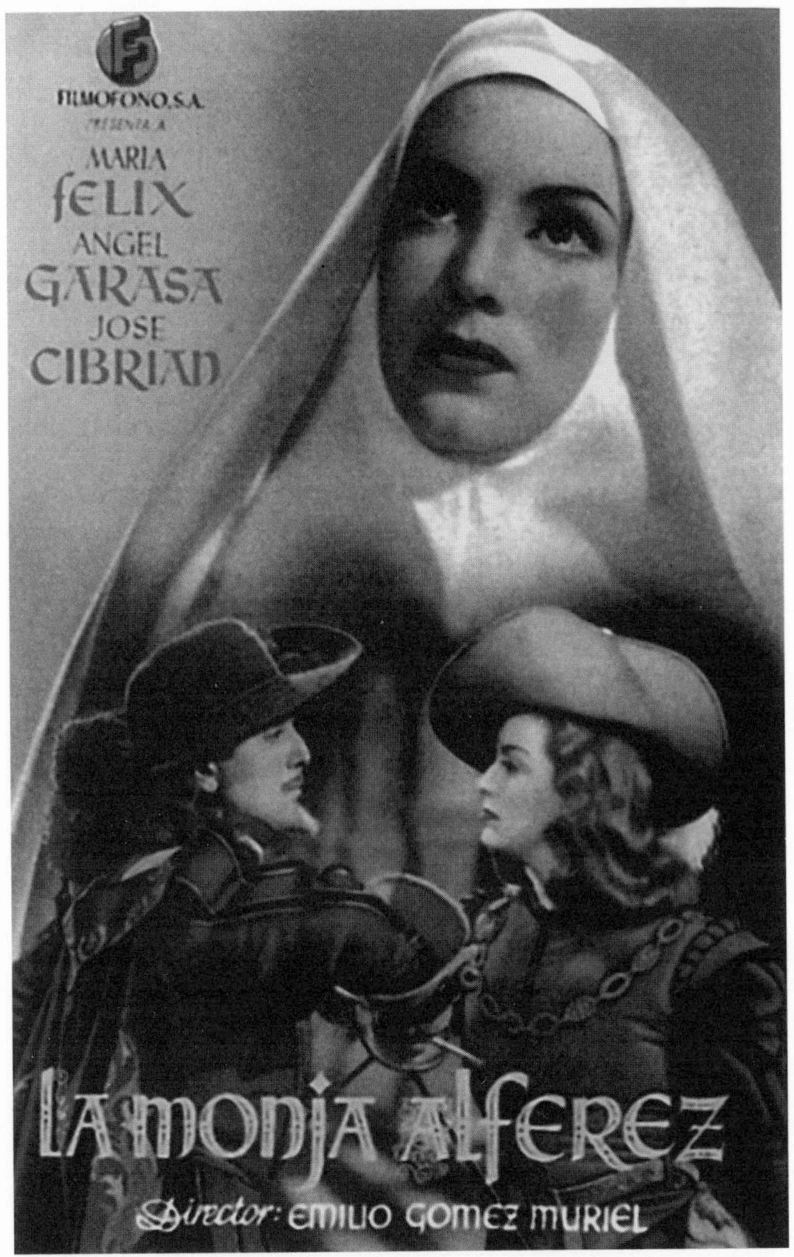

FIGURE 8. Advertisement for Gómez Muriel's *La Monja Alférez*. Courtesy of Dirección General de Actividades Cinematográficas, Mexico City.

side the orthodox filter of heterosexuality, similar to the cross-dressed Marlene Dietrich in *Morocco* (1930) and the subversive kiss in *Queen Christina* (1933) between Garbo and Elizabeth Young that is not explained or corrected by the film's end.[22] In either case, María Félix's performance is conceived and advertised using strategies centered on the selling of heterosexual desire through the femininized masculine woman.

The Lieutenant Nun as a Model for Educating Women

The image of the Lieutenant Nun presented to female readers during Franco's fascist regime in Spain (1939–1975) attempts to reconcile Erauso's transgression by evoking nationalism, religion, and patriarchal superiority. During a period in which the "mission" of books published in Spain was to guide "la nueva raza" (the new race), special attention was devoted to female children: "The less educated and all women required greater vigilance. Children, of course, required the greatest care of all, and female children regardless of their age, more than male" (Nichols 216). Accordingly, Fernando Velasco's 1956 publication destined for female adolescents, *Cuando las grandes heroinas eran niñas* (When the Great Heroines Were Young Girls), articulates the ideal model of behavior for young women in terms of silence, resignation, and suffering.[23] Given this definition of female heroism, it is curious to note that the text's presentation of Erauso's life fails to demonstrate the feminine submission exalted in the book's introduction. In fact, the text first characterizes Catalina as a rebellious and mischievous girl who was influenced by her father's stories of military adventure and victory, while her adult life is described in terms of bravery and violence, both on the battlefield and in personal fights, such as the deadly altercation with Reyes. The image of a rebellious, violent, and manly woman hardly seems congruent, initially at least, with Franco's ideal model of feminine domesticity, which was articulated through cultural mechanisms such as La Sección Femenina (Women's Section), founded in 1934. The Women's Section of the Falange became the institution charged with educating and preparing women for "their new role as rebuilders of the Spanish nation, the dedicated, self-denying heart of the Catholic family and mainstay of Franco's deeply authoritarian patriarchal regime" (Brooksback Jones

1–2). The message of the Sección Femenina for women was "back to the home," promoted in an attempt to undo the progressive social reforms of the early decades of the twentieth century (Graham 105). The nineteenth-century ideal of the "angel del hogar" (angel of the hearth) had been transformed in the 1910s and 1920s, and what emerged was the "Nueva Mujer Moderna" (New Modern Woman): "The shift from the old traditional model of femininity to the innovative *Nueva Mujer Moderna* allowed women to adjust to the process of modernity. . . . The 'New Modern Woman' challenged women's restriction to the home and contested discriminatory practices toward women" (Nash 1999, 31–32). Conversely, in Franco's vision of women's role in a new Spanish empire (encouraging the participation of the "passive, pious, pure, submissive woman-as-mother"), the Women's Section was reminiscent of both Fray Luis de León's *La perfecta casada* (1583) and the nineteenth-century "angel of the hearth" ideal for women. Not surprisingly, Renaissance treatises on the education of Christian women (such as Juan Luis Vives's *La instrucción de la mujer cristiana* [1523] and Fray Luis's *La perfecta casada*) were republished during the 1940s and 1950s (Morcillo Gómez 56). Although Fernando Velasco's 1956 text may seem at odds with the domestic mission for women, its suppression of lesbian desire and the focus on Erauso's masculine courage ultimately prove the superiority of the male gender role: "Sometimes she used to think that women were a bit cowardly for not wanting to imitate men in the great feats and deeds that they achieved throughout the world" (43).[24] Moreover, through her imitation of superior men, Erauso was able to contribute to the construction of the early modern Spanish Empire, which was frequently evoked by Franco in his own project of Spanish nationalism: "In particular, they focused on the period of the so-called Catholic monarchs in the late fifteenth and early sixteenth centuries, and also on the process of conquest and colonization of America. By establishing an identification between the reign of the Catholic monarchs and the Franco regime, Francoists opened the possibility of an imperial future for Spain" (Escudero 73). In this vein, F. Ximénez de Sandoval, in his 1949 *Varia historia de ilustres mujeres,* likewise mentions Catalina de Erauso in his justification of "feminine patriotism": "Like the Baroness of Albi [the 'Captain of a Spanish resistance movement'], Catalina de Erauso, Isabel de Barreto [the 'Lady Admiral'], Manuela Malasaña, and Agustina Zaragoza, Doña María Pita, the Lieutenant from La Coruña, is an example of how Spanish women, in addition to possessing all the feminine virtues, are capable (when their country requires it) of gloriously demonstrating other virtues, such as energy, courage, boldness, and heroism, commonly attributed exclusively to men" (205).[25] Unlike Ferrer's support of women like Germaine de Staël, Ximénez de Sandoval contrasts the "tenderness, patriotism, or the faith" of Spanish women with the "souls of ice" of other non-Spanish European women such as Staël or Christina of Sweden: "In the Spanish woman there has never been seen such complete perversity" (16).

Cristóbal de Castro's 1941 *Mujeres del Imperio* similarly justifies Erauso's controversial life by emphasizing the commendable way in which Catalina emulates nationalistic values: "No other 'manly woman' comes closer to being a man than she does. Since she feels like a man and talks like a man, she basically becomes one. . . . One could make such a great tribute to her that it would erase all possible opposition. And fighting alongside the men like a Spanish conquistador, nobody discovered she was a woman, and like a Homeric hero rewarded by the gods, she was promoted right on the battlefield" (210–211).[26] Like Castro's account, Blanca Ruiz de Dampierre's 1943 *La Monja Alférez* begins by urging readers to admire Erauso's patriotism but not her gender and sexual nonconformism: "I do not mean that you should use her life as a model or try to imitate her. Unfortunately, she is not always worthy of praise, although she is undoubtedly worthy of the most profound admiration" (3).[27] Despite this vague reference to the protagonist's problematic traits, the text includes no trace of same-sex desire, while it does feature brawling, gambling, and murder. F. Hernández Castanedo's 1944 *Aventura española,* conversely, does mention same-sex flirtation in his account of Erauso's life: "She flirts with and even seduces several upper-class women" (141).[28] Although Jean Grugel and Tim Rees argue that lesbianism (compared to male homosexuality) during Franco's dictatorship was not as fiercely repressed (since the regime assumed it could not exist), Hernández Castanedo justified Erauso's behavior as an attempt "to identify herself more with her role as a man" (141).[29]

Like the ambiguity of the Monja Alférez legend, the popularity of early modern historical figures such as Queen Isabel the Catholic and St. Teresa of Avila during Franco's dictatorship were also problematic "given that they could be read as examples of women with a powerful public role" (Grugel and Rees 135). As Helen Graham notes: "The Franco regime used sanitized versions of certain historical figures to legitimize its values; in particular St. Teresa—'the saint of the race'—was pressed into service to exemplify ideal Catholic womanhood. In the process, the regime had to edit out certain awkward heterodoxies: in this case, St. Teresa's possible Jewish ancestry, independent thought, and active role as a religious reformer" (184–185).[30] This double-bind was likewise evident in the debate over the Sección Femenina, since "it actually offered to women just the kind of public role that they were not supposed to have" (Grugel and Rees 135). In fact, the subsequent interpretations of the Sección Femenina's role for women also reflect this cultural and political ambiguity. Victoria Lorée Enders, for example, has analyzed the debate between scholars on the left who are critical of the Women's Section and women on the right who actually participated in the social program of the auxiliary organization. The latter group sees their historical role as "daringly progressive and their lives as dedicated to improving the condition of Spanish women" while the former criticize the organization for having colluded with a regime "that oppressed and degraded women" (Enders 377–378). Regardless of these conflicting portraits, the contradiction of women working outside the home, instructing other women to restrict their ambitions and remain confined to the domestic sphere, could mirror a similar ambiguity in Erauso's example.

While Erauso's story lent itself to issues of patriotism and female chastity, topics related to independence, Basque nationalism, and sexuality were silenced. Given the need to edit out certain features from the early modern model, it is not surprising that both Francoists and the antifascist Republicans showed interest in the Lieutenant Nun: "During the Spanish Civil War in the 1930's leaders of both sides exhorted their women to emulate Catalina" (Laffin 24).[31] As noted above, Max Aub as well as other liberals were intrigued with Erauso's life, and the image of the "miliciana" (militia woman) was also evoked by the republic as a model for the "new woman" against the fascist regime: "One of the symbols of the revolution and antifascist resistance in the early fervor of the war was the figure of the *miliciana,* the militia woman. Revolutionary art, seen primarily in war posters, portrayed attractive young girls, with rather masculinized silhouettes, clothed in blue overalls . . . guns slung over their shoulders heading off to the front. . . . The message was crystal clear.

La Monja Alférez

1 En el año 1620, en la rica ciudad de Guamanga, del reino del Perú, entra un alférez español. Es arrogante, pendenciero, lleva con soltura la espada, además de un puñal y dos pistolas, una de ellas de tres bocas. Este alférez se llama Alonso Díaz Ramírez de Guzmán y huye perseguido por la justicia de Cuzco, por haber dado muerte a un espadachín terrible llamado el Cid. Una noche intentan detenerle los alguaciles del corregidor de Guamanga. Derriba a uno de un tiro, y cercado por muchos, está a punto de sucumbir, cuando se abre una puerta y aparece el obispo de Guamanga, quien, quitándole las armas, le mete en su casa, salvándole de la muerte.

2 El obispo que ha salvado al belicoso alférez es un fraile agustino, santo varón llamado fray Agustín de Carvajal. Al meterle en su casa le ha puesto en sagrado, donde el fuero civil no puede detenerle. El obispo se encara con el alférez y bondadosamente le hace ver los riesgos de la vida que lleva y el espanto de la muerte si no le sorprende bien apercibido. El bizarro alférez se atusa el fino mostacho, se enternece y, al fin, se arrodilla. Le parece estar en la presencia de Dios.

—Señor —dice—, ¡soy mujer! Cuando tenía cuatro años me entraron en un convento, allí me crié y tomé el hábito. Estando para profesar, me salí con quince años, me corté el cabello, anduve de aquí a acullá, me embarqué, trajiné, maté, herí y maleé, hasta venir a parar en lo presente y a los pies de su señoría ilustrísima.

3 El asombro del obispo es inmenso, si bien se resiste a creer en la insudita confesión del alférez matachín, pero al día siguiente, cuando dos matronas certifican que es mujer, tiene que rendirse a la evidencia: "Hija, ahora creo sin duda lo que me dijiste y creeré en adelante cuanto me dijereis; os venero como una de las personas notables de este mundo y os prometo asistiros en cuanto pueda y cuidar de vuestra conveniencia y del servicio de Dios."

El alférez-monja hace confesión general, y después, el obispo en su misa le da la comunión. Pasados seis días se la ingresa en un convento, y de allí en una litera, custodiada por seis clérigos, cuatro religiosos y seis hombres de espada, es trasladada a Lima.

4 Dos años y cinco meses después de su ingreso en el convento, llega de España razón de que no había sido monja profesa, por lo que se le permite salir libre del convento. Decide volver a España, pero antes, para que consten los servicios prestados por ella a la Corona, pide que figuren en un pedimento que se halla actualmente en el Archivo de las Indias, de Sevilla, y que es uno de los más notables documentos que allí se encierra, al mismo tiempo que es un historial completo de la célebre Monja Alférez. Comienza así: "El alférez doña Catalina de Erauso, vecina y natural de la villa de San Sebastián, provincia de Guipúzcoa, dice: Que en tiempo de diecinueve años a esta parte, los quince ha empleado en servicio de V. M. en las guerras del reino de Chile e indios del Perú, habiendo pasado a aquellas partes en hábito de varón, por particular inclinación que tuvo de ejercitar las armas en defensa de la Fe católica y emplearse en servicio de V. M., sin que en el dicho reino de Chile, en todo el tiempo que asistió, fuera conocida sino por hombre..."

Escribe: MUÑOYERRO **Dibuja: SALINAS**

(En exclusiva para LA GACETA DEL NORTE)

La Monja Alférez

5 A fines del siglo XVI y principio del XVII, les nace siete hijos en San Sebastián al matrimonio Miguel de Erauso y doña María Pérez de Galarraga y Arce. Ambos son de distinguidas familias y él es capitán. Sus tres hijos siguen la carrera militar y las tres hijas profesan monjas. La cuarta hija... empezando a ser monja, como sus hermanas, llegó a ser militar, como sus hermanos. En el claustro fue conocida por su nombre de sor Catalina de Erauso, y en los ejércitos de Chile y el Perú, como el alférez don Alonso Díaz Ramírez de Guzmán. Catalina de Erauso nació el 10 de febrero de 1592, y a los cuatro años de edad, la ingresaron en el convento de monjas dominicas de San Sebastián el Antiguo, siguiendo la costumbre de entonces de decidir los padres lo que van a ser sus hijos.

6 Su tía, doña Ursula de Unzá y Sarasti, prima hermana de su madre, era priora del convento, fundado en 1546 por don Alfonso de Idiáquez, del Consejo de Estado y secretario del emperador Carlos V, y padre de don Juan de Idiáquez, secretario de Estado de los reyes Felipe II y III. Catalina de Erauso no se sentía a gusto vestida de monja ni rezando en el coro los maitines de medianoche. Ella tenía un inclinación irresistible al ejercicio de las armas, y así, una noche, cuando tenía sólo quince años, abrió la puerta del convento y se escapó sin tener ningún plan. Sólo llevaba en el bolsillo tijeras, hilo y aguja. Se ocultó en un castañar cerca del convento y allí estuvo tres días en ayunas, mientras se fabricó, con la ropa que llevaba, una vestimenta de hombre. Se cortó el pelo y echó a andar por monte hasta que fue a parar a Vitoria, cerca de cien Kilómetros, sin comer más que hierbas.

7 En Vitoria se colocó de criado en casa de un catedrático, el cual, viéndole listo, se ofreció a darle carrera, pero ella rehusó porfiadamente y, cogiéndole unos cuartos, escapó, esta vez a Valladolid, donde estaba la Corte. Allí se colocó de paje de don Juan de Idiáquez, secretario del rey, con el nombre supuesto de Francisco de Loyola.

Llevaba siete meses en aquella ocupación, cuando una noche se presentó su padre preguntando por don Juan. Mientras esperaba ser recibido, padre e hija estuvieron juntos, sin que el padre reconociera a la hija tras la cual andaba.

8 Mientras su padre explicaba a don Juan de Idiáquez la fuga de su hija del convento del que don Juan era patrono, Catalina recogió su ropa y, ajustándose con un arriero, se vino a Bilbao, donde su genio vivo tuvo su primera manifestación. Riñó con unos muchachos y de una pedrada hirió a uno, por lo que la tuvieron la cárcel un mes. De Bilbao pasó a Estella, donde estuvo dos años y de allí a San Sebastián, donde ya nadie la conoció; hecho un apuesto galán, se atrevió a volver a su convento y allí oyó misa al lado de su madre, que tampoco la reconoció. Sin saber adónde ir, como pluma que lleva el viento, Catalina apareció en Sanlúcar, donde sentó plaza de grumete en un galeón que marchaba a América, mandado por un tío suyo. Desde que salió del convento, Catalina procuraba servir a vascongados (entonces se decía vizcaínos), ya que hablando vascuence le trataban mejor.

Escribe: MUÑOYERRO **Dibuja: SALINAS**

(En exclusiva para LA GACETA DEL NORTE)

Women were to play a crucial role both in organizing the homefront and in fostering male involvement in the military resistance" (Nash 1995, 50). At the same time, however, a comic-strip version of a contemporary "Monja Miliciana" (Militia Nun) was published in Mexico during the 1940s in the conservative Catholic magazine *Cruzada* in support of the anti-communist ideology of Franco's regime.[32]

While the Militia Nun is evoked in a Mexican comic strip as a Catholic warrior fighting against communism in Spain, sequential art narratives of the 1950s used the de-sexualized Lieutenant Nun to educate readers about Spain's imperial past and the pious role of women. One of the first comics presenting Erauso's story was published in a Basque newspaper, *La Gaceta del Norte,* for adult readers.[33] Published in Bilbao in two installments on August 30, 1959, and September 1, 1959, the comic strips (written by Muñoyerro and illustrated by Salinas) recount a serious and informative version of Erauso's life in eight panels (but misnumbered according to chronology). Unlike most comic strips this example of sequential art lacks dialogue and contains only narrations and pictorial images. Although the written word is crucial in the process of understanding the illustrations, the selection of the specific moments in Erauso's story depicted in the pictorial panels dictates how the reader will interpret the narration (see fig. 9). The eight panels portray the following highlights:

A nun behind bars in the convent (5)
Erauso escaping through a fence surrounding the convent (6)
The protagonist dressing in men's garb (7)
A maritime scene representing the voyage to the New World (8)
A "pistol fight" portraying Catalina in violent conflict with El Nuevo Cid (1)
Erauso in male clothing as she confesses her biological identity to the bishop (2)
Catalina in nun's garb, kneeling and receiving the communion host from the bishop (3)

FIGURE 9. *La Monja Alférez,* a 1959 comic strip printed in the Basque newspaper *La Gaceta del Norte.* The eight panels recount Erauso's life, beginning with panel 5. Courtesy of Biblioteca Nacional, Madrid.

SEÑORAS QUE HICIERON EPOCA

LA MONJA ALFEREZ

Por
JULIO CEBRIAN

Cuando ella nació, en San Sebastián, su padre que era prudente, debió pensar: ¡Qué mejor sitio para la niña que un convento allí resguardada de los peligros y tentaciones del mundo, lejos del tráfico y de los impuestos y sin contacto con la inflación y la subida de los precios! Y así fue. La pequeña Catalina de Herauso, que tal era su nombre, fue enclaustrada a los cinco añitos, pero oiga, aquí viene lo bueno, enseguida la niña dio muestras de inquietud y rebeldía. Quería ver mundo, disfrutar del ruido y leer los artículos de Argos, Emilio Romero y Carandell. La superiora no lograba hacer carrera de ella, y sus compañeras, las monjitas, empezaban a observarla como una novicia rara, dada a fantasías y excentricidiades. Por las noches la niña deliraba y se ensonambulaba creyéndose, ora Alejandro el Magno, ora Manolo Santana. Y llegó un momento en que no pudo más, aquellas paredes monásticas se le venían encima y una noche agarró la pértiga y saltó el muro. Atrás los maitines y la disciplina. ¡Libre! —gritó ella— y acto seguido dio en buscarse una vestimenta de hombre con el fin de disfrazarse. Contaba a la sazón quince años, y ya era toda una mujer, aunque eso sí, plana de pecho, fea de cara y con pelos en las piernas. Hay que comprender a la chica, ella era así y no tenía remedio.

Año 1610. Ya con su nueva personalidad masculina, se hace llamar Francisco de Loyola y entra a trabajar de paje en casa de Don Juan de Idiaquez, secretario del Rey. A todo esto las cosas le iban bien salvo un mal momento que tuvo que pasar al toparse un día cara a cara con su propio

padre. ¿Se imaginan el apuro? Se miraron de hito en hito, pero el buen hombre no reconoció a su vástaga, aunque le quedó un «no se que» por dentro, como preguntándose: ¿Dónde he visto yo esta cara? Superado el trance, tiene a continuación unos días de arrepentimiento y reconsidera su postura ante la vida. Llora, pero su destino ya tenía el signo opuesto al de su sexo y se enrola de grumete en un galeón que zarpa para las Américas recién estrenadas. El capitán del barco tampoco nota nada raro, a pesar de ser su propio tío, don Esteban de Equino, al que Catalina le roba 500 pesos y salta a tierra a disfrutarlos con salud. Capítulo siguiente: Catalina está en Panamá «colocado» de dependiente. Se aburre y se va al Perú. Naufraga, pero se salva. Una vez seca, tiene un altercado con un individuo al que la ex-novicia le corta la cara con una faca. Un amigo del herido le corta el paso cuando huye y ella también se lo carga de un tajo. Perseguida por la justicia llega a Trinidad, donde mata a un forajido que trata de robarla. Catalina es encarcelada, pero el regidor de la localidad es un paisano suyo de Vizcaya y la salva con la condición de que se corrija e ingrese en un convento. Resiste poco en su nuevo encierro e ingresa al servicio de un ricachón. Se siente aburrida y opta por alistarse en los tercios coloniales como soldado. Cambia su nombre de Francisco de Loyola por el de Alonso Díaz Ramírez y durante tres años lucha contra los fieros araucanos, contándose tales hazañas y hechos de armas de la moza, que la superioridad le asciende a Alférez, inaugurándose lo que más ter-

de pasaría a la historia como la increíble vida de la Monja Alférez. Ya con su nuevo grado y mando siguen sucediéndole cosas para ver y contar. Metida constantemente en líos y pendencias, lo mismo ahorca a un jefe indio que quema una casa de juego o mata a media docena de ciudadanos que la provocan. En una ocasión estuvo a punto de ser linchada por una multitud y tuvo que defenderse a mandobles y escapar a uña de caballo como John Wayne.

Después de tal escaramuza tiene su tercera crisis espiritual. Seis meses pasó ella en oración y reposo hasta que un antiguo compañero de armas fue a buscar al alférez para que le sirviera de padrino de un duelo. Las cosas se tuercen, y ella tiene que intervenir matando a los padrinos del contrario y al apuntador. Pero esto no fue lo peor ¡Una de sus víctimas resultó ser su propio hermano, al que no había reconocido.

En el campo de las relaciones sentimentales al alférez Alonso Díaz Ramírez no le faltaron pretendientes. Varias dulces y delicadas mujercitas se sintieron atraídas por su varonil apostura y tuvo que librarse de ellas con la mayor celeridad, como si de indios se tratara.

Por cuarta vez ingresa en un convento, pero, como las antériores, la estancia es corta. La historia se repite, siguen las guerras y sigue aumentando su colección particular de víctimas. En Cuzco cae gravemente enferma y confiesa a un cura que ella no es un alférez, sino una señorita.

A partir de ahí se pone la falda, el corsé y el tapado de armiño y regresa a España. Cuando se entera el rey Felipe IV de sus aventuras, le concede una pensión de 800 escudos y desde entonces vive tranquila y entregada a las faenas del hogar hasta el año 1650.

A scene showing the Archivo de Indias, which houses the historical documents summarizing Erauso's military service to the state (4)[34]

The 1959 comic strip not only avoids specifying Erauso's status as a woman with royal and papal license to live dressed as a man, but depicts her dressed in nun's garb in a final submissive and repentant pose (panel 3 in fig. 9). Likewise, although the narrative describes her before the confession as "arrogant, quarrelsome, she carries her sword with ease, as well as a knife and two pistols" (panel 1),[35] there is no mention of homoerotic desire, which is not surprising given the strict censorship during Franco's dictatorship. Despite the omission of the various scenes of same-sex desire, the narratives accompanying the drawings follow material from the autobiography. This sequential art narrative, although it alludes to some of the sensational aspects of Erauso's life, seeks to provide a more didactic and informational history, without humor or dialogue.[36]

The educational narratives based on the Monja Alférez legend reappear in the 1970s during the gradual "opening up" of Franco's regime, which officially ended with his death in 1975. Despite the continued conservative approach to Erauso's life, these representations reflect the freedom to address issues of same-sex flirtation that earlier adaptations had suppressed. In contrast to the serious sequential art narrative of 1959, Julio Cebrián, the author and artist of a Spanish comic published in 1974 in a weekly women's magazine titled *Miss,* rewrites Erauso's story by using humor while still supporting the traditional role designated for women during Franco's regime.[37] Cebrián's comic art, consisting of six panels in three tiers, includes humorous dialogue and separate narrations accompanying each panel (see fig. 10). While the 1959 newspaper presents Erauso in a more sober yet positive depiction of implied Basque pride (given references to her beneficial relationships with other Basque individuals), Cebrián's use of humor ridicules the transgender figure in a narrative that combines an early modern context with details from Spanish culture during the 1970s. In the first panel, one of the nuns warns: "Girl,

FIGURE 10. "Famous Women in History: The Lieutenant Nun," a 1974 comic that appeared in the Spanish women's magazine *Miss* (see Appendix for translation). Courtesy of Biblioteca Nacional, Madrid.

don't get near that grated window, can't you see that it has an 'R' rating?" ("dos rombos" refers to the rating system under Franco and to the double diamond cutouts near the grated window of panel 1).[38] Other references to names and places in contemporary culture include the Olavide market, the style of Courreges, and the articles of Argos, Emilio Romero, and Carandell.

The implied justification for Erauso's ability to successfully cross-dress is evident in the narration's characterization of the protagonist as a "flat-chested girl with an ugly face and hairy legs. We must try to understand the girl, that's just the way she was and there was nothing that could be done about it" (panel 2).[39] Although initially this depiction may seem to "forgive" her gender transgression by using an essentialist argument reminiscent of Huarte de San Juan's theory of biological transmutation, ultimately the author/artist ridicules and then "tames" the historical figure.

The first panel presents Catalina dressed in nun's habit while she expresses her desire to take a day trip outside the cloister (upper left panel of fig. 10). One nun comments: "Let her go Mother Superior, it's only one day."[40] The second panel portrays Erauso dressed in seventeenth-century military garb while looking in the mirror as her horse tells her to saddle him up so they can show the world what a well-dressed woman is capable of doing (upper right panel of fig. 10). In the third panel, however, the horse is struggling to keep up with the energetic Erauso, traveling across the mountains of the New World with sword in hand (middle left panel of fig. 10). Unlike the 1959 version of Erauso's tale, however, Cebrián's comic strip includes a humorous homoerotic scene portraying a woman's aggressive romantic pursuit and Erauso's preference for military battle. The scene, nonetheless, is ultimately justified by the character's trust in deceptive appearances. The woman is reaching for Catalina as the latter proclaims: "Leave me alone, you crazy girl. I can't attend to you because duty calls," to which the woman answers: "I want to marry you, my dear little conquistador" (middle right panel of fig. 10).[41] Even the panel's colonial-biased narration clarifies Erauso's aversion to same-sex relations with women in the New World: "In the field of personal relationships, the lieutenant Alonso Díaz Ramírez did not lack interested women. Various sweet and delicate little women felt attracted to her because of her masculine attitude, and she had to free herself from them with great speed, as if they were Indians" (below last panel).[42] Even though Erauso is now de-lesbianized, the text hints at the possibility of same-sex desire. Nonetheless, Erauso's real transgression is suggested by her violent pugnacity. In the fifth panel, surrounded by injured bodies on the ground, she wounds another with her sword as she shouts: "Now this is my kind of sport!" (lower left panel of fig. 10).[43] By the last panel, however, the Lieutenant Nun is dressed in the garb of a secular woman, not in nun's habit. She is bowing to the king, who tells her, "What you have done is very good but now take this generous pay and go settle down at home."[44] The last statement in the story is made by one of the king's attendants, who adds, "And may she learn to sew the back-stitch" (see lower right panel of fig. 10).[45] Cebrián's version converts Erauso into a feminine and traditional woman who not only returns and then remains in Spain but, according to the final episode, "lives a peaceful life dedicated to her domestic duties until the year 1650."[46] Unlike the 1959 comic strip, which attempts to portray Erauso's life according to the autobiography and historical documents from the seventeenth century, Cebrián's adaptation rewrites the end of Catalina's life as an edifying example of feminine domesticity.

In addition to these pictorial narratives of 1959 and 1974, which were targeted toward adult readers, two books based on the Lieutenant Nun and designed for adolescents were published during the last few years of Franco's dictatorship. Even though both works take advantage of a national historical figure to teach young adults a lesson about Spain's imperial past while appealing to the readers' preference for adventure, independence, and tales of rebellion, the novels are markedly more open about Erauso's activities than earlier versions published in the 1950s. Given the target audience of these adaptations, perhaps one of the most interesting aspects of the portrayal of Erauso's life is found in the interpretation of the homoerotic episodes. *La Monja Alférez,* written in 1970 by María del Carmen Ochoa and illustrated by Francisco Blanes, makes no attempt to avoid Erauso's attraction for other women. While an episode in chapter 5 of the original autobiography is explicitly homoerotic ("I had my head in the folds of her skirt and she was combing my hair while I ran my hand up and down between her legs" [17]), the same scene is described by Ochoa in terms of innocent games: "the girl with whom I would play and have fun on many occasions, as it was a natural thing due to our young age" (45).[47] Despite this initial attempt to normalize same-sex eroticism, when the author continues to include other homoerotic episodes, she feels obligated to offer an explanation for the transgressive desire: "The Lieutenant Nun's habit of flirting with women is not so strange; we have already seen that she had done it on various occasions and we will even see her do it again. One of two reasons could explain what motivated her to do it: the first, that perhaps she started to believe that she was really a man and as such she would behave accordingly; the second, and the most probable, by acting in this way she prevented people from suspecting her true sex, which from the beginning was her biggest worry" (50–51).[48]

Ochoa does not deny the intimacy between women, but she interprets it as either a performance used to convince others of her masculine role or, the less likely case, as a sign that Erauso really began to believe she was a man. "Genuine" lesbian desire is denied since the protagonist must either perform something she does not feel or she must become a man in order to love another woman. Moreover, since the author intuits the subversive potential in seeing Erauso flirt with other women, she encourages her audience to read the protagonist as a man when "he" is attracted to women: "Considering all these things, it was difficult to think that she was a woman" (51).[49] However, none of the twenty illustrations included in Ochoa's adaptation portray the homoerotic flirtation that is suggested in certain episodes, while in Armonía Rodríguez's 1975 version titled *De monja a militar* (From Nun to Soldier), one of the fifteen drawings by Pilarín Bayés depicts Juana (Erauso's admirer and future fiancée) nursing her back to health.[50] Like Ochoa's adaptation, Rodríguez's work presents Erauso's sexuality in ambiguous terms as she seems genuinely attracted to Juana ("I like to gaze at Juana" [85]),[51] although the "heterosexual" expectations of the girl's mother creates both anxiety and humor: "But I know that I can't behave how they expect me to" (86).[52] Later, when the girl's mother discusses the possibility of marriage, the protagonist "felt like laughing" (90). Despite the vague suggestion of same-sex desire in Rodríguez's novel, the theme is ambivalent as it is neither confirmed nor denied in the narrative.

While Ochoa ends Erauso's life story with the protagonist choosing to live as a man in Mexico, Rodríguez's work concludes with Erauso's melancholic reaction to her new identity as public spectacle, which the protagonist compares to the imprisonment of the convent: "I feel like a prisoner. A prisoner of the people who want me to tell them my story . . . people are surprised, astonished. They find my story amazing and they invite me to their palaces, to their country homes, so that I can entertain their guests with my stories. . . . I feel as furious as when the nun guarding the entrance to the convent wouldn't let me open the door so I could follow my blue butterfly" (118–119).[53] Even though she affirms her plan to escape the public's curious gaze ("they will never find me . . . never!" [121]),[54] the final illustration of the text shows the butterfly, which previously had symbolized her desire for freedom, now dead and pinned down as if on display in a collection.

While the most recent Lieutenant Nun sequential art narrative published to date was possibly modeled after the first comic book inspired by Erauso (the one published in Mexico in 1956), it provides a good example of how mainstream transvestite narratives can be used both to disrupt and police sexual borders. On January 2, 1991, an issue of the comic book *Hombres y Héroes* (Men and Heroes), featuring the life of the Lieutenant Nun, was published in Mexico. Like most mass-produced comic books, *Hombres y Héroes* was marketed to adolescent consumers and was undoubtedly designed to teach young readers about historical figures while appealing to the audience's tastes and interests. In reference to the use of real-life individuals in American comics, Joseph Witek notes that comics attempting "to tell true (or ostensibly true) stories were usually either didactic efforts to edify the adolescents or sensational real-life analogues to the comic-book industry's pulpy stock-in-trades" (13). Since action and violence are part of the formula for most comics, the episodes from Erauso's autobiography were easily adapted to the comic-book format. Roughly half of the comic book's ninety-four pages feature the protagonist engaged in violent fights, whether in gambling houses, in the streets, or on the battlefield (see fig. 11). Like the characterization of Erauso in the autobiography, the protagonist is again depicted as hot-tempered, independent, deceitful, and violent, yet brave. Unlike the life narrative, however, the comic book presents a protagonist who is remorseful for her numerous crimes and sins. This repentance implies a transformation or conversion; and once Catalina confesses her true identity the sequential art text abandons the violence featured in the first eighty-seven pages.

While Catalina's transgenderism is justified as a heroic effort to achieve

FIGURE 11. Lieutenant Nun in fight sequences from the 1991 Mexican comic book *Hombres y Héroes* (see Appendix for translation). Reprinted by permission of Novedades Editores, Mexico City.

freedom from early modern Spain's restricting role for women, this gender rebellion does not include the transgressive desire featured in her autobiography. In the Mexican comic book of 1991, the scenes of homoerotic flirtation and petting from the *Vida* are either excluded or reinterpreted as a resistance to the consequences created by the masculine disguise. Unlike the autobiography's most explicit scene of same-sex desire, which portrays Catalina caressing the inner thigh of one of the sisters-in-law of her boss (Diego de Solarte), the corresponding episode in the comic-book version reveals a protagonist who seems resistant to becoming involved with the other woman (see fig. 12). The narration as well as the dialogue show Erauso's innocence in the "compromising" situation: "Those two young women were very charming. I made friends with them without anticipating that they would see me as a man" (60).[55] When one of the women starts to hug Catalina, declaring "I love you! I would do anything for you. Take me as your wife and let's run away!" (61), Catalina, visibly shocked, can only respond with "Me?? . . . Oh

God!" (61).[56] Likewise, the illustrations demonstrate the aggression of the other woman while Catalina's facial expressions reveal confusion and fear (right panels of fig. 12).

Even in the drawing that portrays Erauso trapped in the forceful embrace of the other woman, the latter appears to be on top of the former in a dominant position, as Catalina seems to be the passive recipient of the sexual desire of her admirer (upper left panel of fig. 13). The illustration allows her boss as well as the reader to ponder the homoerotic/ambivalent embrace, but the narration insists that the unwanted harassment was brief, as it was concurrent with the entry of Erauso's boss in the room: "At that exact moment . . ." (62). Despite the conclusion that clarifies Erauso's rejection of the opportunity to enjoy the favors of another woman, if the reader perceives the panel according to the comic-book pattern described by Lawrence L. Abbot, the "preliminary visual impact" would focus on the homoerotic embrace (161). Although the eye soon moves from the drawing to the text (to the narration and then to the dialogue balloon) for explanation of the pictorial elements, the brief moment of alternative desire provides diegetic as well as extradiegetic shock or pleasure before the text imposes a non-lesbian reading on the ostensibly disruptive picture.

This potential ambiguity is apparent at other times, most notably when Catalina is willing to play the role of heterosexual male voyeur. The dialogue as well as the position of the pictorial elements in a brief encounter between Erauso and Beatriz de Cárdenas demonstrate the protagonist's unprovoked willingness to flirt with other women.[57] The reader's attention is drawn to Beatriz's chest, which is accentuated by its relatively large size and central position in the panel (upper right panel of fig. 14). Just below, in the next panel, we see a closeup of the two women, as if to indicate intimacy and secrecy in proximity while Erauso tells her: "You have open credit, ma'am. These are orders from my boss, which I follow with pleasure, since it is for such a beautiful woman" (45).[58] The possibility of reading these episodes in terms of a visual lesbian spectacle is intensified by the distinction between the drawings of Catalina as man and those of the biological men. Although in general terms she is not drawn to look like an obvious cross-dresser, there are subtle signs of her female identity. In many illustrations, her eyelashes are more defined than those of

FIGURE 12. Scenes of the homoerotic complications from *Hombres y Héroes* (see Appendix for translation). Reprinted by permission of Novedades Editores, Mexico City.

FIGURE 13. Romantic and military scenes from *Hombres y Héroes* (see Appendix for translation). Reprinted by permission of Novedades Editores, Mexico City.

FIGURE 14. The Lieutenant Nun as dedicated employee serving her female customer in *Hombres y Héroes* (see Appendix for translation). Reprinted by permission of Novedades Editores, Mexico City.

the men, her hair always covers her ears (unlike most of her male companions), she lacks the beard frequently worn by the men, and the lines in her face seem less severe than the men's features (see figs. 11–14).

Regardless of temporary moments of ambiguity, these episodes ultimately seek to de-lesbianize the protagonist. The final example of this attempt is evident in the comic book's conclusion, as it eliminates the central lesbian love story from the third broadside published in Mexico, even though it includes all other activities detailed in the 1653 text. Catalina no longer falls desperately in love with a woman while accompanying her on a trip. The comic-book narrative explains only that the protagonist was frequently entrusted to escort women who were traveling alone (93).

The last line of the comic establishes the protagonist's identity as the embodiment of a "woman who overcame the limits imposed on her by the society of her time and who achieved a free and adventurous life" (94).[59] The image that accompanies this narration in the panel, like the cover illustration, again combines the dual religious-military elements: a cross is placed diagonally against a sword and Erauso is depicted in nun's habit with a soldier's helmet.[60] Most superheroines of comic books fight against evil: Warrior Nun Areala, for example, combats the devil and his representatives on Earth (such as the Nazis). The Lieutenant Nun in the Mexican comic book is also a freedom fighter, but her cause promotes a brand of transgenderism that does not disrupt the conservative ideology that endorses religious and sexual conformity. In this sense, it is not surprising that she does not resemble her American comic counterpart, the Warrior Nun Areala, who is presented as a sexual object with revealing curves for adolescent or adult voyeurs (see fig. 15). Although their fighting techniques may share certain features, Erauso is not depicted as an eroticized Warrior Nun, as was María Félix in the 1940s. Erauso's attraction in *Hombres y Héroes* resides in her sensational life adventures and in her hybrid nature. As a result, the Mexican comic-book adaptation of Erauso's life entertains as it also serves to teach young readers about historical figures and geographical locations in Spain and Latin America, which are printed in bold letters in the text to underscore the edifying function of the sequential art.

Although the message to young readers may imply a positive yet asexual model for women's equality in the 1990s, the images cannot escape other possibilities of reception. Despite the attempt to silence same-sex desire, inherent in the unconvincing disguise of the transvestite narrative is the unavoidable lesbian reading, which is intensified by the viewing pattern of sequential art. As the reader privileges the illustration over the text, a new lesson about female sexuality emerges and, given the enduring appeal of the Lieutenant Nun for almost four hundred years, it is precisely this ambiguity that ensures the continued success of the transvestite spectacle for such a wide variety of curious viewers.

The Lieutenant Nun as Pornographic Spectacle

Whereas the prose and sequential art narratives in Spain during the 1970s (as well as the 1991 Mexican comic book) hint at same-sex flirtation but ultimately silence any detailed expression of this desire, two historical novels published in Chile in 1938 and 1972 eroticize Catalina de Erauso

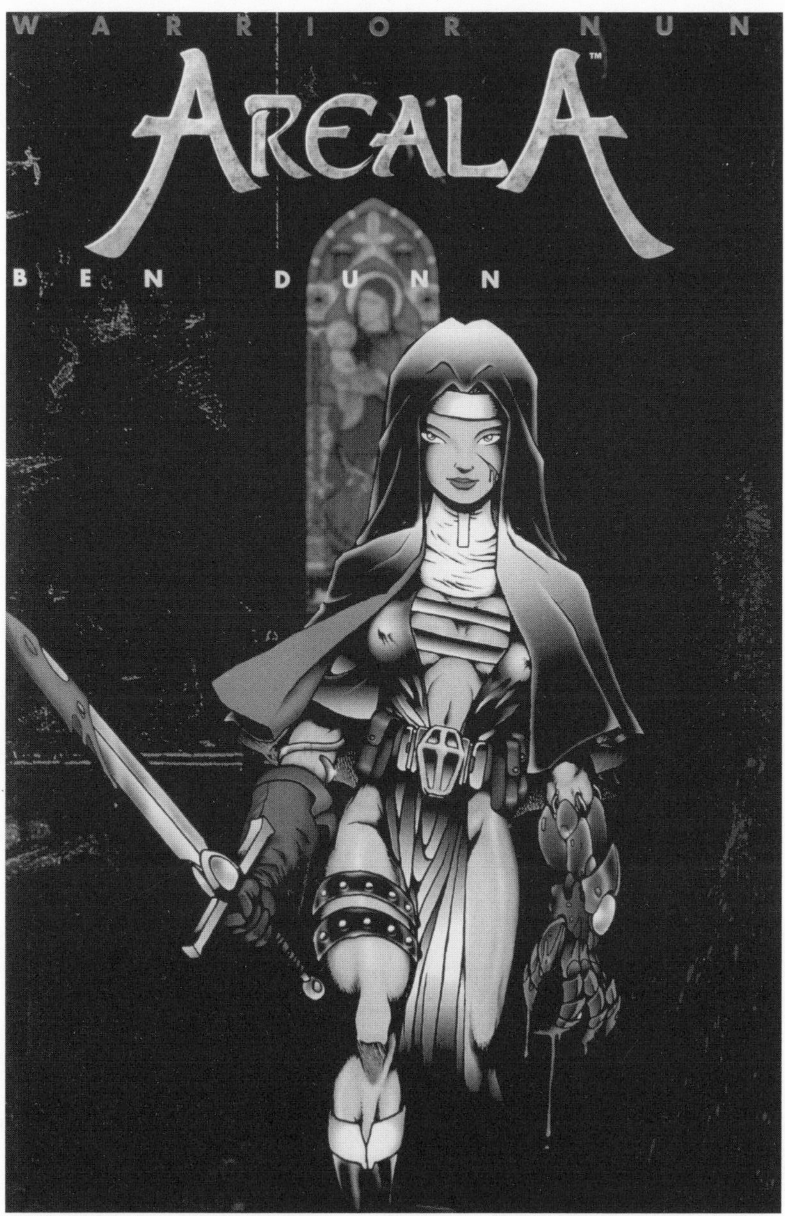

FIGURE 15. Areala, the "warrior nun" from the American comic book *Warrior Nun Areala* (San Antonio: Antarctic Press). Reprinted by permission of Ben Dunn.

and her adventures in South America. More than thirty years separate the two novels, written by Raúl Morales-Alvarez and Carlos Keller respectively; yet politically and socially they share significant and somewhat comparable moments in Chile's history. The year 1938 marks the beginning of the radical Pedro Aguirre Cerda's administration, which sought to restore constitutional rule, civil liberties, and basic social reforms after the conservative government of Arturo Alessandri. In 1972, when Keller's novel appeared, Chile was governed by Salvador Allende in his goal to achieve socialist reform in his country. A year later, however, marks the start of one of Chile's most violent dictatorships, lead by Augusto Pinochet.[61] As a result, the two erotic historical novels are products of liberal cultural contexts that escape the strict censorship imposed during more repressive periods.

Raúl Morales-Alvarez's 1938 *La Monja Alférez (crónica de una vida que tuvo perfil de romance)* manipulates the protagonist's desire in terms of both heterosexual and lesbian attraction in order to convert her experiences into erotic spectacles for the reader. Although Morales-Alvarez does not hesitate to reprove same-sex flirtation by describing it as "sadistic pleasure," "poison," and "perverse enjoyment," the author refrains from abbreviating the details of the erotic scenes between the women: "And leaning against the smitten Beatriz, she kissed her madly on her white and sensual neck, on her feverish mouth, and on her small and transparent ears" (56).[62] While these scenes may provide the reader with the same intermittent "pastimes" that, according to the author, the protagonist enjoyed between fights and battles, he ultimately transforms Erauso into a heterosexual figure by inventing a romantic episode with a monk named Fray Lope. Although they never actually engage in sexual relations, through fantasy and dream sequences the text feminizes and heterosexualizes Erauso as an object for the reader's pleasure: "A lover to whom she would offer her turgid and burning throat, the nape of her neck, her shoulders, and her hard breasts, which were like two blooming roses, or better yet like two wounded doves. A lover who would take her in his arms to strip her, petal by petal, causing endless sweet and painful pleasure" (42).[63] The author concludes his novel by inviting the reader to join him in his voyeuristic contemplation of Catalina: "Observe her from a visual perspective. Look at her tumultuous, burning, wild, and always beautiful life. Reader: with this spirit you must ponder the version of the

Lieutenant Nun that you have just read. It is possible, then, that you will come to love her, as I do" (112).[64]

Similar passages are found in Luis Angel Rodríguez's historical novel *Vida y hazañas de la Monja Alférez,* published in Mexico in 1937. Rodríguez includes the same homoerotic episodes featured in the autobiography and the Mexican broadside of 1653, and like Morales-Alvarez he highlights the erotic imagery for his readers. For example, Rodríguez's version of the physical flirtation described in chapter 5 of the autobiography contains much more explicit and sensual details than does the original: "Francisco [Erauso] was lying on an elegant tapestry rug with her head resting on the lap of Doña Mencia, who was caressing her curly locks of hair and was occasionally lowering her delicious fleshy lips to the nun's mouth, giving her loud and passionate kisses, while the suitor's hands did not remain still but were skillfully exploring below the skirt of the beautiful and carefree young woman" (51).[65]

Carlos Keller's 1972 historical novel, like Morales-Alvarez's 1938 adaptation, reveals the voyeuristic pleasures in viewing both the eroticized national landscapes (in Latin America and Spain) and the lesbian adventures described by the protagonist. In *Las Memorias de la Monja Alférez,* Erauso's objectification of and desire for other women become a voyeuristic spectacle for the bishop as well as for the readers of the novel. When the protagonist describes the sexual enjoyment experienced by watching, hugging, and kissing women, the bishop acts shocked but is clearly titillated, as he asks questions to ensure the continuation of the narrative:

> "Her entire body was like a harmonious rhythm that moved in such delicate figures, delicate as the arabesques of the Alcázar of Seville. . . . And so we went from playing a simple word game to becoming involved in a true, hot, and passionate love. We would hug each other and kiss each other. . . ."
>
> "Jesus, Mary, and Joseph!" cried out the bishop.
>
> "With good reason Your Excellency is shocked," I answered, "since I was like a crazy person and had forgotten my true condition. The fact is that during one of these hot nights in Saña, Beatriz, after much fondling, confessed to me: 'Francisco, love me more! I am yours, I want you to possess all of me, to penetrate me. Please join your body with mine in one immense blaze of fire that will consume us both.'

She flung herself on my cot and dragged me with her as she undressed herself. . . ."

"And what did you do, Catalina?" my investigator asked. (70–71)[66]

This pattern is repeated throughout the text. Catalina describes her sexual attraction for other women, which eventually leads to hugging and kissing; the bishop listens with fascination, justifying his curiosity by referring to his role as the spiritual examiner of Catalina's soul:

> "The young woman had sat down on my lap and was combing her hair, which was brown and silky. I was caressing her beautiful body. . . . Suddenly Diego interrupted, . . . without mincing words, he fired me on the spot and ordered me to leave the house. . . ."
>
> "He gave you a well-deserved punishment!"—the bishop commented, adding: "But I would like us to examine your aberrations with more detail, Catalina. Come back the day after tomorrow. I will meditate on this a bit." (77)[67]

The structure of Keller's version of Catalina's narrative engages a strategy comparable to Elizabeth Rhodes's interpretation of early modern nuns' life narratives, which present a "pornographic" mystical spectacle to please the male confessor's voyeuristic gaze: "The *vida,* then, is expected to reconfirm men's control and superiority over a woman who was about to escape from the shackles of the fleshly object and turn herself into a legitimate, spiritual subject. Consequently, she is exposed by the same cultural dynamic which bares the woman of the sex flick: turned into an object, forced to adopt a posture she knows will please whether it is her own or not, because her very life depends on her ability to appease the masculine ego and look like what she is supposed to be" (15).

Keller, however, converts the bishop into a homosexual voyeur who is attracted to the masculine appearance of Erauso: "As a woman, you have a masculine component; and as a man I have a feminine part. You have been a witness of the fondness that in this sense I have for you. I will confess to you also that I would have been happy to have been loved by you, since you seemed to embody masculine beauty" (79).[68] Catalina later discusses her own "aberrations" as well as the bishop's homosexual desires as she describes her feelings of being a man in a woman's body and then intuits that her listener must likewise feel like a woman in a man's body: "There are those who possess female organs, such as myself, and who nonetheless feel like a man; and there are those with whom the opposite occurs. . . . (I paused a second, but I resisted the temptation to allude to him)" (82).[69] Despite the numerous possibilities for explaining the bishop's desire for Catalina (heterosexual attraction of a biological man for a biological woman, of a man who feels like a woman who desires a woman who feels like a man; the homoerotic desire of a man for an individual who looks, acts, and feels like a man, and so forth), the text explains the homosexuality of both characters in terms of a traditional heterosexual configuration: Catalina loves women because she really feels like a man; and the bishop loves men because he feels like a woman. Not surprisingly, this "sexual inversion" is slowly corrected and by the end of the novel the text attempts to transform Erauso's lesbian desire from the carnal instinct of her youth into a spiritual maternal love: "I loved her terribly, with a madness that I had never known . . . but was it a carnal feeling like before? No. I was already approaching older age, I was peaceful. I loved her but not as a lover but like a mother" (449).[70] Just as lesbian desire is transferred to the maternal realm, the protagonist's sexual attraction for an image of the Virgin is also converted into spiritual devotion: "I will confess to you that at first I was pierced physically, above all, by the sight of the exquisite image of the Virgin of Tolsa. . . . But it is also true that that image no longer has a carnal meaning for me but rather it embodies the divine strength that I needed to renew myself" (467).[71]

As the final proof of Catalina's conversion from transgressive lesbian to reformed believer, the last scene in the novel depicts a struggle between the pre-Columbian goddess Coatlícue and the image of the Virgin mentioned above. In Keller's novel, Coatlícue symbolizes the terrifying and horrible hybridity of Erauso's lesbian instincts, and, as expected, the pagan goddess is defeated by the Virgin: ". . . the terrible goddess Coatlícue. Above her immense tiger's claws there lies a pile of serpents. They have dismembered the body and its parts are kept by the vipers, along with the sacrificed hearts. Oh, it is horrifying! . . . then the Virgin absorbed Coatlícue, she dominated her, and covered her" (482–483).[72] While Coatlícue continues to symbolize lesbian desire for some contemporary Chicana feminists such as Gloria Anzaldúa, Keller's image of Coatlícue represents the horrifying monstrosity of homosexuality; Anzaldúa's Coatlícue, on the other hand, portrays the freedom and empowerment of duality: "She represents: duality in life, a synthesis of duality, and a third perspective. . . . I see the heat of anger or rebellion or hope split open that rock, releasing *La Coatlicue.* And someone in me takes matters into our own hands, and eventually, takes dominion over serpents" (Anzaldúa 46, 51).

Despite the efforts in Keller's text to neutralize same-sex desire by defeating it through orthodox religiosity, there is another way of reading the novel's end that could disrupt the heterobiased resolution. Although Catalina insists that her desire for her friend María is purely maternal, the protagonist continues the eroticization of her beloved: "It was a visual pleasure watching her move around my house, her graceful little hands grasping each object to caress it. . . . I savored each movement of her slender body. She had a wave-like walk, and she would approach me as if she were a springtime breeze" (450–451).[73] As a result, the reader is invited to reconsider the sincerity of her conversion from active lesbian to an asexual maternal figure who no longer feels the same "unnatural" passions of her youth. Therefore, when she claims that her carnal attraction for the image of the Virgin was likewise transformed into a "divine force," we may also doubt the success of her "regeneration." The final scene in which the Virgin invites the protagonist to join her in eternal life can be also read as an everlasting story of same-sex love, as the Virgin takes Catalina by the hand and they go off together to live happily ever after: "There is the radiant Virgin. She takes my hand . . . , and asks me to accompany her" (483).[74] Although Catalina dies, she really lives forever with the image of a woman to whom she is carnally attracted.

The Lieutenant Nun as "Carnival" Spectacle

Once Spain achieved its successful transition from a forty-year repressive dictatorship to a democratic socialist government, the Lieutenant Nun adaptations returned to the original portrait of a lesbian military hero. Written in 1986, published in 1992, and performed on stage in 1993, Domingo Miras's theatrical rendition of Erauso's story evokes the Baroque notion of hybridity and the monstrous spectacle. According to the Spanish playwright, the Lieutenant Nun is a theatrical figure because "her hybrid and contradictory condition as a religious and military person, a woman and a soldier, gives her that mysterious attraction usually containing dark and ambiguous aspects, that which combines at the same time two temperaments theoretically opposed and irreconcilable, and this places her outside the norms, outside the normal, conferring to her the disturbing attribute of anomaly, disruption, and the seductive aura of a marvel" (Miras 24).[75]

Miras's play is divided into nine scenes that portray different aspects of Erauso's life, with the first and the last scenes framing the presentation in a portrait of Erauso in 1630. In these scenes the protagonist's autobiography is read by another character (performed by the director Luis Cabañero), whose reading of the memoirs coincides with our viewing/reading of the play. What stands out in the Miras adaptation is the protagonist's self-reflection regarding the popularity of her case: "We cannot know whether the historical person became aware of the role that power had imposed on her; but the dramatic character is definitely aware of it" (Serrano 1994, 36).[76] Just as Castillo Solórzano's 1637 picaresque novel suggests how Erauso might have reacted to Pérez de Montalbán's version of her life, Miras presents a Catalina who has also seen the seventeenth-century play and is annoyed by its plot: "The play *La Monja Alférez* in which all my worries are about whether my friend will marry or not marry his lady was completely invented by the playwright. A lot of ignorance and a lot of lies dominate the stories about me that are circulating" (Miras 56).[77]

In an attempt to include all of the principal features of the Lieutenant Nun icon, each segment portrays a different moment, personality trait, or a key incident in the life of the protagonist. Scene 2, characteristic of numerous versions discussed above, presents Catalina in the convent engaging in physical and verbal fights with an older nun before escaping (see fig. 16).[78] In scene 3 the protagonist, now in Chile, narrates her crimes and numerous conflicts and fights. Likewise, scene 6 showcases Erauso's gambling habits and the fight with El Nuevo Cid, while scene 4 portrays her courage and superiority over other men, as she is the only traveler to persevere in the treacherous trip over the mountains in freezing temperatures (described in chapter 7 of the autobiography).

Scene 5 condenses most of the homoerotic episodes and, like the films by Javier Aguirre and Sheila McLaughlin, converts the episode in which

FIGURE 16. Juli García as Catalina de Erauso before her escape in Domingo Miras's play, *La Monja Alférez,* performed in 1993. Photo courtesy of Luis Cabañero.

Erauso rescues the wife from her violent husband (chapter 13 of the autobiography) into another example of the protagonist's same-sex desire (see fig. 17). Unlike her account of the flirtations with two fiancées in the past (from chapter 7 of the autobiography), her attraction to and love for Doña María Dávalos appear to be genuine: "She is more beautiful than the sun that shines on us, more beautiful than life. . . . María, I adore you like God" (104), while the stage directions specify: "(Catalina hugs her and covers her face and mouth with kisses. María hugs her also, with increasing passion)" (104).[79] Despite the open display of lesbian affection in the play's script, the production tempers the physicality of the women's relationship. In the actual performance the actress portraying Erauso (Juli García) kisses her fellow actress (Elena Belmonte) on the cheeks, usually avoiding the mouth-to-mouth contact noted in the playwright's original text.[80]

One aspect of Erauso's icon that is given prominence in Miras's play is her carnival attraction. The last three scenes are characterized by the protagonist's awareness of becoming the monstrous spectacle of everybody's

FIGURE 17. The Lieutenant Nun (played by Juli García) flirts with María Dávalos (played by Elena Belmonte) in Miras's *La Monja Alférez*. Photo courtesy of Luis Cabañero.

gaze; first the bishop is presented as a curious spectator in scene 7 when Erauso reveals her identity, as is the pope in scene 8, as well as the general public after the revelation. The interaction with the pope reveals, perhaps more than any other representation, the policing capacity of the hybrid spectacle. The pope is clearly entertained by the Lieutenant Nun and is aware of her popularity, which is attributed to the strangeness and rarity of her case. When the cardinal raises his concerns about establishing a potentially negative precedent, the pope responds by describing Erauso as a unique case that does not threaten the system: "A curiosity of nature, Cardinal. A prodigy, a unique phenomenon and nothing more . . . and so she has turned into a prodigy that is outside the system, without helping or hurting it. If there were many Catalina de Erausos, then yes: then, the order would be disturbed" (142–143).[81] In fact, it is the assignment of her identity as a monstrous spectacle, an aberration from the normal, that ensures its control and containment.

The last scene begins with the reading on stage of the final page of

Erauso's life narrative. As the character reads the anecdote describing the prostitutes who seem to tease the protagonist for her transgenderism, Erauso walks into the room and the two discuss the scene. Catalina indicates that the prostitutes' remarks clearly demonstrate the ridicule that she had been experiencing after her biological identity was made public. Other spectator reactions include envy, disbelief, fear, anger, and ostracism. The imagery that Erauso uses to illustrate her perception of others' gaze emerges directly from the carnival attractions or freak shows: "I am a carnival monkey . . . they would watch me as if I were a monkey performing extreme and never-before-seen flips for the amazement and entertainment of those present and nothing else. . . . The bearded lady or the incredibly strong woman at whom the children stare in the public square while a man plays the drum and shows her to the curious spectators" (147).[82] It is Catalina's displeasure with her "carnival" life after the revelation that leads Virtudes Serrano to characterize Miras's protagonist as a tragic heroine: "Catalina is not seen as an absolute triumph but as a tragic heroine up against an unavoidable destiny" (36).[83] Despite the depressive tone in the final scene, the last segment, which describes her plans for the future, reveals a sense of hope and optimism. Catalina reveals her plan to establish a new business in Mexico in order to avoid further fame and recognition. She describes her project as a "new day" and a "new life" (150); the play ends as Catalina looks out the window while the sun rises, creating a halo effect around her head (see fig. 18). Although she is alone in her new journey, she does not die nor does she lose a significant love interest at the end like the versions that incorporate the third broadside. Miras's resolution is perhaps not the triumph that we will see in McLaughlin's film, and although it is not a tragedy, it does reveal a certain pity for the plight of the protagonist that precludes a full celebration of her transgender success.

Tragic Lesbian Love

In the same year that Miras wrote his play about Catalina de Erauso, Javier Aguirre's film adaptation of the seventeenth-century icon was released in Spain as *La Monja Alférez*. However, in a radical departure from the 1944 Mexican film version of the Lieutenant Nun, Javier Aguirre's

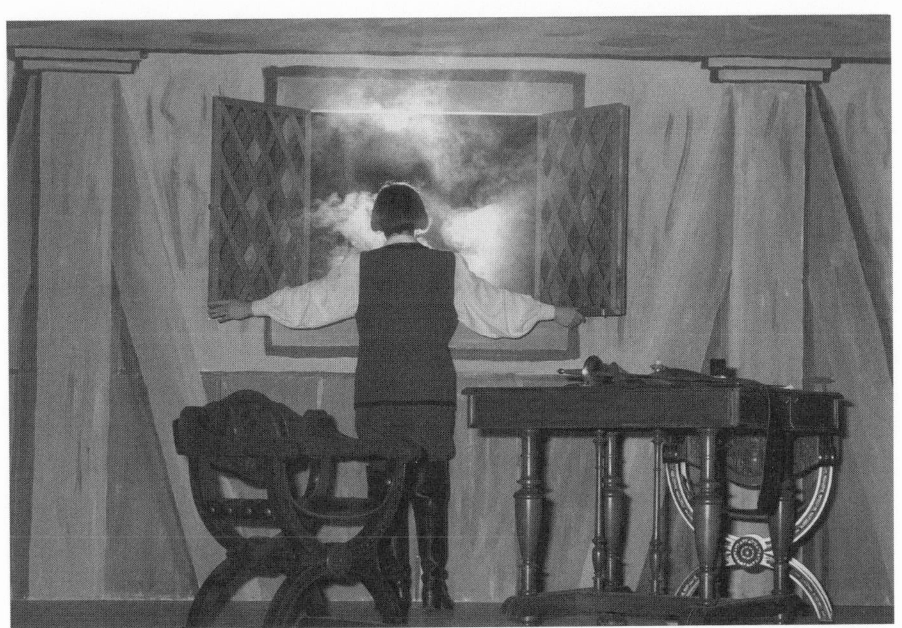

FIGURE 18. Erauso makes plans to start her own business in Mexico in the final scene of Miras's *La Monja Alférez.* Photo courtesy of Luis Cabañero.

1986 Spanish cinematic adaptation restores Erauso's lesbian status and in certain aspects re-masculinizes the protagonist's role (played by the director's wife Esperanza Roy) in accordance with the autobiography. Although Aguirre, himself a Basque, studied the life of Catalina de Erauso in school when he was only twelve years old, he attributes the relative lack of publicity and popularity of Erauso's story in history to her lesbian identity: "For historians, Catalina de Erauso is one of the most unusual characters in history. I think that her status as a homosexual has prevented more publicity" (quoted in Doneil); "If her adventures aren't more popular . . . it is due to the fact that her distinct attraction for other women has prevented her popularity" (quoted in *Fotogramas,* March 1986).[84] According to comments made in interviews and to the script, written by Aguirre and Alberto Insua, which was based on Erauso's autobiography and Thomas De Quincey's nineteenth-century version of her life, it seems that adventure, rebellion, and lesbianism were the main themes motivating the first cinematic adaptation of Erauso's story produced in Spain.

FIGURE 19. Blanca Marsillach as the adolescent Catalina in Javier Aguirre's 1986 film, *La Monja Alférez.* Frame enlargement courtesy of Filmoteca Española, Madrid.

The film begins with a portrait of the oppressive environment in the convent and, in particular, the conflicts with an older nun who physically and emotionally abuses the protagonist. Catalina (portrayed as an adolescent by Blanca Marsillach) first demonstrates her mischievous nature in the convent; there her close relationship develops with another novice, Inés, who eventually becomes the most significant person in the protagonist's life (see fig. 19). Although their friendship is intimate, it is not characterized, initially at least, by homoerotic attraction. Since the relationship between Catalina and Inés is the only positive aspect of convent life for the protagonist, after Inés dies from an undiagnosed illness, Catalina decides to escape and disguise herself as a man.

Once Erauso travels to the New World, however, the same-sex flirtation scenes repeated in previous versions are again used to create tension between Catalina and the women attracted to her, as the protagonist initially seems intimidated by the sexual advances of the more aggressive women. The notations in Aguirre's screenplay reveal a sense of ambiguity with regard to Catalina/Alonso's feelings about the lesbian flirtation. In Trujillo, for example, as Beatriz (one of Erauso's admirers) attempts to seduce "Alonso," the latter reacts passively yet notices the woman's appeal: "It must be clear that Catalina/Alonso's attitude regarding Beatriz's flirtation and insinuations is expectant or even passive, although she never ceases to admire the woman's charms" (51–52).[85] Likewise, when Beatriz exposes her breasts for the visual pleasure of her love interest, Catalina reacts with similar ambiguity; she is immobilized yet continues to gaze at her body: "Catalina/Alonso doesn't know how to respond. Her eyes have focused on Beatriz's breasts and her forehead breaks into a sweat while she watches her with semi-clouded eyes. Nonetheless she is incapable of responding" (53).[86] As Beatriz continues her petting, Catalina "doesn't know what to do, but she enjoys it anyway" (54).[87] When Beatriz unexpectedly kisses her, however, the protagonist reacts with horror: "Suddenly she kisses her. 'He,' taken by surprise, reveals a horrified expression" (60).[88] While the viewer may interpret this horror as a heterosexual sign of resistance to same-sex desire, the script's notations insist on an ambivalence that suggests possible interest: "Catalina/Alonso comes closer and kisses Beatriz through the bars. We don't know if it is out of pleasure or not" (67).[89]

The fact that Catalina does not display the same horror when she initiates the kisses with other women might indicate that the resistance to same-sex flirtation is bound to issues of control and fear of discovery (see fig. 20). When Juana (another admirer) caresses Catalina's inner thigh, slowly moving upward, the latter removes her hand to prevent any genital contact. However, Catalina willingly gives Juana long passionate kisses ("Slowly they fall to the grass. They remain lying down. They kiss and hug in silence" [129]).[90] The protagonist subsequently abandons her on a deserted road in a manner that is described as somewhat "diabolic" but justified nonetheless by her need for freedom: "In her face one can detect an uncontrollable fury. A sudden decision to recover her freedom. In her face underlies something diabolical" (130).[91] Catalina also kisses another woman, Doña Francisca, despite the former's intention of escaping the situation before the relationship develops beyond kissing and hugging (see fig. 21).

The protagonist's gradual willingness to participate in erotic contact with same-sex partners suggests that she slowly discovers and later accepts her desire for other women. When Catalina saves Doña María from her husband's violent revenge for an affair with another man, the pro-

FIGURE 20. Esperanza Roy as the adult Catalina disguised as a man in Aguirre's *La Monja Alférez*. Frame enlargement courtesy of Filmoteca Española, Madrid.

FIGURE 21. Esperanza Roy seducing another woman in Aguirre's *La Monja Alférez*. Frame enlargement courtesy of Filmoteca Española, Madrid.

tagonist shares a tender and passionate kiss that seems to be a sincere demonstration of lesbian desire, since there are no other apparent ulterior motives to justify the action: "They stare at each other for a moment. Then, softly, Catalina/Alonso places her lips on María's mouth. It is a delicate kiss, touching softly" (154).[92] Chris Straayer describes the type of kisses that Catalina shares with Beatriz, Juana, Doña Francisca, and Doña María as paradoxical or bivalent since they allow for heterosexual as well as homosexual interpretations (54). The heterosexual understanding of the paradoxical kiss assumes that it is a mistake caused by the disguise, while identification with the perceived desire of the deceived character charges the kiss and allows for an alternative homoerotic reading. Whereas Catalina's first kiss with Beatriz reflects the heterosexual response of aversion, her final kiss with Doña María exhibits the same desire that the deceived character feels. Moreover, the use of the two-shot (see figs. 20 and 21) instead of the shot-reverse-shot accentuates the bisexed nature of the inadequately disguised character: "The image of the paradoxical kiss requires the viewer to look at the two characters and binds the unconvincing disguise with narrative passing via the two-shot" (Straayer 57).[93]

Like María Felix's celebrity persona in her performance of the Lieutenant Nun, Esperanza Roy is also an important influence on the audience's response to the transgendered character in Aguirre's film. In contrast to the highly feminized Félix, Roy attempted to appear as masculine as possible for the sake of verisimilitude, but because of the inadequacy of the disguise as well as star recognition, the audience would never be "fooled" into believing she was really a man, as were the seventeenth-century observers of the historical Erauso and many mainstream spectators of the 1992 film *The Crying Game.* Roy's preparations included letting her hair and eyebrows grow, taking fencing and horseback riding lessons, and studying men's gestures and movements for months, even though she believed that "what is important is the feeling and the sense that you give to the interpretation, not the image but what you express. For example, Greta Garbo didn't look like Queen Christina either, yet there is the film" (*El Alcazar,* Oct. 12, 1986).[94]

Despite Roy's endeavor to de-feminize her character, the script departs from historical sources and reinscribes the actress's femininity by inventing a fictitious revelation scene in which two monks care for the protagonist after she receives serious wounds in a fight. According to Erauso's memoirs, she was in complete control of the revelation process, first by deciding to confess to the bishop and then by requesting a physical examination to prove her virginity. It is significant to note, however, that in the manuscript of Erauso's *Vida* deposited in the Archivo Capitular in Seville, it is the bishop who first suspects the truth and then questions her directly: "He took me by the hand and quietly and confidentially asked me if I was a woman. I responded yes. He asked me if I was a nun. I said yes, lying about it to free myself from that tight bind" (quoted in Rubio Merino 86).[95] In Aguirre's film, however, Erauso is the passive and unsuspecting victim of the revelation, as the diegetic observers discover her identity by chance while treating the injuries of their unconscious patient. The already suspenseful scene is made even more tense when an "effeminate" monk reacts with disgust and horror upon discovering the large breasts of the protagonist. The unveiling scene is reminiscent of the mummy or monster revelations in horror films: "They begin to remove the bandage carefully. It is soaked with blood. Slowly they become suspicious. Something isn't normal. The friar's hands tremble. He swallows audibly. He removes the last bandage wrap and . . . two beautiful and lovely women's breasts appear. The friar lets out a tremendous effeminate scream. He looks at his companion with terror, as if he had seen the devil" (158).[96] Unlike seventeenth-century comments indicating Erauso's flat chest, Aguirre's film reveals a Lieutenant Nun with large breasts, which results in a re-feminized protagonist in order to produce the shock effect for the film's characters as well as to convert Roy into a sexual object for the film audience's gaze.

Once the protagonist's identity is revealed, she begins to reconcile her past with her present. As a result, the gradual realization of her lesbian identity propels Catalina to reconsider her childhood friendship with Inés in terms of a genuine love affair. Earlier Catalina describes her love for Inés as that between siblings: "Yes, I loved her. As only innocence, beauty, and youth can be loved, . . . I loved her like a brother loves his sister, like one loves children" (120).[97] The screenplay writers, nonetheless, see Catalina's articulation of her past relationship with Inés as an indication of "the primary problematic feature of her personality" (119).[98] Toward the end of the film, the protagonist begins to realize how important her love for Inés was, not only in the past but for her identity in the present. When Catalina is forced once again to live enclosed in a convent after her biological identity is discovered, she meets a young nun, Mercedes, who shares a physical resemblance to Inés. Catalina develops a close relationship with Mercedes and her true feelings about Inés (and perhaps about Mercedes) begin to emerge. When the protagonist is delirious with a high fever, she expresses the passion that had been unacknowledged during her adult years: "Mercedes . . . come . . . I love you . . . only you Inés, only you. Come Inés, come Mercedes . . . No, you are Inés. I love you, I have always loved you . . . since we were children" (170).[99] By the film's final scene, Catalina's life is reinterpreted as a tragic story of lesbian love. The protagonist is now in Mexico, again living as a man, but she cannot forget her first and only true love. The film's final shot is a closeup of Catalina's melancholy face in the present with a superimposed sequence of frames from earlier in the film, portraying her as an adolescent playing with Inés on the beach. Unlike the nineteenth-century anonymous novel from Mexico, which also concludes with an episode of melodramatic same-sex love that is thwarted in the end, Aguirre's film does not use the lesbian episode from the third broadside but invents a new relationship, one that does not exist in any of the previous adaptations. Sheila McLaughlin's is the only other version that includes a similar plot addition by giving Catalina a positive and loving relationship with a young friend in the convent.

Voyeurism and Triumphant Lesbian Desire

Inspired by Thomas De Quincey's 1847 version of Catalina de Erauso's story, the transvestite heroine is reappropriated toward the end of the twentieth century in the United States as a symbol of transgender rebellion for lesbian spectators. Sheila McLaughlin's 1987 film, *She Must Be Seeing Things,* incorporates Erauso's story through the use of the film-within-the film device. Although McLaughlin originally planned to create a film entirely devoted to Erauso's life, because of financial restraints she decided against making another period piece (Butler 1987, 26). The result is a contemporary film set in New York that features an interracial lesbian couple who both directly and symbolically become obsessed with Erauso's life narrative (see fig. 22).

FIGURE 22. Lois Weaver and Sheila Dabney in Sheila McLaughlin's 1987 film, *She Must Be Seeing Things.* Publicity still by permission of First Run Features, New York.

McLaughlin's cinematic adaptation portrays Jo (Lois Weaver), a filmmaker who is making a movie about Catalina de Erauso titled *Catalina,* and her partner Agatha (Sheila Dabney), who is so controlled by her jealous imagination that she becomes a voyeur-detective in an attempt to prove or disprove her suspicions about Jo's sexual desire for men. As the film intercuts between Agatha's jealous obsession and Catalina's story, the viewer becomes aware of the symbolic relationship between these two women:

> It is clear that Catalina represents Agatha, or better; represents what Jo finds attractive in Agatha—her rebelliousness against a repressive, Catholic upbringing; her jealousy and anger at God's and men's claim of exclusive access to women; her lesbian difference; her pain and her defiance: throughout the film, all the scenes with Catalina are crosscut with shots of Agatha; whether imagined by Jo or actually being shot on location, or finally edited by Jo in the cutting room, all the scenes

of the film-within-the-film are intercut with shots of Agatha reading Jo's diary and looking at the pictures in it, or Agatha watching on the shooting stage, or Agatha watching the edited film. In this sense both Agatha and Jo, both spectator and filmmaker, are seeing things. (de Lauretis 1991, 228)

The viewer's first introduction to Catalina is presented by Jo, who describes her as "a seventeenth-century woman who rebelled." The film then cuts to a scene, imagined by Jo while in bed with Agatha, in which a young Catalina is alone in the convent on a dark and stormy night, as Jo comments "she must really have been something." The second scene portraying Catalina is also intercut from a bedroom scene between Agatha and Jo: now Catalina is with another young nun as the former expresses her desire to escape the convent: "I wish we could see the world. I don't remember. I was just a baby when they brought me here. Tell me what it's like." In McLaughlin's film, the two girls sleep side by side as Catalina's companion, Angelina, tells her: "Catalina, I love you." The scene, however, is interrupted by an older nun who accuses them of "committing evil" and threatens to punish them. When Catalina defiantly states that she does not want to become a nun, the older woman lectures her about how some groups, such as women and children, need leadership so they will not lose control and become harmful. Teresa de Lauretis interprets this scene as the original castration fantasy: "The origin of the castration fantasy is also inscribed in the film-within-the-film, in the scene where the young (pre-oedipal) Catalina and her girlfriend in the convent are threatened by a nun with God's punishment for an 'evil' of which they have no knowledge" (1991, 239).[100] Freudian or not, this scene establishes Catalina's early experience with homosocial bonding and the church's fear of such affection.

The third scene featuring Catalina is crosscut from a kitchen scene with Agatha and Jo. Catalina is now a young adult who escapes from the convent during the day, runs through the woods, and rips her nun's habit. The scene cuts to Agatha reading Jo's journal detailing the male lovers from her past and then cuts back to Catalina in the woods at night as she moves a rock and sees a pile of squirming worms. The film then cuts to Agatha arriving on location as Jo is filming the scene in which Catalina removes her religious habit. Jo and Agatha talk, but the former is too busy

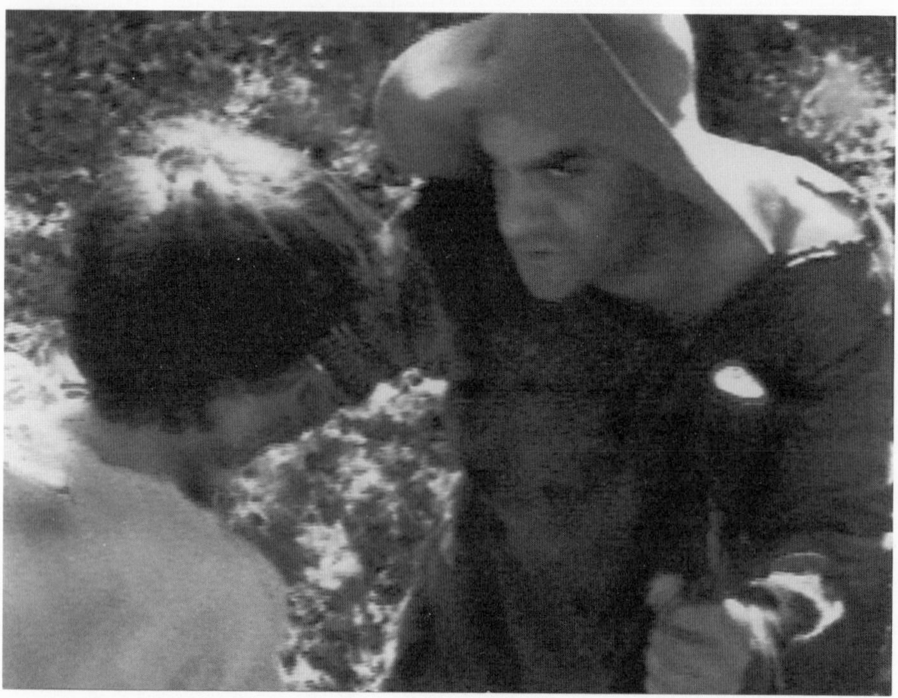

FIGURE 23. Charles Ludlam in the "Lazarillo" scene in McLaughlin's *She Must Be Seeing Things.* Frame enlargement by permission of First Run Features, New York.

and continues to direct the actress portraying Catalina (Kyle de Camp) during the transformation scene. Jo explains to the diegetic actress that Catalina was never able to live as a woman; first she was a nun and then a man in order to hide and survive. She was androgynous at first but then had to forget she was female. Despite the film's explanation of the motivation behind the transformation scene, the viewer never actually sees the change from nun to man. At this point the film cuts to Agatha's fantasies of murdering Jo and then cuts to Catalina in the woods as she no longer actively participates in the action but merely observes a condensation of the two most famous scenes with the blind master in the early modern Spanish picaresque novel *Lazarillo de Tormes* (published in 1554). In this episode the blind man physically abuses the young boy Lazarillo, accusing him of eating the master's sausage (see fig. 23).

Catalina remains unnoticed as she witnesses how the boy takes revenge on his cruel master by guiding him to jump full-force into a tree before abandoning him. While Catalina observes the scene, she not only identifies with the marginalization of both characters but also with the victimization and abuse.[101] These episodes from *Lazarillo* are not included in any of the previous adaptations of Erauso's life, despite the fact that her story has been frequently described as "picaresque." Equally important, nonetheless, is the casting in this scene. For those spectators familiar with classical gay camp and comic theater in New York, this scene provides a queer subtext not directly related to Erauso's story, since the blind man is played by Charles Ludlam. After years writing, directing, and acting, Ludlam became a cult figure of New York's gay community, frequently appearing in female drag (Moore 87).

Catalina is later involved in a duel with a masked man whom she kills. Once she discovers his identity, she cries "Juan, oh no!" and mourns over the body until dawn, at which time two monks arrive as she requests sanctuary. Although many viewers are probably unaware that this scene was most likely adapted from the episode in which Erauso inadvertently kills her own brother in a duel, it nonetheless communicates the "swashbuckling" aspect of Erauso's life as a man while it also humanizes the protagonist. The final sequences of the film-within-the-film (*Catalina*) involve one brief episode from chapter 13 of the autobiography, which is developed with greater detail in De Quincey's adaptation.

In this episode, Erauso reveals that she was requested to save María Dávalos from her irate husband, who had discovered her with another man named Antonio Calderón. Having murdered the lover, the husband also intended to kill his wife to avenge the insult to his honor. The rest of the episode is characterized by action and violence, as Erauso engages in dramatic fights with the husband; in the end she saves the wife, but both Erauso and the husband are wounded in the process. Erauso's self-description in her memoirs, nonetheless, lacks the detective-voyeur themes that are present in both De Quincey's and McLaughlin's versions. In De Quincey's adaptation, Erauso is presented as a voyeur whose curiosity leads her to save the wife from the rage of the cuckolded husband. In this detailed version of the original episode, the protagonist's activities are presented with an abundance of verbs that communicate watching or observing: "Catalina by mere accident had an opportunity of observing, and observed with pain. . . . Kate observed . . . Catalina watching . . ." (225–226). De Quincey also described Erauso in terms of investigative

FIGURE 24. Catalina (Kyle de Camp) as lesbian voyeur in McLaughlin's *She Must Be Seeing Things.* Frame enlargement by permission of First Run Features, New York.

detection and observation: "Catalina noticed a second ill-omened sign that all was not right. . . . Catalina, as usual, had read everything. Not a wrinkle or a rustle was lost upon *her.* . . . Catalina was too well convinced, however, of the mischief on foot to leave him thus. She followed rapidly, . . . Catalina watching circumstances to direct her movements. . . . Catalina followed on his traces" (226). What Erauso observes is the planning and attempted completion of the clandestine meeting between the lovers, but not the specific sexual act and consequent murder that are featured in McLaughlin's film.

McLaughlin explores the ideas of jealousy, violence, and spectatorship from De Quincey and then adds the additional themes of heterosexual sex and lesbian desire to the climactic finale of the film-within-the-film, which also reflects the conflict between Agatha and Jo. In the episode referred to as the "voyeur scene" by the diegetic filmmaker, Agatha watches as Jo explains to the actress the psychological motivation for the scene. Here the actress is instructed that she will be watching a sex scene between a man and a woman; "she is curious, jealous, she sees a penis, realizes it's sex, feels pain, is left out, excited," she sees a knife and runs in. It is not until the end of the film that we see the edited result of this scene when Jo shows Agatha the final cut. In this scene, Catalina is watching from behind a curtain as a woman is kissing Rafael in bed (see fig. 24). The scene then cuts to Agatha imagining Jo making love with a man, and then cuts back to Catalina visibly excited by seeing the woman's legs, then cuts back to Agatha watching Jo, as the film continues, alternating intercuts between Catalina and Agatha. It finally cuts to Catalina, who watches another man enter the room with a knife and stab the male lover repeatedly while the woman runs off with Catalina.

Both the film-within-the-film and *She Must Be Seeing Things* end with two women leaving together, without men. Unlike most Hollywood movies, the women in both films do not die, get married, or end up alone (de Lauretis 1991, 227). While lesbian desire is absent from the corresponding episodes in the autobiography and De Quincey's version, McLaughlin not only emphasizes the homoerotic desire but also suggests that heterosexuality is the real transgression in her film. The filmmaker describes this as the "ultimate lesbian horror, the fantasy of having sex with a man" (quoted in Butler 1991, 22). Unlike the other adaptations of the Lieutenant Nun, McLaughlin's film deemphasizes the masculine disguise in *Catalina;* thus there is an absence of the generic elements featured in most transvestite films that eventually lead to heterosexual coupling. Catalina is not the eroticized object offered for the heterosexual gaze but rather a lesbian subject who desires, objectifies, and observes. Figure 24, for example, demonstrates the frequent closeups of Catalina as voyeur instead of the full-body shots that focus on one particular part of a fetishized manly outfit. In the hands of a lesbian filmmaker, Erauso's story is now recreated as a spectacle for a different viewer. Not surprisingly, McLaughlin's film is the only version to end with the survival of the protagonist in the company of another woman.

Conclusion

WHILE IT MIGHT seem that all three cinematic and dramatic adaptations of the late 1980s (by Miras, Aguirre, and McLaughlin) share little resemblance other than the re-lesbianization of the protagonist, perhaps a comparison of the reception of these works may provide more common ground. The reappearance of a lesbian Lieutenant Nun in Spain is indicative of an eagerness during the post-Franco era to explore those themes previously prohibited during the dictatorship. As Peter Evans describes it, "No longer looking over their shoulders after the abolition of censorship in 1977, Spanish film-makers rushed to speak the unspeakable" (326). But however open Spanish society of the 1980s may seem, these serious portrayals of lesbian desire did not gain mainstream success. Despite an enthusiastic review from theater critic Virtudes Serrano, Miras's play was performed only one weekend in a small urban center (Campo de Criptana) by the local theater group.[1] Aguirre's film, on the other hand, was widely distributed but did poorly at the box office as well as in the film critics' reviews.[2] While Serrano praised Miras's play, she criticized Aguirre's film for "completely distorting the protagonist, who seems ridiculous at times, given the emphasis that the writers have placed on the erotic aspect of her personal relationships" (1991, 288).[3] Spanish film scholar Chris Perriam suggests that mainstream audiences in Spain are still not ready for "cultural production about, by, or for ordinary lesbians and gay men" (394). In other words, the public will pay to see the humorous or absurd portrayals of alternative desire, but a serious representation that ennobles the gay or lesbian has yet to become a box office hit. While Catalina de Erauso is hardly an "ordinary" lesbian, her story does not adhere to the popular comic renditions of queer gender-benders in mainstream cinema.

One might reach a similar conclusion regarding McLaughlin's film. Although hers is an independent film made by, for, and about the lesbian spectator, *She Must Be Seeing Things* did not gain mainstream recognition, nor was it created to do so. In fact, while lesbian flirtation scenes may have been intended to titillate male viewers during the seventeenth century as well as the nineteenth and twentieth centuries, Sheila McLaughlin argues that her film does not participate in the selling of heterosexual desire: "Then couldn't men watching *Seeing Things* get turned on by scenes between Jo and Agatha, and at the same time feel reassured that their cocks remain all-important? McLaughlin thinks not. 'It's difficult for a man to find a way into this movie,' she says. 'There's no nudity in this film, no genital sex, yet if some men get off on it, I can't worry about them. I'm interested in dealing with the issues and in presenting full, complex lesbian characters. If I thought about how men would respond, I wouldn't be able to make anything' " (Solomon 76).[4]

Consequently, at the end of the twentieth century, when we discuss the revival of certain homoerotic connotations regarding the Lieutenant Nun's desire for other women from the seventeenth century, we must also distinguish where these representations appear and how they are received. The selling of Erauso's same-sex desire was marketed for popular culture genres of the early modern period (the *comedia* and the broadsides, for example) while in late-twentieth-century film and stage versions the Lieutenant Nun is most successful with specialized audiences, such as Basque, lesbian, transgender, and academic spectators.[5]

Despite this apparent marginalization of the lesbian Lieutenant Nun, there is something about her transgender image that has kept her legend alive for nearly four hundred years in Europe, Latin America, and the United States.[6] In addition to the exciting adventures of her life narrative, what proves so fascinating for readers of cultural studies is the way in which Erauso's icon as the Monja Alférez has been evoked by such diverse and often opposing ideological groups. During the seventeenth century her hybrid nature allowed the church and state to present her as their symbol of Catholic imperial pride while mainstream audiences reading the news pamphlets and watching the *comedia* were intrigued by the swashbuckling action and erotic nature of both her clothing and her interaction with other women. Conversely, in the nineteenth century when lesbians were interpreted as a perversion of the ideal woman, who was educated for purposes of domestic labor and motherhood, the Lieutenant Nun was reworked into an asexual or heterosexual protagonist and then "tamed" as a lesson for the mainstream audiences of the *zarzuela,* theater, and the historical novel. The Romantics, on the other hand, admired Catalina de Erauso for her passion for adventure, travel, freedom, and rebellion.

By the twentieth century the aggressive yet highly feminine Lieutenant Nun was marketed as a sexy femme fatale for the heterosexual male gaze. However, as the twentieth-century representations gradually reappropriate a lesbian profile of the protagonist, they also display the contradictory politics related to the icon during the seventeenth century. The hybrid nature of the Lieutenant Nun allowed both the liberal Republicans as well as the opposing fascist Francoists to evoke Erauso as a symbol of their political ideology. For the first group, the Lieutenant Nun represented a challenge to repressive patriarchal control while the latter saw Erauso as a symbol of conservative nationalistic and religious ideals. After Franco's death, the Basque government was also motivated to reappropriate Erauso's story as an example of the regional pride that was suppressed under the dictatorship. As a result of the program of *euskaldunización* (Basquification), an adaptation of Erauso's autobiography was published for the first time in *euskera* (the Basque language) in 1976.[7] Likewise, the Basque government subsidized Aguirre's 1986 film *La Monja Alférez:* "If it weren't for the Basque government, my film could not have been made."[8]

In addition to the lesbian, transgender, and Basque interest in Catalina de Erauso in the late twentieth century, a resurgence of scholarly attention to the Lieutenant Nun emerged in 1992, the quincentennial of the Conquest of the Americas as well as the four-hundred-year anniversary of Catalina de Erauso's birth. In an attempt to analyze both peninsular and colonial contexts (with complex issues of gender, ethnicity, race, class, and sexuality), scholars found in the Lieutenant Nun fertile soil for their investigations. It is not by chance that much of the Erauso scholarship in the last decade was published in 1992 or was the result of a conference presentation during the same year.[9]

Just as Catalina de Erauso's story is used to promote Spanish and Basque nationalism, her life is also appropriated to teach Latin American history.[10] This tradition begins in the seventeenth century with Diego de Rosales's chapter on Erauso in his *Historia general del reino de Chile* and continues throughout the twentieth century.[11] For example, despite her Basque origin, Erauso is included in Henderson and Henderson's *Ten Notable Women of Latin America* and Adams's *Notable Latin American Women.* In fact, dozens of publications from Latin America emphasize those geographical and historical features that pertain to the specific country, as is the case with a 1988 publication of her life, edited by the Biblioteca Nacional del Perú, in which most of the footnotes explicate Peruvian historical figures and geography.[12] Likewise, after living in Mexico for two decades under the name Antonio de Erauso and dying there, Erauso is frequently cited in Mexican histories, such as Luis González Obregón's *Leyendas de las calles de México* and Casasola's chapter "The Lieutenant Nun Dies in Mexico" (in his *Seis siglos de historia gráfica de México 1325–1976*), emphasizing Erauso's final years.[13] González Obregón's attempt to analyze Mexico's past through its national legends and anecdotes has been compared to Ricardo Palma's interpretation of Peru's history in his *Tradiciones peruanas,* which not surprisingly includes a chapter featuring Erauso's gambling escapades in Peru (Castro Leal 977). For the Mexican historian Artemio de Valle-Arizpe, however, the Monja Alférez was a "lawless butch . . . the Antichrist" (quoted in Tellechea 253).[14] In Valle-Arizpe's 1933 account of the lesbian episode in the Mexican broadside, Erauso is characterized as a dangerous beast: "The nun turned into a griffin. She roared like an injured bull, raising her wrath up to the stars. . . . She spewed venom from her mouth and bit into the ground out of pure rage" (quoted in Tellechea 257).[15]

While the characterizations of the protagonist may vary, what remains consistent is the national bias in many of the versions of Erauso's life. Although she died in Mexico, in the Chilean publication by Raúl Morales-

Alvarez, Catalina returns to Chile in her mind before she dies: "She believed that she was in Chile again. . . . For two days and two nights she wandered around the Mexican city, which she mistook for Concepción de Chile" (Morales-Alvarez 99, 102).[16] As a result, the text privileges the role of Chile, as it represents the location of her most defining moments, both romantic and heroic.

Of course, in order to remold any of these images of the Lieutenant Nun, certain aspects of her experience must either be highlighted or silenced. Depending on which features of her extraordinary life are evoked, the Lieutenant Nun can be upheld as the hero or enemy of Catholic, transgender, lesbian, heterosexual, feminist, misogynist, racist, classist, and nationalist (Spanish, Basque, or Latin American) ideologies, as well as colonial, Enlightenment, Romantic, liberal, fascist, democratic, and postcolonial politics. While Mary Elizabeth Perry sees Catalina as a "pre-feminist whose rebellion helps to explain the subsequent development of feminist consciousness" (1987a, 246), Michele Stepto notes the contradictions and ambiguities in Erauso's life: "She is an anti-hero we can't help but like, and yet regardless of how much we may like her, regardless of her tongue-in-cheek criticisms of the subordinating masculinist culture, she is not one on whom we can easily hang a sign or banner" (Stepto and Stepto xli–xlii). Equally intrigued but much less enthusiastic about her own feelings toward the popular icon, Angeline Goreau views Erauso as a negative example of patriarchal culture: "What seems remarkable, rather, is the degree to which de Erauso's male persona conforms to the most clichéd version of honor-besotted, trigger-happy machismo—to the point of dueling over being called a 'cuckold.'. . . I can't quite bring myself to like her, but I can't help admiring the sheer effrontery of leaping from a nunnery into the world of colonial Latin America and surviving to enjoy fame, fortune, and absolution" (29).

It is also worth noting that while the general trend in the twentieth century marks a gradual return to a lesbian icon, some of the most recent interpretations of the Monja Alférez are designed for educational purposes and present Erauso as an asexual hero. In Vicki León's 1999 *Outrageous Women of the Renaissance* (marketed for children between the ages of ten and fourteen) the author highlights most aspects of Erauso's controversial legend (including her weakness for gambling, liquor, and brawls) as well as her military feats and her virginity. The only exclusion in León's biography of Erauso is the protagonist's attraction to other women and the multiple false engagements. However, in her *Uppity Women of Medieval Times* León does allude to the homoerotic episodes but fails to consider Erauso's possible desire: "Like other Dirty Harrys, she attracted female admirers but evaded the snare of intimacy—or matrimony" (186). The life story of the Monja Alférez also appears in a 1999 Spanish grammar book, *¡A que sí!,* marketed for U.S. college students. Paraphrased excerpts from Erauso's autobiography are recorded on an accompanying compact disc, as the students can listen to her story and then answer questions in the workbook based on their listening comprehension. In addition to specifics about Erauso's life, the question topics range from sexual liberation and women in the military to the cultural function of cross-dressing (García-Serrano, de la Torre, and Cash 285–287).[17] Again, any mention of same-sex desire is silenced.

Despite the contradictory adaptations of the familiar icon, what allows for the diverse readings is the ambivalence of the transgender figure. Erauso was both a rebel and a conformist, a hero and an outlaw, able to represent either side of any controversy. Because Erauso's experience joins all possibilities, it invites readers and spectators to see what they choose to celebrate or repress. Ultimately her image remains vague and perhaps unsettling for those who seek one unified subject. Not surprisingly, some writers choose to leave Erauso's life open so their readers may end her adventurous tale according to their own preferences. Like De Quincey and Blasco in the nineteenth century, Blanca Ruiz de Dampierre as well as F. Hernández Castanedo conclude Erauso's life with a mysterious disappearance "that permits each reader to finish her life story according to his/her own fantasy" (Ruiz de Dampierre 69).[18] At the same time, Erauso's death has been read as that of both a saint and the devil. The 1653 Mexican broadside describes her burial in terms of holiness, while another legend of Erauso's death from Veracruz evokes the traditional signs of demonic involvement, such as the smell of sulphur (Kress 52–53). In the end, after analyzing so many of the cultural representations of the Lieutenant Nun, perhaps we learn more about ourselves than about the historical individual who was named Catalina de Erauso but who chose, nonetheless, to live as Francisco de Loyola, Alonso Díaz Ramírez de Guzmán, and Antonio de Erauso.

 Appendix

FIGURE 1. "True relation of a monstrous boy, who was born April 14, 1628, in Lisbon. Sebastián de Grajales sent a letter from Madrid to a merchant from this city, enclosed with the true effigy of the monster, which was copied from the one sent to our Majesty the King."

FIGURE 10. *Upper left.* First nun: "It is the grated window to the world." [Since "celosía" means both "grated window" and "jealousy," the nun also implies that Erauso is jealous of those who are out in the world.] Second nun: "Girl, don't get near that grated window; can't you see that it has an 'R' rating?" Lieutenant Nun: "Mother, I want to see the Olavide market before they tear it down." Third nun: "Let her go Mother Superior, it's only one day."

Upper right. Lieutenant Nun: "There's no doubt about it. This is my style and not that of Courreges." Horse: "Saddle me up, you sturdy young lass! Let's show the world what a well-dressed woman is capable of accomplishing."

Middle left. Horse: "This woman is killing me!"

Middle right. Lieutenant Nun: "Leave me alone, you crazy girl.

I can't attend to you because duty calls." Smitten woman: "I want to marry you, my dear little conquistador."

Lower left. Lieutenant Nun: "Now this is my kind of sport!"

Lower right. King: "What you have done is very good, but now take this generous pay and go settle down at home." Lieutenant Nun: "Yes, Your Majesty." King's attendant: "And may she learn to sew the back-stitch."

FIGURE 11. *Upper left.* Narration box: "Suddenly . . ." First swordsman: "Alonso, we don't want your cloth but your blood!" Second swordsman: "We come to avenge the insult against our friend Reyes."

Lower left. Gunman: "I personally will see to it that your pretenses of being a swordsman are over, young man." Lieutenant Nun: "Reyes!"

Right. Narration box: "A kick and a yell were my only response to his arrogance." Gunman: "Oh!" Lieutenant Nun: "Throw the bolt of cloth at them!" Swordsman: "Ouch!"

FIGURE 12. *Upper left.* Narration box: "Like many times before, the church gave me sanctuary. Later Urquizu gave me 2,600 pesos and sent me to Lima to see a merchant named Diego de Solarte." Diego de Solarte: "I am hiring you to run my store, Alonso. Look, here are my sisters-in-law." Lieutenant Nun: "It is a pleasure to meet you, ladies."

Lower left. Narration box: "Those two young women were very charming. I made friends with them without anticipating that they would see me as a man." Young woman: "Alonso, guess who?"

Upper right. Lieutenant Nun: "You shouldn't be in the store so late at night but rather asleep in your room." Young woman: "I prefer to keep you company."

Lower right. Young woman: "I love you! I would do anything for you. Take me as your wife and let's run away!" Lieutenant Nun: "Me?? Oh, God!"

FIGURE 13. *Upper left.* Narration box: "At that exact moment . . ." Diego de Solarte: "Alonso . . . Good Lord! So that's how you repay my trust—by seducing this young lady behind my back! Scoundrel!"

Lower left. Narration box: "De Solarte threw me out and since I didn't have any money, I made a decision . . ." Lieutenant Nun: "I'll enlist as a soldier."

Upper right. Narration box: "I left with Captain Gonzalo Rodríguez for the city of Concepción and there . . ." Soldier: "This is the new recruit Alonso Díaz; he is Basque." Miguel de Erauso: "A fellow countryman! Well, I'm Miguel de Erauso, secretary to the governor. I will recommend you for my company."

FIGURE 14. *Upper left.* Urquizu: "I am leaving to take care of other business. I order you to give Miss Beatriz de Cárdenas anything she asks for in this store." Lieutenant Nun: "I understand."

Lower left. Narration box: "Soon after Urquizu left, the lady in question arrived." Beatriz: "Give me five meters of brocade, fourteen of the twill, and nine of the purple velvet, young man."

Upper right. Narration box: "Later . . ." Lieutenant Nun: "The lad will carry the merchandise to your house, Mrs. . . ." Beatriz: "De Cárdenas. And about the cost . . ."

Lower right. Lieutenant Nun: "You have open credit, ma'am. These are orders from my boss, which I follow with pleasure, since it is for such a beautiful woman."

Notes

INTRODUCTION

1. This passage was taken from James Fitzmaurice-Kelly's translation, reprinted in Vallbona (215). "Allí me crié; que tomé el hábito; que tuve noviciado; que estando para profesar, por tal ocasión me salí; que me fui a tal parte, me desnudé, me vestí, me corté el cabello; partí allí, i acullá, me embarqué, aporté, trahiné, maté, herí, malee, corretee" (110).

2. Advanced praise on the book jacket of the English translation by Michele Stepto and Gabriel Stepto of Erauso's memoirs.

3. León 1997, 186–187, and book jacket promotion.

4. For the most thorough investigations of sources related to Erauso to date, see Vallbona's excellent edition of the autobiography, Tellechea's bio-bibliographic study, Berruezo's bibliography, and Kress's notes.

5. See Vallbona 1–31.

6. Rima de Vallbona edited and published the 1784 copy of the *Vida i sucesos* in 1992, while three years later Pedro Rubio Merino published two manuscript versions of the autobiography deposited in the Archivo Capitular of Seville (one is titled *Vida y sucessos de la Monja Alférez, D[a] Catharina de Erauso* and the other is without title). See also Ferrer 17–35.

7. See also Ortega 7.

8. See Vallbona 227–229, Tellechea, and Berruezo.

9. "Arranqué mi espada y daga y me fuý a ellos y diles una soba de cintarazos y escapáronseme por los pies, y volviendo a ellas, les dí muchas

bofetadas y puntillones y estuve tentada de cortarles las caras" (Rubio Merino 92). All translations are mine unless otherwise noted.

10. "Tomóme de la mano y preguntóme quedo y cerca si era mujer. Respondíle que sí" (Rubio Merino 86).

11. "Me preguntó quién era, i de dónde, hijo de quién i todo el curso de mi vida" (quoted in Vallbona 110). English translation mine. All quotations from the *Vida* in Spanish are from Vallbona's edition; all quotations from Erauso's autobiography in English are from Stepto and Stepto's translation unless otherwise noted.

12. "Allí me crié; que tomé el hábito; que tuve noviciado; que estando para profesar, por tal ocasión me salí; que me fui a tal parte, me desnudé, me vestí, me corté el cabello; partí allí, i acullá, me embarqué, aporté, trahiné, maté, herí, malee, corretee" (110).

13. "Preguntóme en forma quien era. De dónde. Hija de quien. Fuy respondiendo. Apartóme un poco y preguntóme si era Monja y la causa y modo de la salida del convento. Díxesela" (86).

14. "resulta más minuciosa, viva e intimista. En esta versión, el alférez espadachín se deja ganar por la venerable personalidad del anciano prelado, se desploma el castillo de la seudo personalidad masculina en el que se había encerrado durante tantos años y termina abriéndose de par en par" (23).

15. See Merrim 1994, 194. Although the theories of Serrano y Sanz and Menéndez Pelayo were later disproved by James Fitzmaurice-Kelly, controversy still persists with regard to the historical identity of Catalina de Erauso. Ferrer and Luis de Castresana propose that there were two women whose lives were mistakenly confused: a Basque nun and a woman from the New World who used the nun's name in her adventures (Tellechea 8).

16. "Disminuye el interés de este texto como literatura femenina ya que al no coincidir autor y narrador, el autor no tiene necesariamente que ser una mujer" (482).

17. Fitzmaurice-Kelly's English translation is included in Vallbona's edition of Erauso's *Vida*.

18. Nangeroni 11. Although terms such as "transgenderist," "transvestite," "cross-dresser," "gender-bender," "transgender butch," and "transsexual" are often used interchangeably, "transgenderist" was originally evoked by Virginia Prince in reference to the individual who lives full time in the role of the opposite gender, without sex-reassignment surgery; while "transvestite" and "cross-dresser" are generally used either synonymously or to distinguish the success or intention of passing, both permanently and temporarily (Feinberg x). Other critics, such as Annette Kuhn, employ the term "transvestite" in its original medical context, which referred to cross-dressing as a perverse and pathological practice (Kuhn

58–59). Holly Devor uses "transgendered" for persons "who have bodies of one sex and who think of themselves either partially or fully as members of the atypical gender but who do not experience profound sex dysphoria" (xxiv). Devor uses the term "transsexual men" to refer to those individuals "who have begun their lives in their preferred genders as men" and to deemphasize their female origins (xxv). See Garber 1993, Straayer, Feinberg, Bullough and Bullough, MacKenzie, Kuhn, Prosser, Raymond 1996, Halberstam, and Devor.

19. In his review of Diane Wood Middlebrook's biography of Billy Tipton (*Suits Me: The Double Life of Billy Tipton*), Jamison Green discusses his use of masculine pronouns and Middlebrook's compromise: "It is only respectful to refer to Billy with masculine pronouns, using the male gender he so completely inhabited. Middlebrook skillfully interweaves masculine and feminine pronouns to reflect the understanding of the people Billy interacts with, and to acknowledge the reality of Billy's body. In this way, she creates a striking sense of the incongruity of gender and body that Billy lived with, and others like him still live with every day" (22).

20. Leslie Feinberg describes Erauso as a "Basque who cross-dressed and traveled to South America in the early 1600s as a conquistador. S/he and fellow soldiers slaughtered many Native peoples" (33).

21. "En los pasajes de cortejo, flirteo, amor, utiliza el masculino; igual en los de la guerra y los duelos. Sin embargo, cuando el registro es neutro, la narradora-protagonista vuelve al uso del femenino" (52).

22. "Adquirió fama de valeroso: i como no le asomaba la barba, lo tenían y llamaban capón" (127).

23. Martín cites Berruezo's assertion that Erauso's mother included "Antonio de Erauso" among her sons in her 1622 will (Martín 36).

24. "Un hermano de ellos llamado Don Antonio de Erauso, alias Alférez Monja" (quoted in Castillo Lara 322).

25. "Es de subrayar el silencio guardado sobre Catalina en este reconocimiento de los hijos por parte de la madre. Podía haberla mencionado y calificado también como ausente. ¿Acaso tras quince años de ausencia, la daba por desaparecida o muerta? ¿O este silencio significa una manera de eliminación voluntaria de la aventurera de quien no tenía noticias y podía ser la pena y la vergüenza de la casa?" (59–60).

26. See the foreword, written by Marjorie Garber, to Michele Stepto and Gabriel Stepto's English translation *Lieutenant Nun*.

27. "Es un vestigio histórico, vinculado a tantos nacidos a la sombra de esa parroquia, en la yo también fui bautizado" (205).

28. See Kuhn 48–73, Hayward 158–159, and Straayer 42–78.

29. I use "diegetic" spectatorship in reference to the act of looking by the

characters in the narrative, while the "extradiegetic" audience here refers to the actual readers or viewers of the adaptations.

30. See Straayer, chap. 3.

CHAPTER 1

1. "Estando en el estrado peinándome acostado en sus faldas i andándole en las piernas" (51).

2. See Boswell, Murray, Perry 1990, and Yarbro-Bejarano 111–113.

3. Bernadette J. Brooten, in her study of female homoeroticism in early Christianity, uses the term "lesbian" to signify the "medieval sense of a woman who 'behaves like a man' (i.e. usurps a male cultural role) and is oriented toward female companions for sex" (17). Patricia Crawford and Sara Mendelson utilize the same term to refer to "passionate or sexual relationships between women" during the Renaissance (374).

4. Other concepts that suggest possible female homoerotic themes—such as *donna con donna,* tribade, hermaphrodite, romantic friend, Sapphist, fricatrice, particular friend, and so forth—were used throughout the early modern period in Europe. See Brown 1986, Donoghue, Dekker and van de Pol, Crawford and Mendelson, Traub, and Murray.

5. See Donoghue, Dekker and van de Pol, Murray, Simons, Bradbury, and Traub.

6. See Olivares and Boyce for Sor Violante de Cielo's poetry. Of course there are also numerous scenes of homoerotic flirtation on the Golden Age stage due to confusions created by female cross-dressing. See Bradbury.

7. Donoghue 87 and Simons.

8. "la Naturaleza tiende siempre a lo que es más perfecto, y no, por el contrario" (42).

9. See Bradbury for a discussion of the association between Platonism and homosexuality in early modern Spain.

10. See Gossy 1998, Charnon-Deutsch, Delgado Berlanga, and Velasco n.d.

11.

> El alma es toda una en varón y en la hembra, no se me da más ser hombre que mujer; que las almas no son hombres ni mujeres, y el verdadero amor en el alma está, que no en el cuerpo; y el que amare el cuerpo con el cuerpo, no puede decir que es amor, sino apetito, y de esto nace arrepentirse en poseyendo; porque como no estaba el amor en el alma, el cuerpo, como mortal, se cansa siempre de un manjar, y el alma, como espíritu, no se puede enfastiar de nada.
>
> —Sí; mas es *amor sin provecho amar una mujer a otra*—dijo una de las criadas.

—Ese—dijo Estefanía—*es el verdadero amor, pues amar sin premio es mayor fineza.*

—Pues ¿cómo los hombres—dijo una de las hermanas de Laurela—a cuatro días que aman le piden, y si no se le dan, no perseveran?

—Porque no aman—respondió Estefanía—; que si amaran, aunque no los premiaran, no olvidaran. Que amor verdadero es el carácter del alma, y mientras el alma no muriere, no morirá el amor . . .

—Pues según eso—dijo otra doncella—, los hombres de ahora todos deben de amar sólo con el cuerpo, y no con el alma. (317, emphasis mine)

All quotations in Spanish are from Alicia Yllera's edition of the *Desengaños amorosos.* All quotations in English are from H. Patsy Boyer's translation of the *Desengaños amorosos* (*The Disenchantments of Love*).

12. "El poder de amor también se extiende de mujer a mujer, como de galán a dama. Dioles a *todas gran risa* oír a Estefanía decir esto . . . Volviéronse a *reír todas,* confirmando el pensamiento que tenían de que Estefanía estaba enamorada de Laurela . . . Empezaron *todas* a *reírse* . . . en todas ocasiones le daba a entender su amor, *ella y todas* lo juzgaban a locura, antes les servía de *entretenimiento y motivo de risa,* siempre que la veían hacer extremos y finezas de amante, llorar celos y sentir desdenes, admirando que una mujer estuviese enamorada de otra, sin llegar a su imaginación que pudiese ser lo contrario . . . empezóse a *reír* . . . *reían todas*" (306–311, emphasis mine).

13. "Bien me parece—respondió don Bernardo—, pues de tan castos amores bien podemos esperar hermosos nietos" (308).

14. See also Gossy 1998, Charnon-Deutsch, Delgado Berlanga, and Velasco 2000.

15. See Velasco 2000.

16. "solo en mi amor es verdad. / Porque en la aficion mas fuerte, / y de mas divino apremio, / todos quieren por el premio, / y yo por solo quererte" (Act 1).

17. "Nadie avrá que no te crea, / prima, que mal puede aver / entre muger y muger / tal premio, que premio sea" (Act 1).

18. "que a no ser muger / nació monstruoso parto / de naturaleza" (Act 2).

19. "Pues si en toda esta comedia / el Poeta lo ha dispuesto / de suerte, que siempre andamos / a palos, es mucho?" (Act 3).

20. "Necio, / es porque admiren prodigios / en mugeres destos tiempos, / unas dando cuchilladas, / y otras escriviendo versos" (Act 3).

21. "dama con sombrero, jugando la espada con Chacon" (Act 1).

22. "Dionisia es muy intratable . . . Si pero en estremo hermosa, / y aquel nuevo maridaje / de hermosura y valentia, / mucho las almas atrae" (Act 2).

23. See Wheelwright and Donoghue.

24. Cristóbal de Chaves claimed that some female prisoners in Seville "made themselves into roosters" by tying an artificial phallus to themselves (Brown 1986, 166; Perry 1990, 125).

25. Gómez describes a specific case in Granada in which the women "were whipped and sent to the galleys" (Crompton 19).

26. "Mejor amistad será esta que todas las ternuras que se pueden decir, que estas no se usan ni han de usar en esta casa, tal como 'mi vida', 'mi alma', 'mi bien', y otras cosas semejantes, que a las unas llaman uno y a las otras otro. Estas palabras regaladas déjenlas para su Esposo" (Teresa de Jesús 308). Asunción Lavrin cites Fray Félix de Jesús María's bibliography of María de Jesús in which the nun is horrified by the "amor particular" that some of the sisters had for one another (Lavrin 48). See also Ibsen 56.

27. See Archivo Histórico Nacional, Madrid, Sección de Inquisición, legajo 234, expediente 24; Lea 187–188; and Bullough and Bullough 94–96.

28. See Burshatin 1996, 1998, and 1999, and Barbazza.

29. See Merrim 1994 and 1999, Maravall, González Echevarría, and Wilson.

30. For studies on early modern monsters see Daston, Canguilhem, Park, Kappler, Huet, Friedman 1981, Ricapito, Fiedler, Braidotti 75–110, Cohen, Carrete Parrondo, Park and Daston, Ettinghausen 1993 and 1995, Daston and Park 1995 and 1998, Friedman 1993, Niccoli, Long, and Vélez Quiñones.

31. "Y que haya mujeres que, por medio de estas excrecencias o ninfas, abusen unas de otras, es cosa tan cierta como monstruosa y difícil de creer" (40). See Donoghue 25–28, Park, Daston and Park 1998, Jones and Stallybrass, and Long. The association between monstrosities and lesbian desire in the early modern period continued into the modern period. Selvagia's love for Ismenia in Montemayor's *La Diana,* for example, is described by Menéndez Pelayo as "monstrous and unpleasant for the reader" (273). The link between monsters and transgressive gender roles is made by Mateo Alemán in *Guzmán de Alfarache,* vol. 1, at the end of chapter 1 when the text associates the effeminacy of Guzmán's father with his discussion of hybrid monstrous spectacles.

32. Henry Ettinghausen groups the monsters featured in news pamphlets into three divisions—human, fabulous, and allegorical: "The first would include siamese twins and giant children; the second, humans with various bizarre forms of physical deformation, or beings that are part-human and part-animal; and the last, composite creatures endowed with a moral or political meaning" (1993, 127).

33. See also Braidotti.

34. References to "real" and metaphorical hybrids are found in both fictional and didactic Spanish works by early modern writers such as Pellicer, Barrionuevo, León Pinelo, Gracián, Lope de Vega, Cervantes, López Pinciano, Góngora, Calderón, Mateo Alemán, and others.

35. "Han cogido un monstruo con pies de cabra, brazos de hombre y rostro

humano, con algunas cabezas y caras, y que aunque tiene en ellas diversos ojos y bocas, sólo come por una. Dicen que le traen al Rey, y que ya vienen" (262).

36. "El retrato del monstruo anda ya, aunque no impreso. Hele visto" (262).

37. Some of the teratological studies of the period include the following: Konrad Lycosthenes's *Prodigiorum Liber,* Jacob Rueff's *De Conceptu et Generatione Hominis,* Pierre Boaistuau's *Histoires prodigieuses,* Ambroise Paré's *Des monstres et prodiges,* Fortunii Liceti's *De Monstrorum Caussis, Natura et Differentiis,* and Ulysses Aldrovandus's *Monstrorum Historia* (Huet 19). See also Braidotti 75–110 and Cohen.

38. "Monstro. Es qualquier parto contra la regla y orden natural, como nacer el hombre con dos cabeças, quatro braços y quatro piernas" (812). See also González Echevarría 104.

39. See also Merrim 1999, 14.

40. "Muchas veces ha hecho Naturaleza una hembra y lo ha sido uno y dos meses en el vientre de su madre, y sobreviniéndoles a los miembros genitales copia de calor por alguna ocasión, salir afuera y quedar hecho varón. A quien esta *transmutación* le acontesciere en el vientre de su madre, se conoce después claramente en ciertos movimientos que tiene, indecentes al sexo viril: mujeriles, mariosos [afeminados], la voz blanda y melosa; son los tales inclinados a hacer obras de mujeres, y caen ordinariamente en el pecado nefando [sodomía]. Por lo contrario, muchas veces tiene Naturaleza hecho un varón, con sus miembros genitales afuera, y sobreviniendo frialdad, se los vuelve adentro; y queda hecha hembra. Conócese después de nacida en que tiene el aire de varón, así en la habla como en todos sus movimientos y obras" (608–609, emphasis mine).

41. "Es de estatura grande i abultada para muger, bien que por ella no parezca no ser hombre. . . . De rostro no es fea, pero no hermosa, . . . Los cabellos son negros i cortos como de hombre" (quoted in Vallbona 128). "Era de buen cuerpo, no pocas carnes, color trigueño, con algunos pocos pelillos por bigote" (quoted in Vallbona 126). English translation from Stepto and Stepto xliv.

42. "dezimos marimacho la muger que tiene desembolturas de hombre" (790).

43. "puede ser causa la frialdad y falta de calor," "ay otros que sin necessidad capan los niños para venderlos, o aprovecharse dellos afeminándolos" (295).

44. "hombres capados valerosos y eminentes, assí en armas como en letras, muy prudentes y grandes siervos de Dios" (294).

45. See also Kuefler and Fiedler 144–145.

46. " 'Andrógeno', (El que tiene ambos sexos de hombre y muger)" (118), " 'Hermaphrodito' (Damos este nombre al que tiene ambos sexos de hombre y muger, dicho por otro término andrógyno)" (530–531).

47. Cited in Vallbona 173.

48. "No tiene pechos: que desde mui muchacha me dixo haver hecho no sé qué remedio para secarlos i quedar llanos, como le quedaron: el qual fue un em-

plasto que le dio un Ytaliano, que quando se lo puso le causó gran dolor; pero después, sin hacerle otro mal, ni mal tratamiento, surtió el efecto" (quoted in Vallbona 128).

49. See Bullough and Bullough 23–73 and Bullough 1996, 223–242.

50. See Bravo-Villasante 146.

51. See Dekker and van de Pol 13, Donoghue, and Delpech.

52.

> que me diste siete hijas,
> y entre ellas ningún varón!
> Allí habló la más chiquita,
> en razones la mayor:
> —No maldigáis a mi madre,
> que a la guerra me iré yo;
> me daréis las vuestras armas,
> vuestro caballo trotón.
> . . .
> Dos años anduvo en guerra
> y nadie la conoció,
> . . .
> Madre, sáqueme la rueca,
> que traigo ganas de hilar,
> que las armas y el caballo
> bien los supe manejar. (203–206)

See also Castro 1924, 259–280, and Flores and Flores 2–7.

53. See Velasco 1997 and Marín Pina.

54. Huarte de San Juan and Torquemada cite other cases of miraculous appearances of the phallus in young women.

55. See Delpech.

56. "Mujeres vivid alerta, / Que a quien anda en malos pasos / Este es el fin que le espera" (367).

57. "desvainando la espada los mató a todos con tan varonil ánimo como si fuera un Roldán o un Rui-Díaz" (82).

58. "peleando valerosamente con tanta furia y ánimo, que excedía al esfuerzo de cualquier varón, por esforzado y animoso que fuera, que a los propios nuestros ponía espanto" (84).

59. "Se fué al campo de Italia, donde sirvió en el mesmo hábito de soldado, y algunas vezes a cavallo, . . . sin ser conoçida por muger. Vino a Barcelona, donde estava el Emperador, a pedirle merçedes por le aber servido en la guerra, y mandóle dar doze mil maravedís cada año de por vida" (106). See also Delpech.

60. "Zayas parece recrear las cualidades y virtudes más sobresalientes de la

monja Alférez en Estela, ejemplo perfecto de una mujer varonil" (Jiménez 120). See also Yllera's introduction to her edition of Zayas's *Desengaños amorosos* (41).

61. See also Bravo-Villante, Yarbro-Bejarano, and Perry 1987a.

62. "mujer casi hombre, y la amazona de las farsantes de su tiempo, que mal hallada con la debilidad de su sexo, usaba ordinariamente el traje de hombre, andando casi siempre a caballo, al que sabía dominar tan bien como el más ejercitado jinete. Este carácter feroz por decirlo así le ayudaba grandemente para ejecutar con general aplauso ciertos papeles en los teatros" (quoted in Díaz de Escovar 218). See also Daniels 116.

63. See McKendrick, Inamoto, Bravo-Villasante, Romera-Navarro, Ashcom, Porro Herrera 121–142, and Bergmann.

64. See also McKendrick, Inamoto 137, Bravo-Villasante 128, and Luna 38.

65. Cotarelo y Mori 1904, 521, 424, 381, 431, 250, 51, 268, and 124.

66. "Una cosa tan vedada y detestable por las leyes divinas y humanas, como es que la mujer se vista en traje de hombre. Si representar la mujer en su propia hábito pone en tantos peligros la castidad de los que la miran, ¿qué hará si representa en traje de hombre, siendo uso tan lascivo y ocasionado para encender los corazones en mortal concupiscencia? . . . Y si en las historias eclesiásticas se lee de algunas mujeres que usaron de este hábito, no fue para ser vistas, sino para estar encubiertas; no para salir al tablado a ser ocasión de culpas, sino para esconderse . . . las vírgenes cristianas que usaron de ajeno hábito, pues iban huyendo de los robadores de su pureza y del naufragio de su virginidad" (381).

In 1614 Francisco Ortiz likewise describes the erotic appeal of female cross-dressing for the male viewer: "Well, a man must be made of more than ice not to burn from lust upon seeing a forward and uninhibited woman, and at times, to acheive this effect, dressed as a man" (Pues ha de ser más que de hielo el hombre que no se abrase en lujuria viendo una mujer desenfadada y desenvuelta, y algunas veces, para este efecto, vestida como hombre [quoted in Cotarelo y Mori 1904, 494]). Likewise, seventeenth-century statements such as "what a dangerous situation for a young man to be looking at one of these women when she is with her guitar strumming away and dancing" and "what a lewd and provocative thing to see a woman . . . dressed as an elegant man, offering to the gaze of so many men, her entire body that nature itself intended to be hidden from sight?" emphasize the sexual and hybrid aspect of women dressed in men's clothing and its effect on male spectators ("¿qué ocasión más peligrosa estarse un mancebo mirando á una de estas mujeres cuando está con su guitarrilla en la mano porreando, danzando? . . . ¿Qué cosa más torpe y provocativa que ver á una muger . . . salir dentro de un instante vestida de galán airoso, ofreciendo al registro de los ojos de tantos hombres todo el cuerpo que la naturaleza misma quiso que estuviese siempre casi todo retirado de la vista?" [quoted in Cotarelo y Mori 1904, 252, 124]). See also Luna 41 and McKendrick 321.

67. "Que las mugeres representen en hábito decente de mugeres, y no salgan a representar en faldellín sólo, sino que por lo menos lleven sobre él ropa, baquero o basquiña suelta o enfaldada, y no representen en hábito de hombres" (quoted in Cotarelo y Mori 1904, 626); "mandando a las mujeres, cuando se hubiesen de vestir de hombre, fuese el vestido de modo que cubriese la rodilla" (quoted in Cotarelo y Mori 1904, 51); "ni las mujeres se vistiesen de hombres y que sacasen las basquiñas hasta los pies" (quoted in Cotarelo y Mori 1904, 164).

68. In 1653, however, the king found a solution to the objection that certain plots required the male disguise. He stated that under no circumstance should an actress dress as a man and thus have to reveal her legs or feet. However, if the plot required such a device, her character should be differentiated from the waist up and thereby avoiding the revealing nature of women's legs in tight hose (Cotarelo y Mori 1904, 635).

69. "Guzman con un penacho en el sombrero con plumas blancas y verdes" (Act 2, scene 2).

70. "Sale Guzmán con el penacho en el sombrero."

71. "[Francisca] me quiso ver jugar las armas, y, visto, me pidió la enseñase, como también a bailar en hábito de hombre, cosa que yo acepté de muy buena gana. . . . Vistióse en hábito de hombre, que verdaderamente lo parecía, por ser justa estatura, ancha de espaldas, ceñida de cintura, pequeño pie y bien proporcionada de pierna, al contrario común de las mujeres; grande frente y ojos hermosos, rasgados y negros; hermosa y proporcionada boca y dientes blanquísimos sobremanera, nariz bien hecha y hermosos colores, sin invención de afeites; cabello negro, que, sobre una blancura sin igual, resaltaba; extremada cara y de perfectísimas manos. Hacía mayor su hermosura una dulce y compuesta armonía, deleitosa a la vista y más al miserable que, como yo, estaba ya preso con sus gracias, que cada día descubría alguna nueva, salsa del apetito del amor" (348–349).

72. "Y tanto se aficionó / a este joven, Don Anselmo, / Que llegó a dudar si acaso / Pertenecía al bello sexo" (Durán 363).

73. "¿Quién es este mozo tan galán? . . . Mejor será del cielo, que cierto es como un ángel; ¡hermoso mozo!" (355).

74. "¿Quién es ese caballero tan chiquito, tan galán y tan favorecido de Vuecencia?" (356). The Duque de Fonteguerra in Beatriz Bernal's romance of chivalry *Cristalián de España* (1545) is also worried about his physical attraction for the handsome warrior, who is later revealed to be a woman disguised as a man. See Marín Pina 91–94.

75. "Otras acciones mímicas indecentes; a que se añade el vestirse de hombres las mujeres contra el recato y la modestia del sexo, y esto delante de todo género de personas y edades frágiles: todo lo cual es de suyo provocativo a lujuria, de tal suerte que es moralmente imposible dejen de seguir de allí muchos pecados" (268).

76. "pisaba recio y airoso y traía el sombrero calado de medio lado; la capa, cruzada sobre la espada, la mano en ella y la otra hecha jarra, y todo con tanta temeridad y desenfado, que nadie la juzgaba por mujer" (354).

77. Andrea Weiss, for example, highlights the importance of Dietrich and Garbo for lesbian spectators during the 1930s (32–39). See also Dyer 192–193.

78. "¿a quién no causará horror y le parecerá mal y cosa indecente y desproporcionada . . . . que una mujer claramente adúltera y infame, cuales regularmente suelen ser las que andan en ese oficio, represente la persona de la purísima Virgen nuestra Señora? . . . Añádese a esto, el representar estas mujercillas en hábito de hombre" (250–251).

79. For an insightful study on early modern actresses in Spain, see Daniels.

80. The name Guzmán originates from the historical Erauso's choice to call herself Alonso Díaz Ramírez de Guzmán for a number of years while living in the New World.

81. Góngora's sonnet:

> Quedando con tal peso en la cabeza,
> bien las tramoyas rehusó Vallejo,
> que ser venado y no llegar a viejo
> repugna a leyes de naturaleza.
> Ningún ciervo de Dios, según se reza,
> pisó jurisdicciones de vencejo;
> volar, a sólo un ángel lo aconsejo,
> que aun de Robles supone ligereza.
> Al céfiro no crea más ocioso
> toro, si ya no fuese más alado,
> que el del Evangelista glorioso.
> "No hay elemento como el empedrado",
> dijo: y así el teatro numeroso
> volar no vió esta vez al buey barbado (88).

82. "¿No viste a tu hija antes que viese comedia con una dichosa ignorancia de estos peligros que vivía como inocente paloma? ¿No la viste después, que abriendo los ojos a la malicia, supo lo que debiera ignorar? Ya pide galas, ya desea salir, ya quiere ver y ser vista" (83).

83. See also Yarbro-Bejarano and Straub.

84. See also Donoghue 89.

85. "Déjame mirarte toda a mi voluntad, que huelgo . . . qué gorda y fresca que estás! ¡Qué pechos y qué gentileza! Por hermosa te tenía hasta agora, viendo lo que todos podían ver; pero agora te digo que no hay en la ciudad tres cuerpos tales como el tuyo en cuanto yo conozco. . . . ¡Oh quién fuera hombre y tanta parte alcanzara de ti para gozar tal vista!" (161, 162).

CHAPTER 2

1. Tellechea describes the *relaciones* as stories published separately, similar to a newspaper, to spread and celebrate important events, war victories, and incredible, shocking, or miraculous happenings (73). See also Ettinghausen 1984 and 1993, Niccoli 30–60, and Friedman 1993.

2. See also Vallbona, Merrim 1990 and 1994, Martín, Perry 1987a, 1987b, 1990, and 1999, and Juárez 1995, 1997, and 1998.

3. In an unpublished paper José Cartagena-Calderón argues that Erauso's actions participate in a cultural program aimed at recuperating a lost tradition of masculine heroes in Spain.

4. See Vallbona 131: "Aunque el andar en hábito de varón es cosa prohibida, ya que ha sucedido, y con él ha servido tantos años y con tanto valor en guerra tan porfiada y continua, y recibido heridas, será muy de la real mano de vuestra majestad hazella merced con que pueda sustentarse y recogerse."

5. "será bien que buelba al ábito de mujer" (132). All quotations from the petitions are from Vallbona's edition.

6. "haviendo oydo algunas cossas, havía respondido en decoro y reverencia de vuestra majestad, la maltrataron, assí de palabara como de manos" (133).

7. Ottavia Niccoli analyzes the news items related to monsters in the broadsheets of Renaissance Italy in terms of political propaganda (30–60). Similarly, Jerome Friedman examines the sensational newsbooks and pamphlet literature from 1640 to 1660 to assess how ordinary English people conceived of the English Revolution.

8. *Relaciones* made up 71 percent of all 1625 publications from Seville, where two of the *relaciones* concerning Erauso were published by Simon Faxardo in 1625 (Ettinghausen 1984, 6). See also Stradling.

9. "las victorias y hazañas que los varones ilustres alcanzan en nombre de su Rey y Señor, y si con justo título las corónicas eternizan su memorias y engrandecen sus hechos" (160). All quotations from the *relaciones* are from Vallbona.

10. "pero que una muger, con apariencia de hombre, siendo por naturaleza todas tan flacas y de ánimo pusil, obrase tanto y tan varoniles hechos que para el más valiente soldado eran dignos de memoria, más es de admirar" (160).

11. "peleó la muger valentíssimamente, y mató de su parte muchíssimos Indios," (163) "peleó varonilmente, no valiéndose de arcabuz para pelear, sino de espada y rodela, siendo de los primeros que saltaron en la nao del enemigo" (168).

12. In Ettinghausen's study on the *relación* in Spain, he unknowingly refers to Erauso when he mentions two news pamphlets published in Seville in 1625 that "recount the valorous deeds performed in America by a young woman who dressed as a soldier. The lady, whose name was not disclosed, must have become quite a celebrity, for at least one other Seville printer reproduced the second *relación*" (1984, 12).

13. For a discussion of picaresque tone and plot structures in Erauso's memoirs, see Vallbona 47–48, 52, 87, 124.

14. "Era robusta, i yo muchacha, me maltrató de manos, i yo lo sentí" (34). All quotations from Erauso's *Vida* are from Vallbona's edition; the English translations are from Stepto and Stepto unless otherwise indicated.

15. See Vallbona 10, James Fitzmaurice-Kelly xxxix, and Juárez 1998 for connections between the autobiographies of early modern soldiers and that of Erauso.

16. "Hasta venir a ponerme la mano" (36).

17. "con el cuchillo picado le dió una cuchillada . . . y le dió una estocada al amigo del Reyes, que cayó por muerto" (162).

18. "Me dixo que mentía como cornudo: yo saqué la espada i entrésela por el pecho" (62).

19. "Entréle yo una punta por baxo, según después pareció, de la tetilla izquierda, pasándole, según sentí, coleto de dos antes, i cayó: "—Ha, traidor!, que me has muerto!" (65).

20. In an attempt to prove that Pérez de Montalbán's play was not a probable source for the autobiography, Vallbona analyzes the differences between the two works, in particular, the episode involving the character "El Nuevo Cid" (22). While Erauso kills "El Nuevo Cid" in both versions, the scene described in the autobiography emphasizes the sensationalized violence, contrasting with the more subtle version of Pérez de Montalbán. Vallbona concludes that Pérez de Montalbán's *comedia* attempts to aggrandize the protagonist by emphasizing the "bravery, bravado, and skill of the protagonist as a swordsman" (20), while the autobiography presents Erauso as a "hardened gambler, insensitive, arrogant, proud, quarrelsome, able swordsman, and rash" deviant ("valentía, fanfarronada y destreza del protagonista como espadachín," "empedernido tahur, insensible, altivo, soberbio, pendenciero, hábil espadachín, temerario" [21]).

21. For Carvajal's letter, see "De una monja que en Vizcaya se huyó del convento y fue soldado en Chile: Su vida, caminos y su conversión hasta que se entró en un convento," in *Historia general del reino de Chile* (Valparaíso, Chile: Mercurio, 1877–1878), 451–455, reprinted in Berruezo 15–19 and Vallbona 179–183, 227. See also the edited version by J. T. Medina in *Biblioteca Hispano-Chilena* (Santiago, Chile, 1897), 221–225, reprinted in Tellechea (65–71). Given the success of the *relaciones* with printers in Seville during the first few decades of the seventeenth century, it is not surprising that Juan Serrano de Vargas published Carvajal's letter in 1618: "A number of Seville printers stand out as having quite clearly regarded *relaciones* as more than just a way of using up odd stocks of paper and increasing their turnover. Several of them—including Juan Gómez, Juan de Cabrera and Juan Serrano de Vargas—had their premises close to Correos (the post office), so

that they must have had easy access to the latest news from abroad" (Ettinghausen 1984, 11).

22. See also Inness and Munt.

23. "Y un día le pidió el hermano que no entrasse en casa de una muger conocida suya, y ella no lo quiso hazer, que fue causa que sacassen las espadas, y pelearon gran rato, hasta que el Capitán Don Francisco de Ayllón los metió paz" (163).

24. "Fue luego muy amiga de su hermano; mas, por la mesma moza de antes, se enemistaron, y en dos años no se hablaron" (163).

25. "Fui con él algunas vezes a casa de una Dama que allí tenía, i de ahí algunas otras vezes me fui sin él: él alcanzó a saberlo, i concibió mal, i díxome que allí no entrase. Acechóme, i cogióme otra vez: esperóme, i al salir, me embistió a cintarazos, i me hirió en una mano. Fueme forzoso defenderme" (57).

26. "Salía de noche e iva a casa de aquella señora, i ella me acariciava mucho, i con son de temor de la Justicia me pedía que no bolviese a la Yglesia de noche, i me quedase allá, i una noche me encerró i se declaró en que a pesar del diacho havía de dormir con ella, i me apretó en esto tanto, que huve de alagar la mano i salirme" (47).

27. "A pocos más días me dio a entender que tendría a bien que me casase con su hija que allí consigo tenía, la qual era una Negra fea como unos diablos, mui contraria a mi gusto que fue siempre de buenas caras" (70).

28. Mary Elizabeth Perry also notes that "here Erauso may have made an allusion to racism in the ideal of female beauty held by most Spanish men at this time. However, she did not simply leave the dark-skinned mestiza, but continued to keep her company until she could no longer delay the marriage" (1999, 400).

29. "Era mi esposa negra y fea, cosa muy contraria a mi gusto, que fue siempre de buenas caras, por lo qual se puede creer que los quatro meses que estube con esta señora fueron para mí quatro siglos" (68).

30. "un negro tan atezado, que parecía hecho de un vocací su rostro . . . un fiero demonio . . . del endemoniado negro . . . el demonio no podía serlo tanto" (Zayas 1988, 134–135).

31. "¿Qué me quieres, señora? ¡Déxame ya, por Dios! ¿Qué es esto, que aun estando yo acabando la vida me persigues? No basta que tu viciosa condición me tiene como estoy, sino que quieres que cuando ya estoy en el fin de mi vida, acuda a cumplir tus viciosos apetitos. Cásate, señora, cásate, y déxame ya a mí, que ni te quiero ver" (Zayas 1988, 135).

32. See also Stolcke, Silverblatt, and McClintock.

33. See McClintock 27 for an engaging discussion of "porno-tropics" (women as imperial boundary markers).

34. "Vide a la moza, i parecióme bien" (70).

35. "Tenía en casa a dos doncellas hermanas de su muger, con las quales, i más con una, que más se me inclinó, solía yo más jugar i triscar: i un día, estando en el estrado peinándome acostado en sus faldas i andándole en las piernas, llegó acaso a una rexa por donde nos vido" (51).

36. This episode was briefly mentioned in Carvajal's 1617 letter, but it did not include the erotic detail that we see in the autobiography.

37. "caminando con ella de su hermosura enamorada" (172).

38. "teniendo por menor daño tenerla embidia a los ojos, que morir de ausencia de los de su querida" (173).

39. "Bolcanes arrojava nuestra Peregrina por los ojos" (174).

40. "sabida la bizarría de su despejo, se celebró mucho de los que la conocían" (174).

41. "parece un mal novelón . . . un frenético y descarado lesbianismo . . . sarta de burdas incoherencias y torpes desatinos" (325, 327).

42. See Tellechea 60–65, Berruezo 15–19, and Vallbona 223. For the connection between Seville printers and the *relaciones,* see Ettinghausen 1984.

43. "porque se regodeaban con ella unas cuñadas del dicho Olarte que eran muy mozas, y ella con ellas, la despidió" (63).

44. "Salí de la reclusión, ajusté mis cuentas, visité muchas vezes a mi Monja i a su madre, i a otras Señoras allí, las quales, agradecidas, me regalaron mucho" (91).

45. "Fui abrazando i fuéronme abrazando las Monjas . . . entregáronme las Monjas con mucho sentimiento" (113); "se me permitió salir del Convento con sentimiento común de todas las Monjas. . . . Partí luego a Guamanga a ver i despedirme de aquellas Señoras del Convento de Santa Clara, las quales me detuvieron allí ocho días, con muchos agrados i regalos i lágrimas a la partida" (114).

46. "Montalbán tal vez escribió esta comedia únicamente porque era asunto tan popular en su día y porque sabía mejor que nadie lo que pedía el público para ser entretenido" (961).

47. "Pude yo (siendo quien soy) / darte señales mas claras / de mi amor?" (Act 1, scene 1).

48. "Esta cadena recibo / mas que por sus eslabones / manifiesten las prisiones / en que enamorado vivo" (Act 1, scene 1).

49. "pero no he de declararme / aunque me cueste la vida" (Act 1, scene 18).

50. "Buelve, buelve, Catalina" (Act 1, scene 18).

51. "Mas al braço primero, / su persona corpulenta, / de la ruina delicada / me ofreció la diferencia, / y para certificarme, / tocole el rostro, y las señas / varoniles, hallo en él, / que tu poca edad te niega" (Act 2, scene 5).

52. "Que yo soy a quien hurtaste / la ocasion, yo quien estava / en la calle, y aguardava / la gloria que vos gozasteis . . . pues que yo en su pensamiento / alcancé solo el intento, / pero vos la execucion" (Act 2, scene 7).

53. "si a vos Guzman os dio / nombre de marido suyo, / y aquella noche os abria / su casa, con esa fe, / como me aseguraré / de que otra vez no haria / el mismo amoroso exceso / con vos?" (Act 2, scene 7).

54. "si adorais / a doña Ana he de creer, / que amais, siendo muger, / otra muger? no querais / acreditar imposibles" (Act 2, scene 7).

55. "Pero mis padres mirando / en mi condicion tan fiera, / en un Convento, que es freno / de semejantes sobervias, / me metieron: ay don Diego, / quien explicarte pudiera / la rabia, el furor, la ira, / que en mi corazon se engendra / en ocasion semejante" (Act 2, scene 7).

56. "publicar que soy muger D. Diego, / primero moriré que lo permitir" (Act 2, scene 7).

57. "Muger yo? / miente, mande su Excelencia / executar la sentencia, / que don Diego se engañó / por escusarme la muerte. . . . Para que quiero vivir / si saben que soy muger?" (Act 2, scene 15).

58. "he padecido y padezco, / por no averme vos guardado / la palabra del secreto" (Act 3, scene 8).

59. "Mentis, que no soy muger / mientras empuño este azero, / que ha vencido tantos hombres" (Act 3, scene 9).

60. "Si lo eres, de que te agravias?" / Guz. "Si lo soy, ni lo confieso, / ni quiero sufrir que nadie / me lo llame, y vos don Diego, / pues padezco estas afrentas por vos" (Act 3, scene 9).

61. "Escucha, señora, / que pues tu agradecimiento, / y tu honor pudieron tanto / en mi pecho, que me hizieron, / solo porque su sospecha / satisfaciese Don Diego, / descubrir, que era muger, / quando estava tan secreto. / Ahora, puesto, Doña Ana, / que es publico, y hago menos, / y que satisfize ya / mi enojo, y cesa con esto / la ocasion, porque mi engaño / le impidió tu casamiento, / mejor lo confesaré / por dar a tu honor remedio, / y no malograr fineza, / que tan a mi costa he hecho. / Y así don Diego, ya es justo / restituir lo que devo / a doña Ana, declarando, / que solo cupo en su pecho / mi amor, y pues aveis visto / de negaroslo el intento, / dadle la mano, que yo, / si acaso consiste en esto, / porque ni vos repareis / en la ofensa que os he hecho, / ni ella, se case con quien / tenga el menor sentimiento. / Y para que efeto tenga / segunda vez os confieso, / que soy muger, pues deshago, / y satisfago con esto / vuestro agravio, pues dezis, / que soy muger, es lo mesmo, / que confesar que no pude / agraviaros, ni ofenderos: / Y si esto no os satisfaze, / haga mi agradecimiento / lo que no hiziera la muerte / en ese invencible pecho, / (Arrodillase.) rindiendome a vuestros pies, / y confesandome en ellos / vencida, y que a merced vuestra / vivo, pues quedais con esto, / mucho mas que con matarme, / ventajoso, y satisfecho" (Act 3, scene 9).

62. "Con aquesto, y pidiendo / perdon, tenga fin aqui / este caso verdadero, / donde llega la Comedia / han llegado los sucesos; / que oy está el Alferez Monja /

en Roma, y si casos nuevos / dieren materia a la pluma, / segunda parte os prometo. / Fin."

63. "su decantada castidad sería de cuerpo, pero no de alma ni de manos" (127).

64. "esta inclinación singular de esta muger, que aun hablando de buena fe con sus lectores, parece quiere llevar adelante su manía de pasar por hombre, afectando una pasión decidida por el bello sexo" (70).

65. "mientras ella esté en las primeras etapas de la caricia y el flirteo, colabora hasta hacer concesiones a las mujeres que la pretenden creyéndola hombre" (48).

66. "Un aspecto desatendido de la composición psicológica de Catalina de Erauso es su probable lesbianismo. . . . Su sexualidad es obliterada, y si se la interpreta no es como lésbica sino reticentemente como un intento de ella por hipermasculinizarse" (36–37).

67. "Aunque es muy posible que existieran también motivos de índole sexual, hay que tener en cuenta que en ese tiempo no existía el concepto de homosexualidad tal y como lo entendemos hoy y, mucho menos, el de lesbianismo" (187).

68. "Estos episodios que relatan sus contactos con otras mujeres con[s]tituyen la prueba límite de su supercherería, aunque ocultan más que una mera intención de sacar partido de la situación y de hacerlos pasar como unas hazañas más. Están narrados con la tirantez causada por el fraude sexual y por la imposibilidad de consumación de la relación, lo cual fricciona con la obvia atracción homoerótica de la protagonista" (190).

69. If we follow Devor's distinction between transgender and transsexual, which argues that transgenders do not experience profound sex dysphoria, Erauso's decision to alter her breasts permanently through the use of a poultice could justify using the term "transsexual man" in reference to the historical individual. See Devor xxiv–xxvi.

70. "No se oyrán en este papel cosas malsonantes, ni que causen deshonor, á la persona de quien van hablando, pues no es digna dél, antes en su favor se dirán cosas loables, y dignas de eterna memoria" (165).

71. While Erauso's memoirs are distinguished by their rebellion against and transgression of societal expectations, some readers continue to highlight those aspects of her life that function in terms of traditional religiosity. As Pedro Rubio Merino, archival canon of the Cathedral of Seville, argues: "Throughout her life, Catalina remained faithful to the religious practices she learned in her childhood" ("A lo largo de su vida, Catalina se mantuvo fiel a las prácticas religiosas, aprendidas en su infancia" [43]).

72. See Bullough and Bullough for a discussion of warrior-saints.

73. According to Tellechea, Rosales was born in 1605 and died in 1657 (65), while Vallbona claims that he was born in 1601 and died in 1677 (179).

74. "recogimiento, ejercicios espirituales y virtud" (66). All quotations from Rosales's account are from Tellechea's study.

75. "una vehemente tristeza y tentación" (66).

76. "tormento y trabajo mayor que traía con su conciencia . . . los tormentos de su conciencia y a las batallas de el que interiormente la hería su alma" (68–69).

77. "Su honestidad era grande, teniendo los ojos bajos y clavados en el suelo, sus palabras muy compuestas, su proceder virtuoso, y aunque no sabían que era mujer, siempre andaba cubierta con el velo de la virginal vergüenza" (68). Rosales's version is based on the unpublished notes of Domingo Sotelo Romay, a Jesuit chronicler of the seventeenth century (Vallbona 181).

78. "Tenía algunas devociones por las cuales se conservaba en virtud, azotábase cada tres noches, ayunaba días en la semana, traía un cilicio de ordinario ceñido a las carnes, rezaba el oficio de Nuestra Señora, y mediante estas devociones la conservaba y sufría la gran paciencia de aquel Señor que espera y llama al pecador con gran paciencia y longanimidad" (68).

79. "Quien principalmente le dió estas heridas fue su divino esposo, que como amante, la hirió en el pecho para traspasarla el corazón con la herida de el amor que tan olvidado tenía, y como solícito pastor, hizo lo que el pastor hace con la oveja fugitiva que errada huye por los montes" (69).

80. "Dormía de noche con calzones y nunca se los quitaba ni bañaba, y cuando le venía el mes se retiraba al monte hasta que pasaba. Conservó siempre su virginidad con señalada virtud" (67).

81. "tenía todos los días por costumbre rezar lo que es de obligación, a las Religiosas professas, ayunava toda la Quaresma y los advientos y Vigilias, hazía todas las semanas, Lunes, Miércoles y Viernes tres deciplinas, y oya todos los días missa" (174). See Merrim 1994, 191, and Kress 21–22. Likewise, Nicolás León notes that during the nineteenth century in Orizaba, the town in which Erauso died, the people believed Erauso to be a person of great holiness (132).

82. Andrea Stulman Dennet argues that "the most obvious modern form of the freak show is the television talk show, an environment in which dysfunctional human beings parade themselves in front of an audience" (320).

83. "Estuve tres días, trazando i acomodándome i cortando de vestir: corté i híceme de una basquiña de paño azul conque me hallava, unos calzones de un faldellín verde de perpetuan, que traía debaxo, una ropilla i polainas: el hábito me lo dexé por allí por no ver qué hacer de él. Cortéme el cabello i echélo por allí" (35).

84. María de Zayas also describes in detail how a young man transformed himself into a woman: "[He] bought everything necessary to turn himself into a damsel. He had no need to buy a wig because men have always cherished their locks and at no time more than the present. He did purchase a razor to remove the light beard that might belie his dress. . . . Then he dressed and made himself

up so that no one would suspect that he wasn't a woman" (1997, 208). ("Compró todo lo necesario para transformarse en doncella, y no teniendo necesidad de buscar cabelleras postizas, porque en todos tiempos han sido los hombres aficionados a melenas, aunque no tanto como ahora, apercibiéndose de una navaja, para cuando el tierno vello del rostro le desmintiese su traje, . . . se vistió y aderezó de modo que nadie juzgara sino que era mujer" [1983, 298].)

85. See Merrim 1994, 193, and 1999, 23–26, for a discussion of the popularity of the "monstrous" in the seventeenth century in relation to Erauso.

86. "Muger? / valor que supo vencer / en campaña al enemigo / tantas vezes, que aun excede / al credito a la opinion, / y esperanza del varon / mas valiente, como puede / ser hijo del fragil pecho / de una mugeril flaqueza?" (Act 2, scene 7).

87. "Que ha de verme; soy acaso / algun monstruo nunca visto? / o la fiera que inventaron, / que con letras, y con armas / se vio en el Reyno Polaco? / no ha visto un hombre sin barbas?" (Act 3, scene 3).

88. "Ser una muger soldado, / y una Monja Alferez es, / el prodigio mas estraño, / que en estos tiempos se ha visto" (Act 3, scene 3).

89. "quanto mi propio ser aborrezco. . . . Dos horas son dos mil años" (Act 3, scene 3).

90. "Quitase la capa con rabia" (Act 3, scene 3).

91. Guz. "Estoy tan acostumbrado." / Mac. "Acostumbrada." / Guz. "Tambien / lo estoy de tratarme hablando / como varon" (Act 3, scene 3).

92. Mac. "Ponte ahora / el manteo, que es bizarro." / Guz. "El mas bizarro manteo / me iguala al calçon mas llano." / Mac. "No aciertas la coyuntura?" / Guz. "Que he de acertar? que los diablos / inventaron estos grillos." / Mac. "Buelvele de estotro lado." / Guz. "Pese a mi, que he de bolver? / no ves que me viene largo?" / Mac. "Pues ponerte los chapines." / Guz. "Chapines, estás borracho?"

93. "Pese a las faldas" (Act 3, scene 3).

94. "Que he de aguardar? / todo es cansarme, y cansaros; / lo que no puedo conmigo; / necedad es intentarlo" (Act 3, scene 3).

95. "tiene solamente / de muger lo porfiado" (Act 3, scene 3).

96. "La verdad es ésta: que soi muger; que nací en tal parte, hija de fulano i sutana; que me entraron de tal edad en tal Convento con fulana mi tía; que allí me crié; que tomé el hábito; que tuve noviciado; que estando para profesar, por tal ocasión me salí; que me fui a tal parte, me desnudé, me vestí, me corté el cabello; partí allí, i acullá, me embarqué, aporté, trahiné, maté, herí, malee, corretee, hasta venir a parar en lo presente i a los pies de Su Señoría Iustrísima" (110).

97. "El Santo Señor entretanto que esta relación duró, que fue hasta la una, se estuvo suspenso, sin hablar ni pestañear escuchándome: i después que acabé, se quedó también sin hablar i llorando lágrima viva" (111).

98. "Vino a decir que tenía éste por el caso más notable en este género que havía oído en su vida" (111); "No se espante que inquiete la credulidad su rareza" (111).

99. "Hija, hora creo sin duda lo que dixistis i creeré en adelante quanto me dixereis; i os venero como una de las personas notables de este mundo" (112).

100. "Con concurso tan grande, que no huvo de quedar persona alguna en la ciudad que no viniese. . . . Corrió la noticia de este suceso por todas las Yndias, i los que antes me vieron, i los que antes i después supieron mis cosas, se maravillaron en todas las Yndias" (112–113).

101. "No podíamos valernos de gente curiosa que venía a ver a la Monja Alférez" (113).

102. "Escondiéndome quanto pude, huyendo del concurso que acudía a verme vestida en hábito de hombre" (118).

103. "Los que antes me vieron, i los que antes i después supieron mis cosas, se maravillaron" (113). English translation by James Fitzmaurice-Kelly, quoted in Vallbona 216.

104. See Hammond and Pérez Sánchez.

105. "Pues cómo os dexástis vos robar!" (120).

106. "Referíle en breve, i lo mejor que supe, mi vida i corridas, mi sexo, i virginidad" (122–123).

107. "Mostró Su Santidad extrañar tal caso i con afabilidad me concedió licencia para proseguir mi vida en hábito de hombre" (123).

108. "Hízose el caso allí notorio, i fue notable al concurso de que me vide cercado de Personages, Príncipes, Obispos, Cardenales, i el lugar que me hallé abierto donde quería, de suerte que en mes i medio que estuve en Roma, fue raro el día en que no fuese combidado i regalado de Príncipes. . . . Y todos, o los más, me mostraron notable agrado i caricia, i me hablaron muchos" (123).

109. See Hammond 102–103. A letter written by Pedro de la Valle in 1626, included in his travel narrative *De' Viaggi di Pietro della Valle* (published in Rome 1650–1653, 1657–1658, 1658–1659; Venice 1661, 1667; Bologna 1677; with translations in French, Dutch, German, English and Persian), also provides an additional version of the protagonist's life story, told to him by Erauso during various visits to his house in Rome. Tellechea notes a similarity between de la Valle's letter and the *relaciones:* "The event narrated continues to agree with the published broadsides. It explains Catalina's turbulent and sexually ambiguous past" ("El hecho narrado sigue concordando con las Relaciones conocidas. Aclara el pasado turbulento y sexualmente ambiguo de Catalina" [133]).

110. "Ella es de estatura grande i abultada para muger, bien que por ella no parezca no ser hombre. No tiene pechos: que desde mui muchacha me dixo haver hecho no sé qué remedio para secarlos i quedar llanos, como le quedaron: el qual fue un emplasto que le dio un Ytaliano, que quando se lo puso le causó gran do-

lor; pero después, sin hacerle otro mal, ni mal tratamiento, surtió el efecto. De rostro no es fea, pero no hermosa, i se le reconoce estar algún tanto maltratada, pero no de mucha edad. . . . En efecto, parece más capón, que muger" (quoted in Vallbona 128). Similarly, the *comedia* plays with the eunuch image by joking about Erauso's lack of *bigote* or facial hair. "El Nuevo Cid" interprets Guzmán's lack of mustache as a sign of inferiority, as "strength is derived from the mustache" ("el vigor se deriva del vigote") (Act 1, scene 6). Guzmán responds by claiming that bravery comes from within and not from appearances (external facial hair), and accordingly, she has her mustache within: "And so that my strength is more centered I have my mustache growing inside" ("Pues porque esté el vigor mas en su centro hecho yo los vigotes azia dentro" [Act 1, scene 6]).

111. Pacheco's portrait was painted in 1630 in Seville while Erauso was waiting to return to the New World. Although Francisco Crescencio also painted Erauso's portrait in Rome in 1626, no existing copy has been located. Pacheco's portrait (22 × 18 inches) is titled *El Alférez Doña Catalina de Herauso Natural de San Sebastián.* Since Pacheco was a close friend of Pérez de Montalbán, who had written a play based on Erauso's life four years before Pacheco would paint her portrait, it is probable that the two friends had discussed their reactions to the "Monja Alférez." An additional portrait of Catalina de Erauso in military garb was painted in 1941 by J. L. Villar. This painting, which portrays Erauso's image full torso, is on display in Madrid's Museo del Ejército in the room featuring female military heroes. A reproduction of this portrait was also used on the cover of Luis de Castresana's 1996 reprint of his *Catalina de Erauso.*

112. "Por él vemos que era de facciones varoniles, más propias de soldado que de doncella" (Serrano y Sanz 390); "la mirada dura e inexpresiva . . . nos da la idea de que pertenece a un hombre y no a una mujer" (León 125); "a nosotros nos parece todo lo contrario de la idea que tenemos de una mujer. Todo el rostro tiene la apariencia de un hombre" (Sánchez Calvo 227); "la singularidad de sus condiciones físicas, manifiestamente varoniles, como lo prueban su retrato" (Sánchez Mogel 6–7).

113. "bien podemos calificar de retrato sicológico de la Monja Alférez" (9).

114. "apoyándonos en un retrato y en unas memorias escritas por nuestra heroína . . . el cuadro neuro-endocrino relatado parece corresponder a un hiperfuncionamiento hipófiso-suprarrenal, encuadrado en el término del virilismo y acompañado de ciertas anormalidades eróticas, tan frecuentes en la psicosomática del tal cuadro" (224, 228).

115. "Esta que acabais de ver, de aspecto claramente hombruno, gesto indiferente, ojos aquilinos, labios gruesos, sensuales, insinuando un rictus irónico, . . . atuendo poco femenino y mucho militar, con un aire entre ausente e introspectivo, como si desde la altura de su fama—fama desde luego bien ganada—nos mirase con pura condescendencia" (7).

116. "no solo en la voz, el rostro, y talle / me parece muger; mas me parece / que las facciones, que su rostro ofrece / las del retrato son, quiero mirarle / unas con otras partes confiriendo" (Act 1, scene 6).

117. "Que falta para que entienda / que es mi hermana Catalina, / este fingido Guzman / que un moço a quien solicitan / la ocasion bella muger, / y la edad mas encendida. / Por el voto no es creible / que a los impulsos resista / de los deleites de Venus; / y mas quando de su vida / en lo demas sus costumbres / de santo no lo acreditan" (Act 1, scene 15).

118. For examples of homoerotic episodes in early modern soldiers' autobiographies, see Duque de Estrada 379–380 and Castro 1956, 576.

119. "Vuesa merced, señor mío, tiene delante de sus ojos el portento, el prodigio, la maravilla, el exorbitante milagro de nuestra España y aun puedo decir de las estranjeras naciones. Tiene por objeto a quien, . . . ha seguido su profesión con tal afecto que ha sido el pasmo de sus adversarios, el asombro de los infieles y el espanto de los opuestos a las banderas filípicas" (175). For a discussion of the advertising techniques of freak shows, see Bogdan 23.

120. "Bien pudiera el poeta que la hizo informarse primero de mí, que yo le dijera hazañas verdaderas mías y escusara ponerlas fabulosas, como lo ha hecho" (177–178). In his edition of Castillo Solórzano's novel, Jacques Joset also notes the possible reference to homosexual relations in the passage: "It is also possible that the episode is less 'innocent' than it seems. In fact, during the life of the author there were rumors and jokes about the possible homosexuality of Catalina de Erauso. . . . Was perhaps Castillo discretely alluding to similar relations between Pernia and Trapaza or just to the homosexual tendencies of his heroine?" ("También es muy posible que todo el episodio sea menos 'inocente' de lo que parece. En efecto, en la época del autor corrían rumores y chistes sobre la posible homosexualidad de Catalina Erauso. . . . ¿Quisiera Castillo aludir discretamente a relaciones parecidas entre Pernia y Trapaza o, por lo menos, a tendencias homosexuales de su héroe?" [178]).

121. Documents describing payments made to the famous Brígida del Río, "la barbuda de Peñaranda" (the bearded lady from Peñaranda), for showing her rare condition seem to suggest that people with physical anomalies traveled and displayed themselves to make a living (Pérez Sánchez 68).

122. "reparé en las risadas de dos Damiselas que parlaban con dos mozos, i me miravan. Y mirándolas [yo], me dixo una: 'Señora Catalina, dónde es el camino?' Respondí: 'Señora puta, a darles a vuestras Mercedes cien pescosadas i cien cuchilladas a quien lo quisiere defender.' Callaron i fuéronse de allí" (124). As noted in the introduction of this study, in the first of two manuscripts housed in the Archivo Capitular in Seville (edited by Rubio Merino), the protagonist physically attacks the women: "I pulled out my sword and dagger and went toward them

with a beating of sword-swipes and they escaped from me by running away. Turning to the women, I gave them many slaps and kicks and I was tempted to cut their faces" ("Arranqué mi espada y daga y me fuy a ellos y diles una soba de cintarazos y escapáronseme por los pies, y volviendo a ellas, les dí muchas bofetadas y puntillones y estuve tentada de cortarles las caras" [Rubio Merino 92]).

123. Stepto sees this end as a parody of masculinist culture (Stepto and Stepto xxxviii).

124. "que el Oidor querrá / verme en el mismo [traje] que traigo; / mas la novedad es esta / que le obligue a desearlo. / Que en el otro, que ay que ver? / es por ventura milagro / ver una muger vestida / de muger?" (Act 3, scene 3).

CHAPTER 3

1. See Tellechea 159, 207, and Vallbona. Pedro Rubio Merino's recent publication of two manuscript copies of Erauso's *Vida i sucesos* dates them to the late seventeenth century or early eighteenth century (18).

2. "Catalina, figura netamente española, no preocupó a ninguno de los escritores de este siglo" (63).

3. More than twenty editions, translations, references, or adaptations of Erauso's story appear between 1829 and 1894 in prose, theatrical, and iconographic images. See Tellechea, Vallbona, Kress, and Berruezo.

4. See Kirkpatrick 1989a, 360, and 1989b, 57.

5. See Andreu, Aldaraca 1989 and 1991, Kirkpatrick 1989a and 1989b, and Blanco.

6. Kirkpatrick 1989a, 361. See also Aldaraca and Llanos.

7. "Mas, por desgracia, la doña Catalina de Erauso está muy distante de ser un modelo de imitación. Mezcla extraña de grandeza y de funestas inclinaciones, su valor es las más veces irascibilidad ciega y feroz, su ingenio travesura, y sin merecer el nombre de grande tiene que contentarse con el de mujer extraordinaria y peregrina, y no puede reclamar aquella admiración, aquella especie de culto que las generaciones reconocidas tributan sólo al empleo útil de los talentos, al uso justo y benéfico de la fuerza, al heroísmo de la virtud" (13).

8. "adquirir y sentir las inclinaciones y deseos del sexo opuesto" (14).

9. "¡Legisladores! La educación, la educación debe ser el asunto más serio de vuestras meditaciones, como el primer interés de la sociedad, como la única base de las leyes" (14).

10. "Si cultivado su ingenio por la educación, no habría sido dirigida por la piedad una santa Teresa de Jesús, inclinada a la elocuencia y la política una Aspasia, exaltada por el entusiasmo patriótico una Porcia, o dada a la literatura una Staël? ¡Qué de graves consideraciones para el legislador que con este espíritu examina los hechos, los materiales que le suministra la historia de tales fenómenos!

Para promover este examen y llamar su atención, harto más que para contentar una curiosidad estéril o para ofrecer un pasatiempo a lectores frívolos y ociosos, he creído conveniente dar a luz esta obrilla que felices casualidades que voy a referir, unidas al deseo de ser útil, de mostar a mi patria cuánto me interesa lo que puede aumentar sus glorias o contribuir a su instrucción" (16–17).

11. Staël, for example, during the late eighteenth and early nineteenth centuries defends the ideals of motherhood, domesticity, and education for women. See Trouille 193–236. For a concise history of Aspasia, see González Suárez. For an excellent study on St. Teresa's rhetorical strategies, see Weber.

12. Julio Didot, the first to print *Historia de la Monja Alférez,* also published other Golden Age works during the nineteenth century, including *El diablo cojuelo, Lazarillo de Tormes,* and *Don Quijote de la Mancha* (Berruezo 32).

13. In 1854 the title was changed to "The Spanish Military Nun." De Quincey's version is believed to be a reworking of the 1847 French adaptation by Alexis Vallon, which was translated into Spanish in 1881 by Felix Rodriguez (Berruezo 51).

14. See Faderman 239–241 and Chauncey.

15. Antonio Sánchez Moguel, "El alférez doña Catalina de Erauso," *La Ilustración Española y Americana* 36 (July 8, 1892): 6–7, quoted in Tellechea. Dorothy Kress cites a version of this article published in Mexico in *La Ilustración Española y Americana* 25 (1892): 77. Pedro Rubio Merino mistakenly cites this author as "Antonio Sánchez de Miguel" in his bibliography (49).

16. "espadachín o perdonavidas adocenado, más bien, un guapo o jaque vulgar, sin talento, sin grandeza, hasta sin gracia, cuyas aventuras, toscamente referidas, están siempre lejos de despertar interés, y mucho menos simpatía. Pasajes hay en ese libro, tan repugnantes los unos, tan chabacanos los otros, que sólo con sólidas pruebas podrían ser atribuidos a la verdadera Monja Alférez" (6).

17. For a list of some of the nineteenth-century publications that include information from the autobiography and the broadsides, see Tellechea 208–209.

18. " 'hija de padres nobles, hidalgos y personas principales', como ella misma nos dice, y de quien sus antiguos jefes aseguraban a una voz 'haberle conocido siempre con mucha virtud y limpieza' " (6).

19. "Solamente la doncella de Orleans es comparable con la doncella donostiarra" (7).

20. "La fe y la patria, he aquí los grandes sentimientos que despertaron las energías varoniles de aquella mujer extraordinaria" (7).

21. "La más poética, sin duda, es la de Coello, quien, con su admirable instinto dramático, atribuye al amor el secreto de la mudanza operada en Catalina" (7).

22. According to Dorothy Kress, Coello's 1866 *zarzuela* was so sucessful in Mexico that it made its way to Spain and was performed in Madrid in 1873 and then published there in 1875 (77) as *"La Monja Alférez." Zarzuela histórica en tres*

actos y en verso Original de Carlos Coello, con músico del Maestro Marqués, y un prólogo de José Gómez de Arteche, Teatro de Jovellanos, 24 de noviembre de 1873. According to Manuel García Franco and Ramón Regidor Arribas's study of the *zarzuela, La Monja Alférez* opened at the Teatro de la Zarzuela on November 24, 1875 (54).

23. "¿Mujer? Decimos mal: demonio parece" (vii).

24. "soldado, jugador, pendenciero, y hasta galán de cuantas hermosas encuentra en su tortuoso y siempre ensangrentado camino" (viii).

25. "la exaltación religiosa, el sentimiento de la patria, una pasión vehemente, una fantasía" (viii).

26. "tan cruel para sus camaradas y el propio hermano como para los indios de quienes llegó a ser terror y espanto, hay la distancia de la fe al descreimiento, del valor a la crueldad, de las aspiraciones más o menos vagas pero disculpables a las que por absurdas y repugnantes, rechaza la Naturaleza" (viii).

27. "y los enredos y amoríos de las damas con ellos relacionadas y no pocas veces comprometidas por la diabólica monja en su nuevo carácter de galán emprendedor y caprichoso" (x).

28. "Porque en lo que Catalina de Erauso se deleita sobre todo, es en demonstrar hasta qué punto llevó su fingimiento, informándonos de las ocasiones de su salida de las casas, siempre extrañas y, no pocas veces, por atrevimientos con las mujeres aposentadas en ellas" (x).

29. "Pocas eran las cualidades que adornaban a Catalina de Erauso para hacerla recomendable a sus contemporáneos si a la posteridad . . . No hay más que leer su escrito, y se observa que ese denuedo era resultado de una índole que no puede menos de calificarse de perversa" (xvi).

30. "Sólo una condición la abona, la de castidad, . . . Sin esa cualidad, todo su cuidado en disfrazarse, sus hombradas y su procacia, quedaban ineficaces para proporcionarle la libertad de acción a que aspiraba. No es, sin embargo, el amor pasión que puede ocultarse durante una vida, y la Monja Alférez debió desconocerlo de todo punto; lo cual es también prueba de su temperamento arisco, rudo e inhumano" (xvi–xvii).

31. "¿Puede con tales caractéres trazarse una acción dramática que interese y conmueva? Una jóven desacordada, sin sentimiento alguno de los de su sexo, viviendo tan sólo en la sociedad de hombres dedicados al lucro y al pillaje, tahures o matones" (xvii).

32. "repugnancia que habría de inspirar su heroína" (xvii).

33. "de no atribuirle rasgos que desfigurasen su carácter conocido de todos en la corte. No se atrevería a tanto, viviendo ella, aun cuando lejos a la sazón; y, por el contrario, sin apartar de la vista y de la penetración del auditorio el defecto que más la afeaba, la adornó con otros no menos repugnantes" (xvii–xviii).

34. "A quien haya leído la comedia del celebrado amigo del Fénix de nuestros

ingenios, le parecerá imposible, y sin embargo es la verdad, que se haya representado no hace mucho en uno de los principales teatros de España sin protesta alguna y, por el contrario, con repetición y estrepitosamente aplaudida. ¿Cómo los oídos de las damas del siglo XIX han podido escuchar la confesión bochornosa de Doña Ana al que decía ella amar y consideraba enamorado todavía de su candor y gracias?" (xix).

35. "El amor era para la ex-monja repulsivo"; "hacerle soportable a los espectadores" (xix).

36. "Es una obra músico-teatral, cuyo texto es hablado y cantado alternadamente sin ruptura de su desarrollo argumental" (7).

37. "la malevolencia o la envidia de los unos y de la presuntuosa necedad y antiespañolismo de los otros" (1934, 17).

38. "ha encarnado en 'La Monja Alférez' de la historia y la tradición un ser que si hubiese germinado sobre un terreno más idóneo que el escenario de la Zarzuela y hubiera nacido acompañado de otros elementos más artísticos, hubiera sido tal vez una de las producciones más bellas del poeta y una de las más felices concepciones dramáticas de nuestro teatro contemporáneo" (xxiii–xxiv).

39. The popularity of the "woman dressed as a man" theme in the nineteenth-century musical theater is also confirmed by the success of cross-dressed actresses such as Carolina Di-Franco, who performed in the 1855 *zarzuela El sargento Federico.* Cotarelo y Mori praises the engaging performance of Di-Franco: "dressed in men's clothing with much grace she expressed herself and sang with charming self-assurance" ("vestida de hombre con mucho garbo, se produjo y cantó con graciosa desenvoltura" [1934, 531]).

40.

En San Sebastian nació
una hembra, desde muy moza,
tan fuerte como un castillo . . .
y tan terca como todas.
Esperando corregirla,
su padre la metió monja;
pero ella dijo una noche:
"¡Vuelvo! . . ." y no ha vuelto hasta ahora.
. . .
De repente se ha sabido
que Lucifer en persona
se la ha llevado al infierno
queriéndola por esposa.
Y este romance que digo,
no es romance, que es historia

de Catalina de Erauso,
por todo el mundo famosa. (16–17)

41. "(burlándose): '¡Ay, qué mozo tan valiente! / Ay, qué miedo que nos dá! / ¡Ay, de oirle solamente, / ti . . . ti . . . ti . . . ritamos ya!' . . . (El coro, y sobre todo las mujeres, celebra de cuando en cuando con sus risas las palabras del alférez)" (32, 25).

42. "y para Lope se guarda / toda mi ternura entera. / Pensando me vuelvo loco / con qué cariño le amo, / porque, si amistad le llamo, / pienso que le llamo poco. / ¿Amor de hermano? Tampoco. / Lope es aun más para mí, / y hace tiempo desistí / de saber qué nombre tiene / su afecto que contiene / todos los demás en sí" (29).

43. "las conozco bien / y sé lo poco que valen" (36).

44. "Me violentaron mis padres" (36).

45. "A mí, el hombre que no ama, / ni hombre me parece casi" (36). "Quien a su madre no amó, / ¿qué mujer quereis que ame?" (37).

46. "Hay que buscarse una dama. / —Una dama . . . / Sí; cualquiera. / Doña Elvira, su favor / me mostró de una manera / indudable. . . . ¡Catalina, cobra aliento! / Diego Guzmán es mi nombre; / vicios adquirir intento / y fingir lo que no siento . . . / —¿Quién dudará que soy hombre?" (41–42).

47. "¡Ingrato! ¡Y yo / no pensaba más que en él! . . . !Lo que siento en mi alma / es amor . . . es amor!!!" (94, 98).

48. "Ya lo empiezo a vislumbrar: / la desgracia, me hizo amar . . . / es el amor, me hace mujer. / Sin mis penas, pensaría / que me despierto en mi infancia . . . / —¡Mujer! ¡Cuán larga distancia / he recorrido en un día! . . . Me rinde el traje de guerra" (117).

49. "No: ¡has sentenciado a tu hermana! (sorpresa general)" (137).

50. "¡Ahora comienza mi vida!" (140).

51. "Si mi amo, en quien se admiró / tan varonil proceder, / ha resultado mujer . . . / ¿qué voy a resultar yo?" (141).

52. "(con gracia y coquetería) / que no soy hombre. / Ya no esgrimo el montante, / ¡zis-zas, zis-zás!; / mujer tierna y amante / soy nada más" (141).

53. See Díaz y de Ovando xxx. Mateos's play opened on April 27, 1879, at the Teatro Nacional in Mexico City and was presented later at the Teatro Abreu (Vallbona 228).

54. "¡Qué violencias, qué arrebatos, / una furia es del infierno! / Desde que ha pisado el claustro / es un desórden tremendo. / La regla nunca obedece, / y con ademan severo / nos domina y aturrulla; / vamos, la tenemos miedo" (1).

55. "¡El demonio os desvanece! / ¡Satanás os aconseja! . . . Es un demonio católico" (4, 8).

56. "lindos ojos . . . labios de rosa . . . tez blanca, como el hielo" (3).

57. Alguacil: ¡Esta sí es la Monja Alférez; / y ya en mi poder la tengo! / ¡Venid por aquí, señora! . . .

Machete: ¡Que señora, ni que cuerno! / Si yo tengo unos bigotes / más ariscos y más . . . tiesos!

Alguacil: Que os oculteis, es en vano, / se adivina vuestro sexo.

Machete: ¿Mi sexo? ¡Voto va Judas! . . . / ¿Si sabré yo lo que tengo?

Alguacil: Hace dos meses, dejásteis / las paredes del convento.

Machete: ¡Alcalde . . . no me saliera / si yo viviera allá dentro!

Alguacil: No os descompaseis, señora, / que este es asunto muy serio. / Llevais el traje de hombre, / pero yo soy juez esperto / y declaro ser la monja, / que sin humano respeto / abandonásteis el claustro.

Machete: ¡Qué claustro, ni qué podenco! / ¡Yo soy el mismo Machete! . . .

Alguacil: ¡Señora, guardad silencio; / y en nombre del Santo Oficio / daos a prisión! (28)

58. "Voy como sombra perdida, / voy como fantasma errante, . . . Sin que un labio con ternura / ni con cariño me nombre! . . . ¡Sueños que no volverán / a mi loca fantasía / . . . Voy como en la mar salvaje / una barca hecha pedazos! / Ahogar quiero entre mis brazos / el fantasma de mi suerte; / que inmóbil, callado, inerte, / ve incierto mi rudo afán! . . . ¡Aquí me espera la muerte!" (29–30).

59. "En mi pecho / la prueba de su inocencia / encontrareis" (31).

60. "Don Félix busca la herida y se apercibe de que Don Carlos es Andr[e]a" (31).

61. "¡Ah! soy feliz, porque muero / ¡en tus brazos! . . . ¡compasión!" (31).

62. "¡Yo que en mi . . . postrer aliento . . . / traigo el . . . arrepentimiento . . . de mis faltas!" (31).

63. See also Vallbona 4 and Kress 89–96.

64. "Que las enamoraras y las dejaras cuando nos vallamos de aquí? Eso importa muy poco, todos lo hacen así, y no debes de escandalizarte por tan poca cosa. Enamora a la que mas te guste, a la que mas te simpatice, y cuenta conmigo. Cuando nos vayamos a Madrid, alli yo te presentaré a otras mas guapas, y de la que hayas dejado aqui no te vuelves a acordar en toda tu vida ya verás" (14v).

65. "os amo con la mayor ternura . . . que hasta hoy no había yo visto a una joven tan amable y encantadora que me inspirara tanto amor y tanto interes con el que vos habeis hecho nacer en mi corazon" (42v).

66. "para poder sostener con Matilde una conversación tan dificil, como era la que se vio obligada a seguir para representar el muy dificil papel que había aceptado" (44v).

67. "Que dificil y fastidioso es querer uno representar lo que no es! Soy muger

y he querido hacerme hombre! . . . Oh! esto es horrible, insoportable, inadmisible" (59v, 60).

68. "falsa y engañosa" (59v), "fingido amor" (79v), "muy sincera y franca amistad" (146v), "en Joaquina verdaderas, mas en Catalina falsas y engañosas" (176).

69. "le tomó la cara con las dos manos y le estampó con sus labios un ardiente y amorosísimo beso" (79).

70. "hablar y mas hablar es facil a toda hora, y hoy me he persuadido que es imposible sostener mi engaño y una mentira hasta sus fines se puede muy bien disimular en todo, mas llega siempre un termino en que ya no se puede pasar adelante" (69v).

71. "Catalina abrasando cariñosamente a Clotilde . . . a quien amaba apasionadamente con todo su corazon" (316v, 317v).

72. "Los hombres solo saben engañar a las pobres mujeres. . . . El amor de los hombres casi siempre es fingido, engañoso, aparento e interesable . . . mi amor es sincero, real y verdadero" (319, 319v).

73. "pensamientos de que solo sería capaz un verdadero hombre" (92).

74. See Vallbona 4.

75. "el haber vivido intimamente entre hombres de todas clases y condiciones, no obstante todo esto, supo mantenerse firme y constante en la pureza de sus costumbres femeninas, sin que ni aun el mas ligero pensamiento hubiera manchando su honra y su reputación" (367, 367v).

76. See Faderman 271.

77. Also cited in Kress 72.

78. "Y extremando las precauciones necesarias para que su verdadero sexo no fuese descubierto, creyó que ninguna le vendría tan bien como una aventura amorosa" (1:193–194).

79. "Catalina, que no podía estar enamorada de la hija de Perales" (1:210).

80. "Catalina había querido engañar al mundo con falsas apariencias, y encontrábase con que, para sostener su engaño, tenía que realizar actos que queremos creer repugnábanla en su fuero interno. Sea como fuere, es el caso que, con repugnancia o sin ella, desempeñó su cometido a la perfección" (2:516).

81. "Y ya no sabemos más, ni más podemos decir a nuestros lectores sobre tan extraño y curioso personaje. . . . Dejemos, pues, que el lector suponga, respecto al indicado punto, lo que más le cuadre" (2:774–775).

CHAPTER 4

1. As Jorge Galindo notes, it is the combination of aggressiveness and beauty in Félix that "raises her to the category of film goddess, together with figures like Greta Garbo or Marlene Dietrich" ("la eleva a categoría de diosa del cine junto a figuras como Greta Garbo o Marlene Dietrich" [59]).

2. "Era sólo un divertimiento. Una ocasión para que María Félix apareciera

como espadachín, muy bien vestida y muy extravagante. . . . La mujer que se viste de hombre lleva por dentro siempre un drama muy serio, una historia que merece ser estudiada y escrita con cuidado. La Monja Alférez no es un personaje pintoresco, sino una mujer apasionante que daría motivo a todo un ejercicio literario y a una adaptación para teatro o cine que me interesaría mucho" (quoted in Taibo 66–67). For Max Aub in exile, see Ugarte 113–151.

3. "plana, estática, lenta, solemne y confusa" (124).

4. "verdaderamente una estampa gallarda, un vestuario bellamente diseñado y la ambigua belleza de María tocada con sombrero de plumas y calzada de pantalones y botas de montar" (69).

5. "el público quería a María Félix vestida de hombre. La sabía desde que la vieron en *Doña Bárbara* con pantalones" (67).

6. "los pantalones y María van hermanándose de tal forma y tan seguido, que se convertirán, con otros pocos elementos, en uno de sus símbolos más pertinaces" (71).

7. "su encuentro con la Monja Alférez le abrió una serie de perspectivas. . . . A lo largo de su vida social, irán apareciendo los sombreros tipo Tercio de Flandes, las plumas airosas, los pantalones de piel, las largas botas por encima de la rodilla, los cinturones de los que parece necesario dejar que cuelgue un arma, los guantes de manopla. Toda una parafernalia que nace con este film y que más o menos encubierta engalanará de manera periódica a la actriz en su vida privada" (Taibo 69).

8. "Resulta curioso y apropiado para investigaciones psicoanalíticas el hecho de que la visión de una María Félix amachada en sus pantalones y en sus gestos de espadachín o de azotadora de hombres venezolanos, aumentara el entusiasmo masculino del país" (65).

9. See De Lauretis 1994, Grosz 1995, Stanley 8, Gossy 1995, and Steele.

10. "La devoradora de hombres se convertía en el objeto de sus propios apetitos y, ante su transformación masculina, eran las mujeres las dispuestas a ser devoradas" (124).

11. See also Stacey 153–154.

12. According to Chris Straayer, a paradoxical kiss involves a cross-dressed character whose disguise is unbelievable for the film's audience but believable for the diegetic participant who is attracted to the character of the "opposite sex" (57–60).

13. "¡Qué linda se ve vestida de hombre! Demasiado linda, porque con esa cara no parece posible que se le tomase por alférez" (quoted in Taibo 71).

14. See also Landy and Villarejo 33, Halberstam 1998a, 211–213.

15. See Bullough and Bullough 97, San Juan 22, Simons 89, and Harris 11–17.

16. "Llegó la Reina de Suecia a Amberes vestida de hombre, a caballo, con gran séquito de los suyos. . . . Dícese hace mal a un caballo, como si fuera hombre,

y por esto el Rey le envía estos caballos y aún se dice que es más que mujer, no porque sea hermafrodita, sino porque no es para poder ser casada" (quoted in Bravo-Villasante 144–145).

17. See San Juan 22 and Bravo-Villasante 145–146. See Barrionuevo 192–193 for news items regarding Calderón's play about Queen Christina (*Aviso* dated June 7, 1656).

18. "La única gente del cine que he admirado fue la Garbo, fui su fan desde que entró al cine, de ahí en fuera . . . nadie!" (quoted in García Fernandez). For a discussion of the relationship between Garbo and Queen Christina, see Landy and Villarejo 27.

19. Possible exceptions include popular comic "drag king" performances by female entertainers such as Lily Tomlin and Tracey Ullman.

20.

Muchacha arisca de corcel y espada,
sintióse en el convento desolada.
Fue allí por orden de una tía,
que negra infamia con sigilo urgía;
pero saltó las tapias del convento
y huyó para cobrar un testamento.
Antes cambióse de ropas Catalina
adoptando figura masculina.
Y en tierras del Perú, dulces mujeres
suspiraron de amor por el alférez (quoted in Taibo 65).

21. "El sexo ha desaparecido en ambas actitudes y lo que queda es una pose a beneficio de un observador que de ser agudo bien pudiera asombrarse antes un doble hedonismo tan ajeno a las pasiones que cabría pensar despiertan en la parte contraria bellezas semejantes" (Taibo 70).

22. See Garber 1993, 337, Straayer 60, Gaines, Landy and Villarejo 42–43, Russo 64, and Halberstam 1998a, 211–213.

23. I would like to thank Ana Rossetti for sharing her copy of this book with me.

24. "Algunas veces había pensado que las mujeres eran un poco cobardicas por no querer imitar a los hombres en las gestas y hazañas que éstos realizaban por todo el mundo" (43).

25. "Al igual de la baronesa de Albi, Catalina de Erauso, Isabel de Barreto, Manuela Malasaña y Agustina Zaragoza, doña María Pita, Alférez de la Coruña, es un ejemplo de cómo las mujeres españolas, además de atesorar todas las virtudes femeniles, son capaces, cuando la Patria lo requiere, de exhibir gloriosamente aquellas otras—energía, valor, audacia y heroísmo—que comunmente son atribuídas de manera exclusiva a los varones" (205).

26. "Ninguna otra 'mujer-hombre' más proxima al hombre que ella. Que se siente hombre, y hablando como hombre, se trata de tal. . . . De ella se haría un elogio—tan grande que borraría todas las impugnaciones posibles—. Y es que combatiendo al lado de hombres como los conquistadores españoles, nadie la descubrió mujer, y como un héroe homérico, recompensado por los dioses, fué ascendida sobre el mismo campo de batalla" (210–211).

27. "No quiero decir que su vida la debáis tomar como modelo, ni tratéis de imitarla; por desgracia, no siempre es digna de elogio, aunque lo es, sin duda, de la más profunda admiración" (3).

28. "Galantea y aun requiere de amores a varias y encopetadas damas" (141).

29. "Quiere identificarse más con su papel de varón" (141). See Grugel and Rees 134.

30. See Di Febo, Morcillo Gómez, and Enders.

31. There are dozens of adaptations of and references to the Monja Alférez published in Francoist Spain between 1939 and 1975. See bibliographies in Berruezo and Vallbona.

32. *Cruzada* 60, no. 2 (1940), cited in Aurrecoechea and Bartra 111–112.

33. The first comic featuring Catalina de Erauso was published in Mexico in 1956 in the comic book series *Aventuras de la vida real,* vol. 12 (Berruezo 59).

34. The misnumbering of the panels must have been due to an editorial error. In any event, the two-part series begins with the more sensationalist years of her life (when she dresses as a man and engages in violence), which no doubt attracted reader attention.

35. "arrogante, pendenciero, lleva con soltura la espada, además de un puñal y dos pistolas" (panel 1).

36. See Witek for discussion of history lessons in comic books.

37. *Miss* is a magazine of celebrity gossip and fashion marketed primarily to women.

38. "Niña no te acerques a esta celosía. ¿No ves que tiene dos rombos?" (panel 1).

39. "plana de pecho, fea de cara y con pelos en las piernas. Hay que comprender a la chica, ella era así y no tenía remedio."

40. "Déjela usted Madre Superiora. Un día es un día."

41. "Quita de ahí locuela. No puedo atenderte que están llamando mi quinta"; "Contigo me quiero casar carita de conquistador."

42. "En el campo de las relaciones sentimentales al alférez Alonso Díaz Ramírez no le faltaron pretendientes. Varias dulces y delicadas mujercitas se sintieron atraídas por su varonil apostura y tuvo que librarse de ellas con la mayor celeridad, como si de indios se tratara."

43. "¡Es este mi deporte!"

44. "Muy bueno lo tuyo pero ahora toma esta paga extraordinaria y a sentar cabeza en el hogar."

45. "Y que aprenda la vainica."

46. "Vive tranquila y entregada a las faenas del hogar hasta el año 1650." While Mexican and American comics have long celebrated the sexy masculine woman (such as Sheena Queen of the Jungle and Wonder Woman in the United States, "Adelita y las guerrillas" in Mexico), recently the figure of the Warrior Nun has received extraordinary success (Aurrecoechea and Bartra). Comics such as *Warrior Nun Areala* provide a sexy hybrid for the heterosexual male gaze that does not use the masculine disguise but rather accentuates the female sex traits (see fig. 15). Along the same line, the television program *Xena: Warrior Princess* has gained amazing recognition. Like Areala, Xena is sexually objectified by some viewers, but her sexuality, nonetheless, has remained somewhat ambiguous given her committed relationship with Gabrielle. Although their friendship is not overtly lesbian, the executive producer Rob Tapert reports that the show "has become a favorite with gay women" (quoted in Minkowitz 75), while the lesbian magazine *Girlfriends* is more explicit about Xena's sexuality: "Lucy Lawless isn't a lesbian, but she plays one on TV. The proof lies not so much in what Xena does on camera, but in what she doesn't do. Quintessentially, *Xena: Warrior Princess* is a drama of the open secret, the obvious but unspoken truth that Xena is bent, and Gabrielle is her lover" (Findlay 29).

47. "con la que solía jugar y divertirse muchos ratos, como era cosa natural dada la juventud de ambos" (45).

48. "No es extraña la costumbre que tuvo la Monja Alférez de enamorar a las mujeres; ya hemos visto que lo ha hecho en varias ocasiones y aún la veremos hacerlo más. Uno de dos pueden ser los motivos que a ello la impulsaron: el primero, que acaso llegó a hacerse la ilusión de que era un hombre y como tal debía obrar; el segundo, y el más probable, porque actuando de esta manera recataba más a las gentes su verdadero sexo, cosa que desde el primer momento fue su máxima preocupación" (50–51).

49. "era dificil pensar en una mujer a la vista de todas estas cosas" (51).

50. While these drawings are suggestive, Salvador Pruneda is one of the few artists to illustrate the homoerotic episode in chapter 5 of Erauso's autobiography ("I had my head in the folds of her skirt and she was combing my hair while I ran my hand up and down between her legs" [17]). Pruneda's drawing appears in Nicolás León's *Aventuras de la Monja Alférez* (33).

51. "me gusta contemplar a Juana" (85).

52. "Pero yo sé que no puedo comportarme como lo que se espera de mí" (86).

53. "me siento prisionera. Prisionera de la gente que me pregunta, que quiere que le cuente mi historia . . . la gente se extraña, se maravilla. Encuentra mi historia extraordinaria y me invitan a sus palacios, a sus casas de campo, para que

entretenga a sus invitados con mis narraciones . . . me siento tan rabiosa como cuando la hermana portera no me quiso abrir aquella puerta para que yo puediera perseguir a mi mariposa azul" (118–119).

54. "no me encontrarán jamás . . . ¡Jamás!" (121).

55. "Aquellas dos jóvenes eran muy simpáticas. Hice amistad con ellas, sin prever que me verían como a un hombre" (60).

56. "¡Yo te amo! Haría cualquier cosa por ti. ¡Tómame por esposa y huyamos!"; "¿Yo . . . ? ¡Oh, Dios!" (61).

57. A few days later, Catalina is again situated as a spectator in a theater as she responds favorably by agreeing with a male companion's reference to the beauty of an actress about to perform onstage (46).

58. "Tiene crédito abierto, señora. Son órdenes de mi patrón, que yo con gusto cumplo, al tratarse de una mujer tan hermosa" (45).

59. "La mujer que superó los límites que le imponía su época y logró llevar una vida libre y aventurera" (94).

60. Interestingly, unlike the strictly military garb worn by Catalina in Pacheco's portrait, the hybrid outfit in the comic book is also featured in the panel that depicts the artist painting Erauso's portrait (91).

61. See Keen and Wasserman 323–341.

62. "E inclinándose sobre la enamorada Doña Beatriz la besó rabiosamente en el cuello blanco y sensual, en la afiebrada boca y en las orejas pequeñas y transparentes" (56).

63. "Un amante al que ella le ofrecería la garganta túrgida y ardiente, y la nuca, y los hombros, y los senos duros que eran como dos rosas abriéndose o, mejor dicho, como dos palomas heridas. Un amante que la cogiera entre sus brazos para irla deshojando, pétalo por pétalo, causándole, a la vez un placer doloroso y dulce, sin término" (42).

64. "Observarla desde este ángulo visual. Y ver su vida. Tumultuosa. Ardiente. Alocada. Hermosa siempre. Lector: Deténgase con este espíritu ante esta noticia de la Monja Alférez que acaba de conocer. Es posible, entonces, que llegue a amarla. Como yo" (112).

65. "Estando acostado Francisco sobre una rica tapicería y con la cabeza puesta en el regazo de doña Mencia, la que acariciábale los rizados cadejos del cabello y de vez en cuando bajaba la rica pulpa de sus labios a la boca de la monja, dándole sonoros y apasionados besos, entretanto que las manos del galán no permanecían quietas, pues exploraban sabiamente bajo las sayas de la hermosa y despreocupada jovencita" (51).

66.

> Todo su cuerpo era como un ritmo cadencioso, que se movía en finísimas figuras, tan finas como los arabescos del Alcázar de Sevilla. . . . Y así de un

simple juego de palabras pasamos a representar un amor verdadero, cálido y apasionado. Nos abrazábamos, nos besabamos . . .

—¡Jesús, María y José!—exclamó el señor obispo.

—Con razón se espanta Vuestra Señoría Ilustrísima—le contesté—, pues estaba como loca y me había olvidado de mi verdadero estado. El hecho es que en una de esas cálidas noches de Saña, doña Beatriz, tras mucho manoseo, me confesó: "Francisco, ¡quiéreme más! Yo soy tuya, quiero que me poseas totalmente, que penetres en mi. Hazme el favor de unirte conmigo en una inmensa llamarada que nos abrase a ambos." Se precipitó sobre mi catre y me arrastró consigo, desvistiéndose. . . .

—¿Y qué hiciste, Catalina?—preguntó mi indagador. (70–71)

67.

La joven doncella se había sentado sobre mi falda y estaba peinando su cabello, que era de color castaño y sedoso. Yo le tocaba su lindo cuerpo. . . . Repentinamente irrumpió don Diego, . . . sin perder muchas palabras, me despidió en el acto y me ordenó abandonar su casa. . . .

—¡Bien merecido castigo te dio!—observó el señor obispo, agregando:—Pero quisiera que examináramos con detenimiento tus aberraciones, Catalina. Vuelve pasado mañana. Yo meditaré un poco acerca de ello. (77)

68. "Tú, como mujer, tienes una componente masculina: yo, como hombre, una femenina. Tú has sido testigo de la afición que en ese sentido he tenido por tí. Voy a confesarte, también, que me habría agradado ser amado por tí, pues me pareciste la encarnación de la belleza varonil" (79).

69. "los hay dotados de órganos femeninos, como yo, y que, no obstante, sienten como hombres; los hay en que ocurre lo contrario . . . (me detuve un instante, pero resistí a la tentación de aludir a él)" (82).

70. "La amé terriblemente, con un frenesí que jamás había conocido. . . . ¿Pero fue un sentimiento carnal, como antes? No. Ya me estaba acercando a la edad bíblica, ya estaba tranquila. La amaba ahora, no como querida, sino como madre" (449).

71. "os confesaré que en un principio penetraron en mí carnalmente, sobre todo el conocer a la bellísima imagen de la Purísima de Tolsa. . . . Pero es también cierto que esa imagen ya no representa para mí un valor carnal, sino que encarna la fuerza divina que necesitaba para regenerar" (467).

72. "la terrible diosa Coatlícue. Sobre sus inmensas garras de tigre yace un hacinamiento de serpientes. Han despedazado su cuerpo, y sus partes son sostenidas por las víboras, en conjunto con corazones de sacrificados. ¡Oh!, es horroroso . . . ya la Purísima asimiló a Coatlícue, la dominó, la encubrió" (482–483).

73. "Era un placer estético verla moverse por mi casita, tomando en sus gra-

ciosas manitos cada objeto para acariciarlo . . . Yo saboreaba cada movimiento de su esbelto cuerpo. Tenía un andar ondulante, avanzando como si fuera una brisa de primavera" (450–451).

74. "Ahí está la Purísima, radiante. Me tiende su mano . . . , me pide la acompañe" (483).

75. "Su híbrida y contradictoria condición de religiosa y militar, de mujer y soldado, le confiere ese misterioso atractivo que suele tener lo ambiguo y oscuro, lo que participa a la vez de dos naturalezas teóricamente antagónicas e inconciliables, y ello lo deja fuera de las normas, de lo normal, para otorgarle el turbador atributo de lo anómalo, la inquietante y seductora aureola del prodigio" (24).

76. "No podemos saber si el personaje histórico llegó o no a ser consciente del papel que el poder le había impuesto: pero el personaje dramático sí lo es" (36).

77. "*La Monja Alférez* en la que todos mis cuidados son si se casa o no se casa con su dama un amigo mío que el señor poeta se ha inventado. Mucha ignorancia y mucha mentira hay en esas historias impresas que de mí corren" (56). Carlos Keller's historical novel invents a related scene in which Lope de Vega and the disguised Catalina question Pérez de Montalbán about his characterization of Erauso, which fails to explain why she wanted to live as a man and why she was so aggressive (322–323).

78. Interestingly, a videotape made of one of the 1993 performances in Campo de Criptana reveals repeated audience laughter at seeing two nuns insult each other and eventually engage in a physical fight.

79. "Es más hermosa que el sol que nos alumbra, más hermosa que la vida . . . Doña María, la adoro como a Dios" (101); "(La abraza CATALINA y le cubre de besos la cara y la boca. DOÑA MARÍA la abraza a su vez, con fuerza creciente)" (104).

80. I refer to a videotape of the original performance in 1993 sent to me by the director Luis Cabañero.

81. "Una curiosidad de la Naturaleza, cardenal. Un prodigio, un fenómeno singular, y nada más . . . y así se ha convertido en un prodigio que está fuera del orden, sin beneficiarlo ni perjudicarlo. Si hubiese muchas Catalinas de Erauso, entonces, sí: entonces, ese orden se quebraría" (142–143).

82. "Soy una mona de feria . . . me miraban como a una mona que da extremadas y nunca vistas volteretas para pasmo y diversión de los presentes, y nada más. . . . La mujer con barba o la mujer forzuda que los niños contemplan en la plaza mientras un hombre toca el tambor y la muestra a los curiosos" (147).

83. "Catalina no se verá como un triunfadora absoluta, sino como trágica heroína opuesta a un ineludible destino" (36).

84. "Para los historiadores, Catalina de Erauso es uno de los personajes más insólitos de la historia, creo que su condición de homosexual es lo que le ha restado publicidad" (quoted in Doneil); "si sus aventuras no son tan populares . . . se

debe a que su marcada tendencia hacia las mujeres le restó popularidad" (quoted in *Fotogramas,* March 1986).

85. "Hay que aclarar que la actitud de Catalina/Alonso, ante la coquetería e insinuaciones de Beatriz, es expectante, más bien pasiva, aunque en ningún momento deja de admirar los encantos de la dama" (51–52).

86. "Catalina/Alonso no sabe qué responder. Sus ojos se han ido hacia los senos de Beatriz y su frente se perla de sudor, mientras la mira con los ojos seminublados. Pero es incapaz de responder" (53).

87. "no sabe qué hacer, pero se encuentra a gusto" (54).

88. "Súbitamente, le besa. 'El', tomado por sorpresa, pone cara de horror" (60).

89. "Catalina/Alonso se acerca y besa a Beatriz, a través de la reja. No sabemos si de buena o mala gana" (67).

90. "Lentamente se dejan caer en la hierba. Quedan tumbados. Se besan y acarician en silencio" (129).

91. "En su cara se adivina una incontenible furia. Una decisión rotunda de recobrar la libertad. En su gesto subyace algo de diabólico" (130).

92. "Se miran un momento. Luego, suavemente, Catalina/Alonso posa sus labios sobre los de Doña María. Es un beso suave, a flor de piel" (154).

93. The two-shot is "a medium or close shot in which two people fill the frame. This is the basic shot for most scenes of conversation in a film, showing the characters talking and responding to one another in profile or in a variety of stances" (Konigsberg 433). The shot-reverse-shot is a technique in which "the camera switches between two conversant or interacting individuals" (Konigsberg 360). The shot-reverse-shot is normally "taken from the point of view of the person listening" (Hayward 320).

94. "Lo que importa es el sentimiento y el sentido que des a la interpretación, no la imagen sino lo que expreses. Por ejemplo, tampoco Greta Garbo se parecía a Cristina de Suecia, y ahí está la película" ("Javier Aguirre: 'La monja alférez' es la crónica de una rebeldía," 24). See also " 'La monja alférez' es la nueva película" and "Javier Aguirre rueda 'La monja Alférez.' "

95. "Tomóme de la mano y preguntóme quedo y cerca si era mujer. Respondíle que si. Preguntóme si era Monja. Díxele que sí, mintiendo en esto pero por librarme de aquél aprieto" (86).

96. "Empiezan a quitar el vendaje con precauciones. Está empapado en sangre. Poco a poco, se van llenando de recelo. Aquello no es normal. Las manos del Fraile II tiemblan. Traga saliva. Quita la última vuelta y . . . . . . aparecen unos hermosos y bellos senos de mujer. El fraile II lanza un tremendo chillido de afeminado. Mira a su compañero, con terror, como si hubiera visto al diablo" (158).

97. "Sí, la amaba. Como solo se puede amar la inocencia, la juventud, la belleza . . . la amaba como el hermano a la hermana, como se ama a los niños" (120).

98. "el principal rasgo problemático de su personalidad" (119).

99. "¡Mercedes . . . ven . . . te amo . . . solo a tí Inés, solo a tí. Ven Inés, ven Mercedes . . . No, eres Inés. Yo te quiero, te he querido siempre . . . desde niñas" (170).

100. The other two are the primal scene ("the child's imaging of parental coitus") and seduction ("the origin and upsurge of sexuality" [de Lauretis 1991, 238]).

101. The similarities between this scene and a comparable scene from Luis Buñuel's *Los olvidados* are also worth noting.

CONCLUSION

1. See Serrano 1994.

2. In a review of the film aired on television in 1988, *Tele Indiscreta* categorized the box office success as "poor" and the artistic quality "poor" ("La Monja Alférez"); *Diario 16* gave the program a one-star ("bad") rating (Marinero).

3. "desvirtúa totalmente al personaje, que aparece como un ser ridículo en ocasiones, dado el énfasis que los adaptadores han puesto en la faceta erótica de sus relaciones humanas" (288).

4. According to Alison Butler, McLaughlin's film distinguishes itself even under the broader rubric of feminist cinema: " 'She Must Be Seeing Things' is one of the few films I've seen in this festival [The 1987 Créteil International Women's Film Festival] which doesn't concentrate on the oppression of women by men, either in a personal sense, or socially and culturally under patriarchy. It's a lively, positive film which deals with the areas of some women's lives where questions of power and identity are open to negotiation to some extent" (20–21). Other queer film critics have been more critical of McLaughlin's film. Ellis Hanson notes that it "has been virtually canonized by feminist film theorists despite its amateurishness" (1).

5. In addition to references to the Lieutenant Nun in Sheila McLaughlin's *She Must Be Seeing Things,* Catalina de Erauso has been evoked in numerous lesbian, feminist, and transgender studies and sources such as *The Furies* (a lesbian/feminist newspaper; see Bunch), the Lambda Literary Awards (see Nangeroni), Jeannette H. Foster's *Sex Variant Women in Literature* (41–43), Leslie Feinberg's *Transgender Warriors* (33), Luz Sanfeliú's *Juego de damas* (53–60), Vicki León's *Uppity Women of Medieval Times* (186–187), Jessica Amanda Salmonson's *The Encyclopedia of Amazons* (82–83), Holly Devor's *FTM* (12–16), and so forth.

6. A study of Erauso's autobiography was recently published in German; see Lotthammer.

7. See Azkune. For publishing patterns in the Basque region after Franco, see Lasagabaster 351–355.

8. "Sin la ayuda del Gobierno vasco no se hubiera hecho" ("Javier Aguirre

rueda 'La monja Alférez' "). In the first three decades of the twentieth century, before the start of Franco's dictatorship, there were also numerous Basque publications dedicated to Erauso. See Erauso 1934, López Alen, Sánchez Moguel, and Martín de Anguiozar's *La Monja Alférez en la Novela Vasca* (cited in Frank 58 and Rubio Merino 49). Pío Baroja's study on the Basque region also includes a brief chapter on the Monja Alférez (138–140).

9. Some of these works are Vallbona's excellent edition of Erauso's *Vida,* Tellechea's *Doña Catalina de Erauso,* Miras's *La Monja Alférez,* and the studies of Martín, Taddeo, and Lara. These investigations continued throughout the decade with articles by Merrim, Perry, Juárez, and Vélez as well as other book-length publications, such as Rubio Merino's *La Monja Alférez Doña Catalina de Erauso,* the reprint of *Catalina de Erauso* by the Basque critic Luis de Castresana, a chapter in Antonio Espina's *Audaces y extravagantes,* and Stepto and Stepto's English translation of Erauso's memoirs.

10. The story of the Lieutenant Nun is used in cultural, historical, and literary collections. For example, Roberto González Echevarría's edition of *The Oxford Book of Latin American Short Stories* includes chapter 7 from Erauso's autobiography (translated by Stepto and Stepto).

11. Reproduced in Vallbona 179–183.

12. See Erauso 1988. In fact dozens of adaptations and references related to the Monja Alférez have been published in Latin America, mostly from Chile and Mexico. See bibliographies and notes in Berruezo, Vallbona, Tellechea, and Kress.

13. Elizabeth Salas cites Erauso as a precursor to the Mexican *soldaderas* (women warriors) while Colin MacLachlan and Jamie Rodríguez O. surprisingly propose *La Monja Alférez* as "the first Mexican novel" (240).

14. "desforado marimacho . . . el Anticristo" (253).

15. "la monja se puso hecha un grifo. Bramaba como un toro herido, levantando su iracundia hasta las estrellas. . . . Echaba ponzoña por la boca y mordía la tierra de pura rabia" (257).

16. "Creyó de nuevo estar en Chile . . . Vagó así dos días y dos noches por la ciudad mexicana que ella tomaba por Concepción de Chile" (99, 102).

17. I thank Lourdes Torres for sharing this material with me.

18. "que permite que cada uno la termine según su fantasía" (69). Hernández Castanedo concludes: "Who knows! The story only states that Miss Catalina disappeared, without leaving a trace, on that frightful infernal night in Veracruz" ("¡Quién sabe! La historia sólo afirma que doña Catalina desapareció, sin dejar rastro, en aquella estremecedora, infernal noche de Veracruz" [145]).

Bibliography

Abbott, Lawrence. 1986. "Comic Art: Characteristics and Potentialities of a Narrative Medium." *Journal of Popular Culture* 19 (4): 155–176.

Adams, Jerome R. 1995. *Notable Latin American Women: Twenty-nine Leaders, Rebels, Poets, Battlers, and Spies, 1500–1900*. Jefferson and London: McFarland & Co.

Aguirre, Javier. 1986. "La Monja Alférez." Screenplay, typescript. Biblioteca Nacional, Madrid.

Aldaraca, Bridget A. 1991. *"El Angel del Hogar": Galdós and the Ideology of Domesticity in Spain*. North Carolina Studies in the Romance Languages and Literatures. Chapel Hill: University of North Carolina Press.

———. 1989. "The Medical Construction of the Feminine Subject in Nineteenth-Century Spain." In *Cultural and Historical Grounding for Hispanic and Luso-Brazilian Feminist Literary Criticism*, 395–413. Ed. Hernán Vidal. Minneapolis: Institute for the Study of Ideologies and Literature.

Alemán, Mateo. 1987. *Guzmán de Alfarache*. Vol. 1. Ed. José María Micó. Madrid: Cátedra.

Andreu, Alicia. 1982. *Galdós y la literatura popular*. Madrid: SGEL.

Anzaldúa, Gloria. 1987. *Borderlands/La Frontera: The New Mestiza*. San Francisco: Aunt Lute Books.

Asensio y Toledo, José María. 1867. *Francisco Pacheco: Sus obras artísticas y literarias, especialmente el 'Libro de descripción de verdaderos retratos de ilustres y memorables varones', que dejó inédito.* Sevilla: Litografía y Librería Española y Extrangera.

Ashcom, B. B. 1960. "Concerning 'La mujer en hábito de hombre' in the *comedia.*" *Hispanic Review* 28: 43–62.

Aurrecoechea, Juan Manuel, and Armando Bartra. 1993. *Puros cuentos. Historia de la historieta en México 1934–1950.* Mexico City: Grijalbo.

Azkune, Iñaki, ed. and trans. 1976. *Katalin Erauso.* Bilbao: Ediciones Mensajero.

Barbazza, Marie-Catherine. 1984. "Un caso de subversión social: El proceso de Elena de Céspedes (1587–1589)." *Criticón* 26: 17–40.

Baroja, Pío. 1953. *El País Vasco.* Barcelona: Ediciones Destino.

Barrionuevo, Jerónimo de. 1996. *Avisos del Madrid de los Austrias y otras noticias.* Ed. José María Díez Borque. Madrid: Castalia.

Bell-Metereau, Rebecca. 1993. *Hollywood Androgyny.* New York: Columbia University Press.

Bennett, Paul. 1996. "Lieutenant Nun: Memoir of a Basque Transvestite in the New World" (Review). *Village Voice* 41: 6, 16, February 6.

Bergmann, Emilie L. 1993. "(Re)writing History in Lope: Cross-Dressing and Feminism in *La vengadora de las mujeres.*" *Indiana Journal of Hispanic Literatures* 2 (1): 29–48.

Berruezo, José. 1973. *Catalina de Erauso. La Monja Alférez.* San Sebastián: Grupo de Camino de Historia Donostiarra.

Bilbao, Jon. 1973. "Euskal Bibliographia." In *Enciclopedia General Ilustrada del País Vasco,* 3:158–159. San Sebastian: Aunamendi.

Bird, S. Elizabeth. 1997. "What a Story! Understanding the Audience for Scandal." In *Media Scandals: Morality and Desire in the Popular Culture Marketplace,* 99–121. Ed. James Lull and Stephen Hinerman. New York: Columbia University Press.

Blanco, Alda. 1989. "Domesticity, Education, and the Woman Writer: Spain 1850–1880." *Cultural and Historical Grounding for Hispanic and Luso-Brazilian Feminist Literary Criticism,* 371–394. Ed. Hernán Vidal. Minneapolis: Institute for the Study of Ideologies and Literature.

Blasco, Eduardo. 1892. *Del claustro al campamento o la monja Alferez: Novela histórica.* 2 vols. Barcelona: Antonio Virgili.

Bogdan, Robert. 1996. "The Social Construction of Freaks." In *Freakery: Cultural Spectacles of the Extraordinary Body,* 23–37. Ed. Rosemarie Garland Thomson. New York: New York University Press.

Boswell, John. 1980. *Christianity, Social Tolerance, and Homosexuality.* Chicago and London: University of Chicago Press.

Bradbury, Gail. 1981. "Irregular Sexuality in the Spanish 'Comedia.'" *Modern Language Review* 76 (3): 566–580.

Braidotti, Rosi. 1994. *Nomadic Subjects: Embodiment and Sexual Difference in Contemporary Feminist Theory.* New York: Columbia University Press.

Brantôme, Pierre. 1933. *Lives of Fair and Gallant Ladies.* Translated by A. R. Allinson. New York: Liveright Publishing.

Bravo-Villasante, Carmen. 1976. *La mujer vestida de hombre en el teatro español.* Madrid: Temas.

Brooksback Jones, Anny. 1997. *Women in Contemporary Spain.* Manchester and New York: Manchester University Press.

Brooten, Bernadette J. 1996. *Love between Women: Early Christian Responses to Female Homoeroticism.* Chicago and London: University of Chicago Press.

Brown, Judith C. 1986. *Immodest Acts: The Life of a Lesbian Nun in Renaissance Italy.* New York: Oxford University Press.

———. 1989. "Lesbian Sexuality in Medieval and Early Modern Europe." In *Hidden from History: Reclaiming the Gay and Lesbian Past,* 67–75. Ed. Martin Duberman, Martha Vicinus, and George Chauncey Jr. New York: Penguin.

Brushwood, John S. 1966. *Mexico in Its Novel: A Nation's Search for Identity.* Austin: University of Texas Press.

Bullough, Vern L. 1996. "Cross Dressing and Gender Role Change in the Middle Ages." In *Handbook of Medieval Sexuality,* 223–242. Ed. Vern L. Bullough and James A. Brundage. New York: Garland Publishing.

———. 1976. *Sexual Variance in Society and History.* New York: John Wiley & Sons.

Bullough, Vern L., and Bonnie Bullough. 1993. *Cross Dressing, Sex, and Gender.* Philadelphia: University of Pennsylvania Press.

Bunch, Charlotte. 1974. "Doña Catalina de Erauso: The Nun Ensign." In *Women Remembered: A Collection of Biographies from* The Furies, 42–51. Ed. Nancy Myron and Charlotte Bunch. Baltimore: Diana Press.

Burshatin, Israel. 1996. "Elena Alias Eleno: Genders, Sexualities, and 'Race' in the Mirror of Natural History in Sixteenth-Century Spain." In *Gender Reversals and Gender Cultures: Anthropological and Historical Perspectives,* 105–122. London: Routledge.

———. 1998. "Interrogating Hermaphroditism in Sixteenth-Century Spain." In *Hispanisms and Homosexualities,* 3–18. Ed. Sylvia Molloy and Robert McKee Irwin. Durham, N.C.: Duke University Press.

———. 1999. "Written on the Body: Slave or Hermaphrodite in Sixteenth-Century Spain." In *Queer Iberia: Sexualities, Cultures, and Crossings from the Middle Ages to the Renaissance,* 420–456. Ed. Josiah Blackmore and Gregory S. Hutcheson. Durham, N.C.: Duke University Press.

Butler, Alison. 1987. "'She Must Be Seeing Things': An Interview with Sheila McLaughlin." *Screen* 28 (4): 20–28.

Butler, Judith. 1993. *Bodies That Matter: On the Discursive Limits of "Sex."* New York: Routledge.

Caballero, María. 1996. "Vida i sucesos de la Monja Alférez: Autobiografía atribuida a doña Catalina de Erauso" (Review). *Colonial Latin American Historical Review* 5 (4): 482–483.

Canguilhem, Georges. 1962. "Monstrosity and the Monstrous." *Diogenes* 40: 27–42.

Carrete Parrondo, Juan. 1993. "Estampas fantásticas. Imágenes y descripciones de monstruos." In *Art and Literature in Spain: 1600–1800*, 55–67. Ed. Charles Davis and Paul Julian Smith. London and Madrid: Támesis.

Cartagena-Calderón, José. 1998. " 'No se hace hombre, se llega a serlo': La construcción de la masculinidad en la autobiografía de una travesti del siglo XVII, *Vida i sucesos de la Monja Alférez.*" Paper presented at the Third Annual Conference on Women Writers of Medieval and Early Modern Spain and Colonial Latin America, "(Re)capturing the Female Hispanic Body: Cultural Representations and Discourse." Loyola Marymount University, Los Angeles, September 17.

Casasola, Gustavo. 1978. "Muere en México la Monja Alférez." *Seis siglos de historia gráfica de México 1325–1976*, 1:248. Mexico City: Editorial Gustavo Casasola.

Castillo Lara, Lucas G. 1992. *La asombrosa historia de doña Catalina de Erauso La Monja Alférez, y sus prodigiosas aventuras en Indias (1602–1624)*. Caracas, Venezuela: Planeta.

Castillo Solórzano, Alonso de. 1986. *Aventuras del Bachiller Trapaza.* Ed. Jacques Joset. Madrid: Cátedra.

Castresana, Luis de. 1996. *Catalina de Erauso. La Monja Alférez.* Madrid: Afrodisio Aguado, 1968. Reprint, Barcelona: Ediciones Internacionales Universitarias.

Castro, Américo. 1924. *Lengua, enseñanza y literatura.* Madrid: Victoriano Suárez.

Castro, Cristóbal de. 1941. *Mujeres del Imperio.* Madrid: Espasa-Calpe.

Castro, Miguel de. 1956. "Vida de Miguel de Castro." In *Autobiografías de soldados (siglo XVII).* Biblioteca de Autores Españoles 90:487–627. Ed. José María de Cossio. Madrid: Atlas.

Castro Leal, Antonio. 1964. *La novela del México colonial.* Mexico City: Aguilar.

"Catalina de Erauso o sea la Monja Alferes." (Nineteenth-century anonymous manuscript from a 368-folio novel.) Benson Latin American Collection, G-593, University of Texas at Austin.

Cebrián, Julio. 1974. "Señoras que hicieron época. La Monja Alférez." *Miss,* November 1, 396.

Charnon-Deutsch, Lou. 1999. "María de Zayas y Sotomayor." In *Spanish Writers on Gay and Lesbian Themes: A Bio-Critical Sourcebook,* 188–190. Ed. David William Foster. Westport, Conn.: Greenwood Press.

Chauncey, George. 1982–1983. "From Sexual Inversion to Homosexuality: Medicine and the Changing Conceptualization of Female Deviance." *Salmagundi* 58–59, 114–146.

Coello, Carlos. 1873. *La Monja Alférez. Zarzuela histórica en tres actos y en verso.* Prologue by José Gómez de Arteche. Madrid: T. Fortanet.

Cohen, Jeffrey Jerome, ed. 1996. *Monster Theory: Reading Culture.* Minneapolis: University of Minnesota Press.

Combet, Louis. 1980. *Cervantès ou les incertitudes de désir.* Lyon: Presses Universitaires de Lyon.

Contreras, Alonso de. 1956. "Discurso de mi vida." *Autobiografías de soldados (siglo XVII).* Biblioteca de Autores Españoles 90:77–248. Ed. José María de Cossio. Madrid: Atlas.

Cotarelo y Mori, Emilio. 1904. *Bibliografía de las controversias sobre la licitud del teatro en España.* Madrid: Real Academia Española.

———. 1934. *Historia de la zarzuela o sea el drama lírico en España, desde su origen a fines del siglo XIX.* Madrid: Tipografía Archivos.

Covarrubias, Sebastián de. 1989. *Tesoro de la Lengua Castellana o Española.* Barcelona: Editorial Alta Fulla.

Crawford, Patricia, and Sara Mendelson. 1995. "Sexual Identities in Early Modern England: The Marriage of Two Women in 1680." *Gender and History* 7 (3): 362–377.

Creed, Barbara. 1995. "Horror and the Carnivalesque: The Body-Monstrous." In *Fields of Vision: Essays in Film Studies, Visual Anthropology, and Photography,* 127–159. Ed. Leslie Devereaux and Roger Hillman. Berkeley: University of California Press.

Crompton, Louis. 1980–1981. "The Myth of Lesbian Impunity: Capital Laws from 1270 to 1791." In *Historical Perspectives on Homosexuality,* eds. Salvatore J. Licata and Robert P. Peterson. *Journal of Homosexuality* 6 (1–2): 11–25.

Cruz, Anne J. 1999. *Discourses of Poverty: Social Reform and the Picaresque Novel in Early Modern Spain.* Toronto: University of Toronto Press.

Cubillo de Aragón, Alvaro. *Añasco el de Talavera.* Rare Book Collection, University of Minnesota, Minneapolis.

Cull, John T. 1989. "Androgyny in the Spanish Pastoral Novels." *Hispanic Review* 57: 317–334.

Daniels, Mary Blythe. 1998. "Re-visioning Gender on the Seventeenth-century Spanish Stage: A Study of Actresses and Autoras." Ph.D. diss., University of Kentucky.

Daston, Lorraine. 1991. "Marvelous Facts and Miraculous Evidence in Early Modern Europe." *Critical Inquiry* 18, 93–109.

Daston, Lorraine, and Katharine Park. 1995. "The Hermaphrodite and the Orders of Nature: Sexual Ambiguity in Early Modern France." *Journal of Lesbian and Gay Studies* 1 (4): 419–438.

———. 1998. *Wonders and the Order of Nature: 1150–1750.* New York: Zone Books.

D'Auvergne, Edmund B. 1927. *Adventuresses and Adventurous Ladies.* London: Hutchinson.

Dekker, Rudolf M., and Lotte C. van de Pol. 1989. *The Tradition of Female Transvestism in Early Modern Europe.* New York: St. Martin's Press.

De Lauretis, Teresa. 1991. "Film and the Visible." In *How Do I Look? Queer Film and Video,* 223–264. Ed. Bad Object-Choices. Seattle: Bay Press.

———. 1994. *The Practice of Love: Lesbian Sexuality and Perverse Desire.* Bloomington: Indiana University Press.

Delgado Berlanga, María José. n.d. "Lesbiagrafisis: Exposición y expansión del deseo femenino en 'La traición en la amistad' de María de Zayas y Sotomayor." *Romance Language Annual,* forthcoming.

Delpech, François. 1995. "Muger hay en la guerra: Remarques sur l'exemplaire et curieuse carrièrre d'une guerrière travestie, Juliana de los Cobos." In *Relations entre hommes et femmes en Espagne aux XVI et XVII siècles,* 53–65. Ed. Augustin Redondo. Paris: Sorbonne.

Dennett, Andrea Stulman. 1996. "The Dime Museum Freak Show Reconfigured as Talk Show." In *Freakery: Cultural Spectacles of the Extraordinary Body,* 315–326. Ed. Rosemarie Garland Thomson. New York: New York University Press.

De Quincey, Thomas. 1890. "The Spanish Military Nun." *The Collected Writings of Thomas De Quincey,* 159–250. Ed. David Masson. Edinburgh: Adam and Charles Black. Reprint, New York: Johnson Reprint, 1968.

Devor, Holly. 1999. *FTM: Female-to-Male Transsexuals in Society.* Bloomington: Indiana University Press.

Di Febo, Giuliana. 1988. *La santa de la raza. Teresa de Avila: un culto barroco en la España franquista (1937–1962).* Translated by Angel Sánchez-Gijón. Barcelona: Icaria.

Díaz de Escovar, Narciso. 1924. *Historia del teatro español.* Barcelona: Montaner y Simón.

Díaz y de Ovando, Clementina. 1971. Introduction to *El cerro de las campanas,* by Juan A. Mateos. Mexico City: Porrúa.

Dixon, Wheeler Winston. 1995. *It Looks at You: The Returned Gaze of Cinema.* Albany: State University of New York Press.

Doane, Mary Ann. 1992. "Film and the Masquerade: Theorizing the Female Spectator." In *The Sexual Subject: A Screen Reader in Sexuality/Screen,* 227–243. London: Routledge.

Doneil, Teresa. 1986. "Estreno de 'La monja alférez'" (Review). *Diario Español Tarragona,* October 23.

Donoghue, Emma. 1993. *Passions between Women: British Lesbian Culture 1668–1801.* London: Scarlet Press.

Downing, Christine. 1989. *Myths and Mysteries of Same-Sex Love.* New York: Continuum.

Duberman, Martin, Martha Vicinus, and George Chauncey Jr., eds. 1989. *Hidden from History: Reclaiming the Gay and Lesbian Past.* New York: Penguin.

Dugaw, Dianne. 1996. *Warrior Women and Popular Balladry 1650–1850.* Chicago: University of Chicago Press.

Duque de Estrada, Diego. 1956. "Memorias de D. Diego Duque de Estrada." In *Autobiografías de soldados (siglo XVII).* Biblioteca de Autores Españoles 90:251–484. Ed. José María de Cossio. Madrid: Atlas.

Durán, Agustín. 1861. *Romancero general. Colecciones de romances castellanos anteriores al siglo XVIII.* Biblioteca de Autores Españoles 16. Madrid: Rivadeneyra.

Dyer, Richard. 1998. *Stars.* London: British Film Institute.

Elkins, James. 1996. *The Object Stares Back: On the Nature of Seeing.* San Diego: Harvest Books.

Enders, Victoria Lorée. 1999. "Problematic Portraits: The Ambiguous Historical Role of the Sección Femenina of the Falange." In *Constructing Spanish Womanhood: Female Identity in Modern Spain,* 375–397. Ed. Victoria Lorée Enders and Pamela Beth Radcliff. Albany: State University of New York Press.

Epstein, Julia, and Kristina Straub, eds. 1991. *Body Guards: The Cultural Politics of Gender Ambiguity.* New York: Routledge.

Erauso, Catalina de. 1988. *Historia de la Monja Alférez, Catalina de Erauso.* Ed. Biblioteca Nacional del Perú. Lima: Salesiana.

———. 1996. *Lieutenant Nun: Memoir of a Basque Transvestite in the New World.* Translated by Michele Stepto and Gabriel Stepto. Boston: Beacon.

———. 1934. *La Monja Alférez.* Prologue by B. Estornes Lasa. Esuskaltzaleak: Editorial Itxaropena-Zarauz.

Escudero, María A. 1999. " 'Cortés and Marina': Gender and the Reconquest of America under the Franco Regime." In *Constructing Spanish Womanhood: Female Identity in Modern Spain,* 71–93. Ed. Victoria Lorée Enders and Pamela Beth Radcliff. Albany: State University of New York Press.

Espina, Antonio. 1996. *Audaces y extravagantes y otros aventureros con fondo ambiental.* Madrid: Ediciones Libertarias.

Ettinghausen, Henry. 1984. "The News in Spain: *Relaciones de sucesos* in the Reigns of Philip III and IV." *European History Quarterly* 14 (1): 1–20.

———. 1993. "The Illustrated Spanish News: Text and Image in the Seventeenth-Century Press." In *Art and Literature in Spain: 1600–1800,* 117–133. Ed. Charles Davis and Paul Julian Smith. London and Madrid: Támesis.

———. 1995. *Noticias del siglo XVII: Relaciones españolas de sucesos naturales y sobrenaturales.* Barcelona: Puvill Libros.

Evans, Peter. 1995. "Back to the Future: Cinema and Democracy." In *Spanish Cultural Studies,* 326–331. Ed. Helen Graham and Jo Labanyi. New York: Oxford University Press.

Faderman, Lillian. 1981. *Surpassing the Love of Men: Romantic Friendship and Love between Women from the Renaissance to the Present.* New York: William Morrow.

Feinberg, Leslie. 1996. *Transgender Warriors: Making History from Joan of Arc to Dennis Rodman.* Boston: Beacon Press.

Ferguson, Ann, Jacquelyn N. Zita, and Kathryn Pyne Addelson. 1981. "On 'Compulsory Heterosexuality and Lesbian Existence': Defining the Issue." *Signs* 7: 158–199.

Fernández-Luna, C. 1959. *La zarzuela.* Madrid: Publicaciones Españolas.

Ferrer, Joaquín María de. 1988. Prologue to *Historia de la Monja Alférez, doña Catalina de Erauso, escrita por ella misma.* Ed. Virgilio Ortega. Barcelona: Ediciones Orbis. Reprinted from 1829 Paris edition.

Fiedler, Leslie. 1993. *Freaks: Myths and Images of the Secret Self.* New York: Anchor Books.

Findlay, Heather. 1998. "Xenaphilia!" *Girlfriends* 5 (4): 28–29, 44.

Fitzmaurice-Kelly, James, trans. 1908. *The Nun Ensign.* London: T. Fisher Unwin.

Flores, Angel, and Kate Flores, eds. 1986. *The Defiant Muse: Hispanic Feminist Poems from the Middle Ages to the Present.* New York: Feminist Press.

Foster, Jeannette H. 1985. *Sex Variant Women in Literature.* Tallahassee, Fla.: Naiad Press.

Fotogramas. March 1986. " 'La monja alférez': Una novicia rebelde."

Fradenburg, Louise, and Carla Freccero, eds. 1996. *Premodern Sexualities.* New York: Routledge.

Fraker, Debbie. 1996. "Lieutenant Nun: Memoir of a Basque Transvestite in the New World" (Review). *Lambda Book Report* 5 (1): 40–41.

Frank, Roslyn M. 1978. "Catalina de Erauso: Una mujer varonil." In *Women in the Literature of Medieval and Golden Age Spain,* 51–63. Ed. Barbara Davis. Syracuse: Onondaga Community College.

Friedman, Jerome. 1993. *The Battle of the Frogs and Fairford's Flies: Miracles and the Pulp Press during the English Revolution.* New York: St. Martin's Press.

Friedman, John Block. 1981. *The Monstrous Races in Medieval Art and Thought.* Cambridge: Harvard University Press.

Fuchs, Barbara. 1996. "Border Crossings: Transvestism and 'Passing' in *Don Quijote.*" *Cervantes* 16: 4–28.

Gaines, Jane. "The *Queen Christina* Tie-Ups: Convergence of Shop Window and Screen." *Quarterly Review of Film and Video* 2: 35–60.

Galindo, Jorge Luis. 1997. "El cine mexicano y sus mitos en la novela mexicana reciente (1967–1990)." Ph.D. diss., University of Kansas.

Gamson, Joshua. 1998. *Freaks Talk Back: Tabloid Talk Shows and Sexual Nonconformity.* Chicago: University of Chicago Press.

Garber, Marjorie. 1993. *Vested Interests: Cross-dressing and Cultural Anxiety.* New York: HarperPerennial.

———. 1996. "The Marvel of Peru." Foreword to *Lieutenant Nun: Memoir of a Basque Transvestite in the New World, Catalina de Erauso,* vii–xxiv. Translated by Michele Stepto and Gabriel Stepto. Boston: Beacon Press.

García Fernández, Ruben. 1996. "'Fui fan de la Garbo.'" *Reforma,* March 22.

García Franco, Manuel, and Ramón Regidor Arribas. 1997. *La zarzuela.* Madrid: Acento Editorial.

García Riera, Emilio. 1992. *Historia documental del cine mexicano 3.* Guadalajara: Universidad de Guadalajara.

García-Serrano, M. Victoria, Cristina de la Torre, and Annette Grant Cash. 1999. *¡A que sí!* Boston: Heinle & Heinle.

Goldman, Ruth. 1996. "Who Is That *Queer* Queer? Exploring Norms around Sexuality, Race, and Class in Queer Theory." In *Queer Studies: A Lesbian, Gay, Bisexual, and Transgender Anthology,* 169–182. Ed. Brett Beemyn and Mickey Eliason. New York: New York University Press.

Góngora. 1939. *Poemas y sonetos.* Buenos Aires: Editorial Losada.

González Echevarría, Roberto. 1993. *Celestina's Brood: Continuities of the Baroque in Spanish and Latin American Literatures.* Durham, N.C.: Duke University Press.

———, ed. 1997. "Amorous and Military Adventures." In *The Oxford Book of Latin American Short Stories,* 46–49. New York: Oxford University Press.

González Obregón, Luis. 1973. "La Monja Alférez." *Leyendas de las calles de México. La novela del México colonial,* 1008–1010. Ed. Antonio Castro Leal. Mexico City: Aguilar.

González Suárez, Amalia. 1997. *Aspasia (ca. 470–410 a.C.).* Madrid: Ediciones del Otro.

Goreau, Angeline. 1996. "Cross-Dressing for Success." *New York Times Book Review,* March 17, 24.

Gossy, Mary S. 1995. "Aldonza as Butch: Narrative and the Play of Gender in *Don Quijote.*" In *¿Entiendes? Queer Readings, Hispanic Writings,* 17–28. Ed. Emilie L. Bergmann and Paul Julian Smith. Durham, N.C.: Duke University Press.

———. 1998. "Skirting the Question: Lesbians and María de Zayas." In *Hispanisms and Homosexualities,* 18–28. Ed. Sylvia Molloy and Robert McKee Irwin. Durham, N.C.: Duke University Press.

Graham, Helen. 1995. "Women and Social Change," "Gender and the State: Women in the 1940s." In *Spanish Cultural Studies,* 99–116 and 182–195. Ed. Helen Graham and Jo Labanyi. New York: Oxford University Press.

Graullera, Vicente. 1985. "Mujer, amor y moralidad en la Valencia de los siglos XVI y XVII." In *Amours légitimes, amours illégitimes en Espagne (XVI–XVII siècles),* 113–119. Ed. Augustin Rodondo. Paris: La Sorbonne.

Green, Jamison. 1998. Review of *Suits Me: The Double Life of Billy Tipton,* by Diane Wood Middlebrook. *Transgender Tapestry* 84: 22–23.

Grosz, Elizabeth. 1996. "Intolerable Ambiguity: Freaks as/at the Limit." In *Freak-*

ery: Cultural Spectacles of the Extraordinary Body, 55–66. Ed. Rosemarie Garland Thomson. New York: New York University Press.

———. 1995. *Space, Time, and Perversion.* New York: Routledge.

Grugel, Jean, and Tim Rees. 1997. *Franco's Spain.* London and New York: Arnold.

Guzzo, María Cristina. 1999. "Catalina de Erauso." In *Spanish Writers on Gay and Lesbian Themes: A Bio-Critical Sourcebook,* 60–62. Ed. David William Foster. Westport, Conn.: Greenwood Press.

Halberstam, Judith. 1998a. *Female Masculinity.* Durham, N.C.: Duke University Press.

———. 1998b. "Transgender Butch: Butch/FTM Border Wars and the Masculine Continuum." *GLQ: A Journal of Lesbian and Gay Studies* 4 (2): 287–310.

Hammond, Frederick. 1994. *Music and Spectacle in Baroque Rome: Barberini Patronage under Urban VIII.* New Haven: Yale University Press.

Hanson, Ellis, ed. 1999. *Out Takes: Essays on Queer Theory and Film.* Durham, N.C.: Duke University Press.

Harris, Helaine. 1974. "Queen Christina: Lesbian Ruler of Sweden." In *Women Remembered: A Collection of Biographies from the Furies,* 11–17. Ed. Nancy Myron and Charlotte Bunch. Baltimore: Diana Press.

Hart, Lynda. 1994. *Fatal Women: Lesbian Sexuality and the Mark of Aggression.* Princeton: Princeton University Press.

Hayward, Susan. 1996. *Key Concepts in Cinema Studies.* London: Routledge.

Henderson, James D., and Linda Roddy Henderson. 1978. *Ten Notable Women of Latin America.* Chicago: Nelson-Hall.

Hernández Castanedo, F. 1944. "La Monja Alférez." *Aventura española,* 135–145. Madrid: Editorial Bibliográfica Española.

Herrmann, Gina. 1999. "Amazonic Ambivalence in Imperial Potosí." *Modern Language Notes* 114: 315–340.

Hic mulier: or, The man-woman: being a medicine to cure the coltish disease of the staggers in the masculine-feminines of our times. Exprest in a briefe declamation. 1620. London: Newberry Library, Case K 77.403.

Hillman, David, and Carla Mazzio, eds. 1997. *The Body in Parts: Fantasies of Corporeality in Early Modern Europe.* New York: Routledge.

Hombres y Héroes, no. 176, 1991. Mexico City: Novedades Editores. "La Monja Alférez," Adaptation: R. Bastien, dialogue: Dolores Plaza, and illustrations: José L. Echave.

Hooper, John. 1995. *The New Spaniards.* New York: Penguin Books.

Hotchkiss, Valerie R. 1996. *Clothes Make the Man: Female Cross Dressing in Medieval Europe.* New York: Garland.

Huarte de San Juan, Juan. 1989. *Examen de ingenios para las ciencias.* Ed. Guillermo Serés. Madrid: Cátedra.

Huet, Marie-Hélène. 1993. *Monstrous Imagination.* Cambridge: Harvard University Press.

Ibsen, Kristine L. 1999. *Women's Spiritual Autobiography in Colonial Spanish America.* Gainesville: University of Florida Press.

Inamoto, Kenji. 1992. "La mujer vestida de hombre en el teatro de Cervantes." *Cervantes* 12 (2): 137–143.

Inness, Sherrie A. 1997. *The Lesbian Menace: Ideology, Identity, and the Representation of Lesbian Life.* Amherst: University of Massachusetts Press.

Jardine, Lisa. 1983. *Still Harping on Daughters: Women and Drama in the Age of Shakespeare.* Totowa, N.J.: Barnes and Noble.

"Javier Aguirre: 'La monja alférez' es la crónica de una rebeldía" (Review). 1986. *El Alcazar,* October 12.

"Javier Aguirre rueda 'La monja Alférez', una vida de aventuras y la historia de una rebeldía" (Review). 1986. *Diario 16,* January 13.

Jiménez, Lourdes Noemi. 1990. "La novela corta española en el siglo XVII: María de Zayas y Sotomayor y Mariana de Caravajal y Saavedra." Ph.D. diss., University of Massachusetts.

Johnson, Julie Greer. 1983. *Women in Colonial Spanish American Literature: Literary Images.* Westport, Conn.: Greenwood Press.

Jones, Ann Rosalind, and Peter Stallybrass. 1991. "Fetishizing Gender: Constructing the Hermaphrodite in Renaissance Europe." In *Body Guards: The Cultural Politics of Gender Ambiguity,* 80–111. Ed. Julia Epstein and Kristina Straub. New York: Routledge.

Juárez, Encarnación. 1995. "Señora Catalina, ¿dónde es el camino? La autobiografía como búsqueda y afirmación de identidad en *Vida i sucesos de la Monja Alférez.*" In *La Chispa '95: Selected Proceedings,* 185–195. Ed. Claire J. Paolini. New Orleans: Tulane University Press.

———. 1997. "La mujer militar en la América colonial: El caso de la Monja Alférez." *Indiana Journal of Hispanic Literature* 10–11: 147–164.

———. 1998. "Autobiografías de mujeres en la edad media y el Siglo de Oro y el canon literario." *Monographic Review/Revista Monográfica* 13: 154–168.

Kappler, Claude. 1986. *Monstruos, demonios y maravillas a fines de la Edad Media.* Translated by Julio Rodríguez Puértolas. Madrid: Akal.

Keen, Benjamin, and Mark Wasserman. 1984. *A Short History of Latin America.* Boston: Houghton Mifflin.

Keller, Carlos. 1972. *Las memorias de La Monja Alférez. Novela.* Santiago, Chile: Editorial Jerónimo de Vivar.

Kirkpatrick, Susan. 1989a. "The Female Tradition in Nineteenth-Century Spanish Literature." In *Cultural and Historical Grounding for Hispanic and Luso-Brazilian Feminist Literary Criticism,* 343–370. Ed. Hernán Vidal. Minneapolis: Institute for the Study of Ideologies and Literature.

———. 1989b. *Las Románticas: Women Writers and Subjectivity in Spain, 1835–1850.* Berkeley: University of California Press.

Konigsberg, Ira. 1997. *The Complete Film Dictionary.* New York and London: Penguin.

Kress, Dorothy M. 1931. *Catalina de Erauso, su personalidad histórica y legendaria.* M.A. thesis, University of Texas, Austin.

Kritzman, Lawrence D. 1996. "Representing the Monster: Cognition, Cripples, and Other Limp Parts in Montaigne's 'Des Boyteux.'" In *Monster Theory: Reading Culture,* 168–182. Ed. Jeffrey Jerome Cohen. Minneapolis: University of Minnesota Press.

Kuefler, Mathew S. 1996. "Castration and Eunuchism in the Middle Ages." In *Handbook of Medieval Sexuality,* 279–306. Ed. Vern L. Bullough and James A. Brundage. New York: Garland Publishing.

Kuhn, Annette. 1985. *The Power of the Image: Essays on Representation and Sexuality.* London: Routledge & Kegan Paul.

"La Monja Alférez" (Review). 1988. *Tele Indiscreta,* November 26–December 2.

"'La monja alférez' es la nueva película que reúne a Esperanza Roy y Jesús Aguirre" (Review). 1984. *La Vanguardia* (Barcelona), December 3.

Laffin, John. 1967. *Women in Battle.* London: Abelard-Schuman.

Landy, Marcia, and Amy Villarejo. 1995. *Queen Christina.* London: British Film Institute.

Lasagabaster, Jesús María. 1995. "The Promotion of Cultural Production in Basque." In *Spanish Cultural Studies,* 351–355. Ed. Helen Graham and Jo Labanyi. New York: Oxford University Press.

Lavrin, Asunción. 1993. "La vida femenina como experiencia religiosa: biografía y hagiografía en Hispanoamérica colonial." *Colonial Latin American Review* 2 (1–2): 27–51.

Lea, Henry C. 1907. *A History of the Inquisition in Spain.* Vol. 4. New York: Macmillan.

León, Nicolás. 1973. *Aventuras de la Monja Alférez.* Mexico City: Colección Metropolitana.

León, Vicki. 1999. *Outrageous Women of the Renaissance.* New York, Wiley & Sons.

———. 1997. *Uppity Women of Medieval Times.* Berkeley, Calif.: Conari Press.

Llanos, Bernardita. 1989. "Integración de la mujer al proyecto de la Ilustración en España." *Ideologies and Literature* 4 (1): 199–223.

Long, Kathleen Perry. 1996. "Hermaphrodites Newly Discovered: The Cultural Monsters of Sixteenth-Century France." In *Monster Theory: Reading Culture,* 183–201. Ed. Jeffrey Jerome Cohen. Minneapolis: University of Minnesota Press.

López Alen, Francisco. 1901. "La monja alférez, Catalina de Erauso." *Euskal Erria* 45: 58–62.

Lotthammer, Cornelia. 1998. *La Monja Alférez. Die Autobiographie der Catalina de Erauso in ihrem literarischen und gesellschaftlichen Kontext.* Frankfurt: Peter Lang.

Luis de León. 1992. *La perfecta casada.* Ed. Javier San José Lera. Madrid: Espasa Calpe.

Luna, Lola, ed. 1993. *Valor, agravio y mujer.* Madrid: Castalia.

MacKenzie, Gordene Olga. 1994. *Transgender Nation.* Bowling Green, Ohio: Bowling Green University Popular Press.

MacLachlan, Colin M., and Jaime E. Rodríguez O. 1980. *The Forging of the Cosmic Race: A Reinterpretation of Colonial Mexico.* Berkeley: University of California Press.

Maravall, José Antonio. 1986. *Culture of the Baroque: Analysis of a Historical Structure.* Minneapolis: University of Minnesota Press.

Marco, Joaquín. 1997. *Literatura popular en España en los siglos XVIII y XIX (una aproximación a los pliegos de cordel).* Vol. 2. Madrid: Taurus.

Marín Pina, María Carmen. 1989. "Aproximación al tema de la *Virgo Bellatrix* en los libros de caballerías españoles." *Criticón* 45: 81–94.

Marinero, Francisco. 1988. "La monja alférez" (Review). *Diario 16,* December 1.

Marshall, P. David. 1997. *Celebrity and Power: Fame in Contemporary Culture.* Minneapolis: University of Minnesota Press.

Martín, Adrienne L. 1994. "Desnudo de una travestí, o la 'autobiografía' de Catalina de Erauso." In *La mujer y su representación en las literaturas hispánicas. Actas Irvine-1992. Asociación Internacional de Hispanistas,* 34–41. Irvine: University of California Press.

Mateos, Juan Antonio. 1877. *La Monja Alférez. Drama en tres actos y en verso.* Mexico City: J. M. Sandoval.

McClintock, Anne. 1995. *Imperial Leather: Race, Gender, and Sexuality in the Colonial Contest.* New York: Routledge.

McDonald, Paul. 1998. "Reconceptualising Stardom." In *Stars,* 177–200. Ed. Richard Dyer. London: British Film Institute.

McKendrick, Melveena. 1974. *Woman and Society in the Spanish Drama of the Golden Age: A Study of the Mujer Varonil.* London: Cambridge University Press.

Menéndez Pelayo, Marcelino. 1961. *Orígenes de la novela.* Vol 2. Madrid: Consejo Superior de Investigaciones Científicas.

Menéndez Pidal, Ramón. 1952. *Flor nueva de romances viejos.* Buenos Aires: Espasa-Calpe Argentina.

Merrim, Stephanie. 1990. "Catalina de Erauso: Prodigy of the Baroque Age." *Review: Latin American Literature and Arts* 43: 38–41.

———. 1994. "Catalina de Erauso: From Anomaly to Icon." In *Coded Encounters: Writing, Gender, and Ethnicity in Colonial Latin America,* 177–205. Ed. Francisco Javier Cevallos-Candau, Jeffrey A. Cole, Nina M. Scott, and Nicomedes Suárez-Araúz. Amherst: University of Massachusetts Press.

———. 1999. *Early Modern Women's Writing and Sor Juana Inés de la Cruz.* Nashville, Tenn.: Vanderbilt University Press.

Merwin, W. S. 1985. *From the Spanish Morning.* New York: Atheneum.

Minkowitz, Donna. 1996. "Xena: She's Big, Tall, Strong—and Popular." *Ms.* 7 (1): 74–77.

Miras, Domingo. 1992. *La Monja Alférez.* Ed. Virtudes Serrano. Murcia, Spain: Universidad de Murcia.

La Monja Alférez. 1944. Mexico City: CLASA Film. Directed by Emilio Gómez Muriel.

La Monja Alférez. 1986. Madrid: Goya Films. Directed by Javier Aguirre.

Moore, F. Michael. 1994. *Drag! Male and Female Impersonators on Stage, Screen, and Television.* Jefferson, N.C.: McFarland.

Morales-Alvarez, Raúl. 1938. *La Monja Alférez (crónica de una vida que tuvo perfil de romance).* Santiago: Excelsior.

Morcillo Gómez, Aurora. 1999. "Shaping True Catholic Womanhood: Francoist Educational Discourse on Women." In *Constructing Spanish Womanhood: Female Identity in Modern Spain,* 51–69. Ed. Victoria Lorée Enders and Pamela Beth Radcliff. Albany: State University of New York Press.

Munt, Sally R. 1998. *Heroic Desire: Lesbian Identity and Cultural Space.* New York: New York University Press.

Muñoyerro. 1959. "La Monja Alférez" (Comic Strip). *La Gaceta del Norte,* August 30 and September 1.

Murray, Jacqueline. 1996. "Twice Marginal and Twice Invisible: Lesbians in the Middle Ages." In *Handbook of Medieval Sexuality,* 191–222. Eds. Vern L. Bullough and James A. Bundage. New York: Garland Publishing.

Nangeroni, Nancy R. 1997. "Trans-actions: News and Notes from the Gender Frontier." *Transgender Tapestry,* Fall, 11.

Nash, Mary. 1995. *Defying Male Civilization: Women in the Spanish Civil War.* Denver: Arden Press.

———. 1999. "Un/Contested Identities: Motherhood, Sex Reform, and the Modernization of Gender Identity in Early Twentieth-Century Spain." In *Constructing Spanish Womanhood: Female Identity in Modern Spain,* 25–49. Ed. Victoria Lorée Enders and Pamela Beth Radcliff. Albany: State University of New York Press.

Niccoli, Ottavia. 1990. *Prophesy and People in Renaissance Italy.* Princeton: Princeton University Press.

Nichols, Geraldine Cleary. 1989. "Children's Literature in Spain, 1939–1950: Ideology and Practice." In *Fascismo y experiencia literaria: Reflexiones para una recanonización,* 213–221. Ed. Hernán Vidal. Minneapolis: Institute for the Study of Ideologies and Literature.

Ochoa, María Carmen. 1970. *La Monja Alférez.* Madrid: G. del Toro.

Olivares, Julián, and Elizabeth S. Boyce. 1993. *Tras el espejo la musa escribe. Lírica femenina de los Siglos de Oro.* Madrid: Siglo Veintiuno.

Ortega, Virgilio, ed. 1988. *Historia de la Monja Alférez, doña Catalina de Erauso, escrita por ella misma.* Prologue by Joaquín María de Ferrer. Barcelona: Ediciones Orbis. Reprinted from the 1829 Paris edition.

Paré, Ambroise. 1987. *Monstruos y prodigios.* Translated by Ignacio Malaxecheverría. Madrid: Siruela.

Palma, Ricardo. 1992. "¡A Iglesia me llamo!" *Tradiciones peruanas.* Reprinted in Tellechea 1992, 242–246.

Park, Katharine. 1997. "The Rediscovery of the Clitoris." In *The Body in Parts: Fantasies of Corporeality in Early Modern Europe,* 170–193. Ed. David Hillman and Carla Mazzio. London: Routledge.

Park, Katharine, and Lorraine J. Daston. 1981. "Unnatural Conceptions: The Study of Monsters in Sixteenth- and Seventeenth-Century France and England." *Past and Present* 92: 20–54.

Parker, Jack H. 1970. " 'La Monja Alférez' de Juan Pérez de Montalván: Comedia americana del siglo XVII." In *Actas del Tercer Congreso Internacional de Hispanistas,* 665–671. Mexico City: El Colegio de Mexico.

Peers, E. Allison, trans. 1964. *The Way of Perfection,* by Teresa of Avila. New York: Doubleday.

Pérez de Montalbán, Juan. *La Monja Alférez. Comedia famosa. Spanish Drama of the Golden Age: The Comedia Collection.* [Microfilmed from *Comedias varias de diferentes autores de España.* Spain, 17—?] New Haven, Conn.: Research Publications.

Pérez Sánchez, Alonso E. 1986. *Monstruos, enanos y bufones en la corte de los Austrias.* Madrid: Amigos del Museo del Prado.

Perriam, Chris. 1995. "Gay and Lesbian Culture." In *Spanish Cultural Studies: An Introduction. The Struggle for Modernity,* 393–395. Ed. Helen Graham and Jo Labanyi. Oxford and New York: Oxford University Press.

Perry, Mary Elizabeth. 1999. "From Convent to Battlefield: Cross-Dressing and Gendering the Self in the New World of Imperial Spain." In *Queer Iberia: Sexualities, Cultures, and Crossings from the Middle Ages to the Renaissance.* Ed. Josiah Blackmore and Gregory S. Hutcheson, 394–419. Durham, N.C.: Duke University Press.

———. 1990. *Gender and Disorder in Early Modern Seville.* Princeton: Princeton University Press.

———. 1987a. " 'La Monja Alférez': Myth, Gender, and the Manly Woman in a Spanish Renaissance Drama." In *La Chispa '87: Selected Proceedings,* 239–248. Ed. Gilbert Paolini. New Orleans: Tulane University Press.

———. 1987b. "The Manly Woman: A Historical Case Study." *American Behavioral Scientist* 31 (1): 86–100.

Prosser, Jay. 1998. *Second Skins: The Body Narratives of Transsexuality.* New York: Columbia University Press.

Porro Herrera, María Josefa. 1995. *Mujer "sujeto"/mujer "objeto" en la literatura española del Siglo de Oro.* Málaga, Spain: Atenea.

Pumar Martínez, Carmen. 1991. *Españolas en Indias. Mujeres-soldado, adelantadas y gobernadoras.* Mexico City: Rei.

Ramet, Sabrina Petra. 1996. *Gender Reversals and Gender Cultures: Anthropological and Historical Perspectives.* London: Routledge.

Raymond, Janice G. 1986. *A Passion for Friends: Toward a Philosophy of Female Affection.* Boston: Beacon.

———. 1996. "The Politics of Transgenderism." In *Blending Genders: Social Aspects of Cross-Dressing and Sex-Changing,* 215–223. Ed. Richard Ekins and Dave King. London: Routledge.

Rhodes, Elizabeth. 1994. "Women on their Knees: The Pornographic Nature of Sixteenth-century Religious Discourse." Paper presented at the Wesleyan Renaissance Seminar, Wesleyan University, Middletown, Conn., May 4.

Ricapito, Joseph V. 1993–1994. "Monsters, Demons, and Iconography in *Guzmán de Alfarache:* The Case of the Monster of Ravenna (I,1)." *Journal of Hispanic Philology* 18 (1–3): 141–156.

Rodríguez, Armonía. 1975. *De monja a militar.* Barcelona: La Gaya Ciencia.

Rodríguez, Luis Angel. 1937. *Vida y hazañas de la Monja Alférez. Novela histórica americana.* Mexico City: Ediciones Nucamendi.

Rojas, Fernando de. 1987. *Celestina.* Ed. Dorothy Sherman Severin, with the translation of James Mabbe (1631). Warminster, England: Aris and Phillips.

———. 1982. *La Celestina.* Ed. Bruno Mario Damiani. Madrid: Cátedra.

Romera Navarro, M. 1934. "Las disfrazadas de varón en la comedia." *Hispanic Review* 2: 269–286.

Ruano de la Haza, J. M., and John J. Allen. 1994. *Los teatros comerciales del siglo XVII y la escenificación de la comedia.* Madrid: Castalia.

Rubio Merino, Pedro. 1995. *La Monja Alférez Doña Catalina de Erauso. Dos manuscritos autobiográficos inéditos.* Seville: Cabildo Metropolitano de la Catedral de Sevilla.

Ruiz de Dampierre, Blanca. 1943. *La Monja Alférez.* Madrid: Ediciones Hesperia.

Russo, Vito. 1987. *The Celluloid Closet: Homosexuality in the Movies.* New York: Harper and Row.

Rutter, Chloe. 1998. "Transatlantic, Transsexual, Transhistorical: A Reading of the Monja Alférez Catalina de Erauso." Typescript. November 19.

Salas, Elizabeth. 1990. *Soldaderas in the Mexican Military: Myth and History.* Austin: University of Texas Press.

Salmonson, Jessica Amanda. 1992. *The Encyclopedia of Amazons: Women Warriors from Antiquity to the Modern Era.* New York: Anchor Books.

San Juan, Rose Marie. 1993. "The Queen's Body and Its Slipping Mask: Contesting Portraits of Queen Christina of Sweden." In *ReImagining Women: Representation of Women in Culture,* 19–44. Ed. Shirley Neuman and Glennis Stephenson. Toronto: University of Toronto Press.

Sánchez Calvo, R. 1964. "Interpretación neuro-endocrina de 'La Monja Alférez' (Doña Catalina de Erauso)." *Medicamenta* 42 (408): 224–228.

Sánchez Cantón, F. J., ed. 1956. *Arte de la Pintura,* by Francisco Pacheco. Madrid: Instituto de Valencia de Don Juan.

———, ed. 1948. Prologue and notes to *Floreto de anécdotas y noticias diversas que recopiló un fraile dominico residente en Sevilla a mediados del siglo XVI.* Madrid: Maestre.

Sánchez Moguel, Antonio. 1909. "El Alférez doña Catalina de Erauso." *Euskal Erria* 60: 130–136.

Sanfeliú, Luz. 1996. *Juego de damas. Aproximación histórica al homoerotismo femenino.* Málaga, Spain: Atenea.

Schwarz, Kathryn. 1997. "Missing the Breast." In *The Body in Parts: Fantasies of Corporeality in Early Modern Europe,* 147–169. Ed. David Hillman and Carla Mazzio. London: Routledge.

Serrano, Virtudes. 1994. "Estreno de 'La Monja Alférez' de Domingo Miras." *Primer Acto* 252: 35–36.

———. 1991. *El teatro de Domingo Miras.* Murcia, Spain: Universidad de Murcia.

Serrano y Sanz, Manuel. 1975. *Apuntes para una biblioteca de escritoras españolas.* Madrid: Ediciones Atlas.

She Must Be Seeing Things. 1987. New York: First Run Features. Directed by Sheila McLaughlin.

Shepherd, Simon. 1981. *Amazons and Warrior Women: Varieties of Feminism in Seventeenth-Century Drama.* London: Harvester Press.

Shergold, N. D. 1967. *A History of the Spanish Stage from Medieval Times until the End of the Seventeenth Century.* Oxford: Clarendon Press.

Shergold, N. D., and J. E. Varey, eds. 1985. *Geneología, origen y noticias de los comediantes de España.* London: Tamesis.

Silverblatt, Irene. 1994. "Andean Witches and Virgins: Seventeenth-Century Nativism and Subversive Gender Ideologies." In *Women, "Race," and Writing in the Early Modern Period,* 259–271. Ed. Margo Hendricks and Patricia Parker. London: Routledge.

Simons, Patricia. 1994. "Lesbian (In)Visibility in Italian Renaissance Culture: Diana and Other Cases of *donna con donna.*" *Journal of Homosexuality* 27 (1–2): 81–122.

Smith, Paul Julian. 1989. *The Body Hispanic: Gender and Sexuality in Spanish and Spanish American Literature.* Oxford: Clarendon.

Solomon, Alisa. 1988. "Sheila McLaughlin: Gaze Liberation." *Village Voice* 33: 16, 76.

Stacey, Jackie. 1990. "Femmes Fatales." In *Woman's Companion to International Film,* 153–154. Eds. Annette Kuhn and Susannah Radston. London: Virago.

Stanley, Jo. 1995. *Bold in Her Breeches: Women Pirates across the Ages.* San Francisco: Pandora.

Steele, Valerie. 1996. *Fetish: Fashion, Sex, and Power.* New York: Oxford University Press.

Stepto, Michele, and Gabriel Stepto, trans. 1996. *Lieutenant Nun: Memoir of a Basque Transvestite in the New World,* by Catalina de Erauso. Boston: Beacon Press.

Stolcke, Verena. 1994. "Invaded Women: Gender, Race, and Class in the Formation of Colonial Society." In *Women, "Race," and Writing in the Early Modern Period,* 272–286. Ed. Margo Hendricks and Patricia Parker. London: Routledge.

Straayer, Chris. 1996. *Deviant Eyes, Deviant Bodies: Sexual Re-orientation in Film and Video.* New York: Columbia University Press.

Stradling, R. A. 1981. *Europe and the Decline of Spain: A Study of the Spanish System, 1580–1720.* London and Boston: Allen and Unwin.

Straub, Kristina. 1991. "The Guilty Pleasures of Female Theatrical Cross-Dressing and the Autobiography of Charlotte Charke." In *Body Guards: The Cultural Politics of Gender Ambiguity,* 142–166. Ed. Julia Epstein and Kristina Straub. New York: Routledge.

Taddeo, Sara A. 1993. "'Mentís, que no soy mujer mientras empuño este acero': Verdad, Engaño, and Valor in La monja alférez." In *Looking at the Comedia in the Year of the Quincentennial: Proceedings of the 1992 Symposium on Golden Age Drama,* 111–120. Ed. Barbara Mujica and Sharon D. Voros. Lanham, Md.: University Press of America.

Taibo I, Paco Ignacio. 1992. "A María le sienta bien el pantalón." In *La Doña,* 64–72. Mexico City: Planeta.

Teresa de Jesús. 1988. "Camino de perfección." *Obras completas.* Madrid: Aguilar.

Teresa of Avila. 1964. *The Way of Perfection.* Translated by E. Allison Peers. New York: Doubleday.

Tellechea Idigoras, J. Ignacio. 1992. *La Monja Alférez. Doña Catalina de Erauso. IV Centenario de su nacimiento.* San Sebastián: Grupo de Camino de Historia Donostiarra.

Torquemada, Antonio de. 1982. *Jardín de flores curiosas.* Ed. Giovanni Allegra. Madrid: Castalia.

Traub, Valerie. 1992. "The (In)significance of 'Lesbian' Desire in Early Modern England." In *Erotic Politics: Desire on the Renaissance Stage,* 150–169. Ed. Susan Zimmerman. New York: Routledge.

Trouille, Mary Seidman. 1997. *Sexual Politics in the Enlightenment.* Albany: State University of New York Press.

Ugarte, Michael. 1989. *Shifting Ground: Spanish Civil War Exile Literature.* Durham, N.C.: Duke University Press.

Vallbona, Rima de, ed. 1992. *Vida i sucesos de la monja alférez. Autobiografía atribuida a Doña Catalina de Erauso.* Tempe: Arizona State University.

Valle-Arizpe, Artemio de. 1992. "La Monja Alférez." *Amores y picardías. Leyendas, tradiciones y sucedidos del México Virreinal.* Reprinted in Tellechea 1992, 247–258.

Vega Carpio, Lope de. 1976. *Arte nuevo de hacer comedias.* Ed. J. M. Rozas. Madrid: SGEL.

Velasco, Fernando. 1956. *Cuando las grandes heroínas eran niñas.* Barcelona: Editorial Cervantes.

Velasco, Sherry. 1997. "Mapping Selvagia's Transmutable Sexuality in Montemayor's *Diana.*" *Revista de Estudios Hispánicos* 31: 403–417.

———. 2000. "Early Modern Lesbianism on Center Stage: Cubillo de Aragón's *Añasco el de Talavera.*" In *Lesbianism and Homosexuality in Spanish Golden Age Literature and Society,* 305–321. Ed. María José Delgado and Alain Saint-Saëns. New Orleans: University Press of the South.

———. n.d. "María de Zayas and Lesbian Desire in Early Modern Spain." In *En el ambiente: Queer Sexualities in Latino, Latin American, and Spanish Writing and Culture.* Eds. Librada Hernandez and Susana Chavez-Silverman. Madison: University of Wisconsin Press, forthcoming.

Vélez, Irma. 1996. "Vida i sucesos de la Monja Alférez: Un caso de travestismo sexual y textual." In *La seducción de la escritura,* 391–401. Ed. Rosaura Hernández Monroy and Manuel F. Medina. Mexico City: Impresos Johnny.

Vélez-Quiñones, Harry. 1999. *Monstrous Displays: Representation and Perversion in Spanish Literature.* New Orleans: University Press of the South.

Vicinus, Martha. 1992. " 'They Wonder to Which Sex I Belong': The Historical Roots of the Modern Lesbian Identity." *Feminist Studies* 18: 467–497.

Warrior Nun Areala. 1996. Dialogue and illustrations by Ben Dunn. San Antonio: Antarctic Press.

Weber, Alison. 1996. *Teresa of Avila and the Rhetoric of Femininity.* Princeton: Princeton University Press.

Weiss, Andrea. 1992. *Vampires and Violets: Lesbians in the Cinema.* London: Jonathan Cape.

Wheelwright, Julie. 1989. *Amazons and Military Maids: Women Who Dressed as Men in the Pursuit of Life, Liberty, and Happiness.* Boston: Pandora.

Willemen, Paul. 1980. "Letter to John." *Screen* 21 (2): 53–66.

Wilson, Diana de Armas. 1991. *Allegories of Love: Cervantes' "Persiles and Sigismunda."* Princeton: Princeton University Press.

Witek, Joseph. 1989. *Comic Book as History.* Jackson: University Press of Mississippi.

Ximénez de Sandoval, F. 1949. *Varia historia de ilustres mujeres (veinticinco vidas de españolas).* Madrid: Industrias Gráficas España.

Yarbro-Bejarano, Yvonne. 1994. *Feminism and the Honor Plays of Lope de Vega.* West Lafayette, Ind.: Purdue University Press.

Zayas, María de. 1983. *Desengaños amorosos.* Ed. Alicia Yllera. Madrid: Cátedra.

———. 1997. *The Disenchantments of Love.* Translated by H. Patsy Boyer. Albany: State University of New York Press.

———. 1990. *The Enchantments of Love: Amourous and Exemplary Novels.* Translated by H. Patsy Boyer. Berkeley: University of California Press.

———. 1988. *Novelas amorosas y ejemplares.* Barcelona: Ediciones Orbis.

Zimmerman, Bonnie. 1985. "What Has Never Been: An Overview of Lesbian Feminist Criticism." *The New Feminist Criticism,* 200–224. Ed. Elaine Showalter. New York: Pantheon Books.

Index